THE CLASSIC 1000 DREAMS

D1350526

THE
CLASSIC
1000
DREAMS

foulsham

LONDON · NEW YORK · TORONTO · SYDNEY

foulsham

The Oriel, Thames Valley Court, 183–187 Bath Road,
Slough, Berkshire, SL1 4AA, England

ISBN 978-0-572-01674-6

Printed in Great Britain by
Thomson Litho Ltd, East Kilbride

Preface

No matter how tired or bored a man may be, mystery will always intrigue him. 'Such stuff as dreams are made on' has prior claim to all mysteries and one on which man has speculated since the dawning consciousness of reason.

The exact cause and interpretation of dreams has been, as it always will be, a highly debatable point. The Ancients thought that a man's soul left him during sleep to wander into strange lands, and that during its nocturnal travels it gleaned rare and wonderful knowledge and at times was favoured with messages from the gods. In the Bible, there are endless references to dreams in which God gives advice and guidance. Probably the most famous examples are the dream of Jacob when he saw a ladder reaching up to Heaven on which angels were ascending and descending, and later when Joseph interpreted Pharaoh's dreams and adverted the dangers of famine, pestilence and civil war in Egypt. Some of the dreams both of ancient and modern times, which lay claim to a divine character, are certainly striking and many believe that they had and still have a bearing on the development of God's purposes.

To the medical profession the subject of dreams has always proved to be one of great interest. The psychologist tells us that dreams are the re-embodiment of thoughts which have before, in some form or another, occupied our minds; that they are the broken fragments of our former ideas revived and mixed together. They are certainly of infallible help in enabling the psychologist to understand mental stress.

In this book I have collected together the interpretations of dreams from the most celebrated writers on this subject starting from Artemidorus and right up to the present day.

There is little doubt that the early books were written in all seriousness and faith, with the intention of bringing knowledge and help to the dreamer. The truth of these interpretations can only be decided by the reader, but I hope they will help to shed light on the meaning of your dreams.

Note from the Publisher.

The dreams in this book are based on traditional interpretations. Please be aware that any specific predictions of death or disaster would be considered by a modern dream interpreter as exaggerated and misconstrued. Traditional interpretations of misfortune are now more commonly explained as the end of a phase in the life or perhaps at worst, a general run of bad luck. It is wise to remember that dream imagery is open to analysis of many different kinds, and thus all interpretations should be approached with an open mind.

Bibliography

These books were used as the source material for the dream interpretations, and the descriptions here have been taken from the books themselves. The letters in brackets are quoted after the relevant interpretations in the book.

Artemidorus (A)

The interpretation of dreams by that most celebrated philosopher, Artemidorus. First written in Greek and afterwards translated into divers foreign languages and now made into English by Robert Hood, it being a treatise of great value and esteem and very useful and entertaining for all sorts of people.

Published in London: Printed for S. Crowder & Co, 1644.

Artemidorus was a native of Ephesus, and was known as Daldianus, from Daldis in Lydia, his mother's birthplace, to distinguish him from the geographer of the same name. He lived at Rome in the reigns of Antoninus Pious and Marcus Aurelius (AD 138-180). His work on the interpretation of dreams is in five books which are still extant.

Nostradamus (N)

The signification of dreams, extracted from the translation of *The Mighty Book of Nostradamus* that was iron clasped and iron bound.

Michael Nostradamus or Notre Dame, one of the most singular personages of the sixteenth century, was born at St Remy in the diocese of Avignon on 14 December 1503, of a noble family. He studied philosophy at Avignon and medicine at Montpellier where he took the degree of Doctor in 1529. At Aix in 1546 during the appalling plague of that year he first advanced his claim to divine inspirations of prophesy. He wrote his predictions in verse and the extraordinary fulfilment of some of these prophecies soon made him famous. He died on 2 July 1566 and was buried at Salon in the church of the Cordeliers. (See the work by Theodore Boneys, Paris 1806, on this curious subject.)

Thomas Tryon (T)

A treatise of dreams and visions wherein the causes, natures and uses of nocturnal representations and the communications both of good and evil angels as also departed souls to mankind are theosophically unfolded; that is according to the word of God and the harmony of created beings. To which is added a discourse of the causes, nature and cure of Phrensie, Madness or Distraction, by Thomas Tryon.

Published in London: Printed by T. Sowle, 1695.

Thomas Tryon born at Bilbury near Cirencester on 6 September 1634. He died at Hackney in London on 21 August 1703.

Partridge and Flamsteads (P&F)

Partridge and Flamsteads new and well experienced Fortune book. Delivered to the world from the Astrologer's office in Greenwich Park for the benefit of all young men, maids, wives and widows etc.

Printed and sold in Aldermary Church Yard, London, 1750.

Dreams and Moles (D&M)

Dreams and Moles with their interpretation. To which is fixed a collection of choice receipts concerning love and marriage. First compiled in Greek and now rendered into English by a Fellow of the Royal Society.

Printed in London, 1750.

The High German Fortuneteller (GFT)

The High German Fortuneteller, laying down true rules and direction by which both men and women may know their good and bad fortune.

Printed and sold in Aldermary Church Yard, London, 1758.

Dreams and Moles (D&M2)

Dreams and Moles with their interpretations and significations, made far more manifest and plain than any published to the very meanest capacities by the most ancient as well as the most modern rules of philosophy. To which is prefixed a collection of choice and valuable receipts concerning love and marriage.

Printed and sold by J. Pitts, London, 1810.

The Dreamer's Sure Guide (DSG)

The Dreamer's Sure Guide or The Interpretation of Dreams Faithfully Revealed.
Published in London: Orlando Hodgson, 1830.

Mother Shipton (MS)

Mother Shipton's verses from *The Dreamer's Oracle* being a faithful interpretation of two hundred dreams, to which is added a new method of eliciting from cards the knowledge of our Destiny and future occurrence of events, with a plain explanation of all their determinable combinations by Mother Shipton also the much famed Norwood Circle or Grand Arcana of Fortune. Provided to persons of every age and sex, all matters relating to Love, Courtship and Marriage and other important circumstances of life, past, present and to come. Together with instructions for making the celebrated Dumb-cake and for insuring the efficiency of various charms.
Published in Derby: Thomas Richardson. Simpkin, Marshall & Co, London. S. Hornsey, Portsea and all other booksellers, 1830.

The Golden Dreamer (GD)

The Golden Dreamer or the Universal Guide to the interpretation of dreams with a correct signification of moles on men and women.
Printed and sold by W. Davison, Bondgate Street, 1840.

The Golden Dreamer or Dreams Realized (GD2)

The Golden Dreamer or Dreams Realized, containing the interpretation of a great variety of dreams.
Glasgow: printed for the booksellers, 1850.

Cagliostro (C)

L'Interprète des Songes. Guide infaillible pour l'explication des songes, rêves et visions avec l'indication des numeros de loterie pour chaque songe et un choix très-interessant d'anecdotes relatives aux songes aux rêves et aux apparitions. Par le dernier descendant de Cagliostro.
Paris: Chez les marchands de nouveautes. Imprimerie Charles Blot, 1870.

Consult the Oracle (O)

Consult the Oracle or How to Read the Future. A guide to the interpretations of dreams and to other matters magical and mysterious, being the wisdom of past times and present times as to what will surely come to pass, by Gabriel Nostradamus.
Published in London by C. Arthur Pearson Ltd.

The Modern Dream Book (M)

The Modern Dream Book and Fortune Teller.
Published in London by Aldine Publishing Co. Ltd.

Old Moore's Dream Book (OM)

Old Moore's Dream Book.
Published in London by W. Foulsham & Co Ltd.

Other Books Consulted

A pleasant treatise of the interpretation of sundry dreams gathered part out of the works of the learned philosopher Ponzettus and part out of Artemidorus. By Thomas Hylle, 1576.
On the interpretation of dreams according to the doctrine of the Indians, the Persians and the Egyptians. By Achmet, 1577.
The dreamer's oracle or future revealer, found in the ark of a late celebrated wizard. By Bowman, 1850.
The Universal Dream Book or Ladies Interpreter. Alphabetically arranged. Published by S. Marks & Son, London, 1876.
The Popular Dream Book. By J. Cameron, Glasgow, 1883.
Through the Gateway of Dreams. Their mysteries and interpretations with chapters on omens and superstitions. By 'A Dreamer', London, 1922.

ABBESS
You will be the victim of the malice and spite. *(C)*

ABBEY
To dream of going into an abbey means that your present situation in life will not change. To the lover it indicates that there will be constancy, faithfulness and devotion in all their love affairs. *(M)*

Seeing an abbey signifies loss and affliction; a ruined abbey or one being destroyed signifies that your difficulties are at an end. *(C)*

ABBOT
This indicates danger to you and your affairs; if he is old you will lose your money; if he is a man disguised as an abbot you will lose your health; whilst petits abbés denotes that you will be betrayed by your sweetheart. To see several abbots together signifies approaching dishonour; if they are descending a flight of stairs you will be embroiled in a family quarrel. *(C)*

ABDOMEN
Pains in your abdomen tells of general good health. You can be pleased with your good looks, the strength of your lungs, and the perfect symmetry of your limbs. *(M)*

ABEL
To dream of Abel, Adam's second son who was murdered by his jealous brother Cain, is a favourable omen, and indicates that you are coming up in the world. If you have a law-suit, you will win. If in love, your partner will be kind and faithful. If you are about to go into business, your business will thrive, and you will become rich. In short, expect to rise to high esteem and affluence. If Abel speaks to you in your dream, be very careful to listen to what he says, as otherwise you may reverse every benefit that fortune has in store for you. *(DSG)*

ABORTION
This signifies hopeless heartaches. *(C)*

ABROAD
If a married person dreams that they are in a foreign country it indicates that a fortune will be left to them. To a lover, such a dream signifies constancy and happiness in married life. *(M)*

———————— ♦ ————————

ABSCESS
Undergoing an operation for an abscess is an omen of good health to follow. *(M)*

———————— ♦ ————————

ABSCOND
To dream that an acquaintance has absconded with his employer's money denotes that you must be on your guard against some friend who, while pretending to help you, will do you an injury. *(M)*

———————— ♦ ————————

ABSENCE or ABSENT FRIENDS
To dream of grieving over the absence of anyone is a sure sign that that person will soon return and your love or friendship will be stronger than ever. To dream of rejoicing at anyone's absence denotes that you will shortly receive news you would rather not hear. *(O)*

To dream of the death of a friend living abroad foretells good news. On the contrary, to dream that you have seen some absent friend alive and well foretells bad news. *(M)*

> To dream of any absent friends,
> Good news of them, or ill portends;
> But if at thy beside they seem,
> Their deaths, perhaps, may solve thy dream. *(N)*

———————— ♦ ————————

ABSENTMINDEDNESS
Signifies approaching good fortune. *(C)*

———————— ♦ ————————

ABSINTHE
Drinking absinthe foretells sickness followed by good fortune and good health. *(M)*

Selling absinthe signifies that you will suffer a loss; that you buy it, foretells a love affair. *(C)*

———————— ♦ ————————

ABSOLUTION
To dream that you are granting absolution signifies that you will be robbed; that you have been granted absolution denotes that you will be scorned. *(C)*

———————— ♦ ————————

ABSTINENCE
For a man to dream he has signed the pledge indicates success in business; for a woman, happiness in some undertaking dear to her heart. *(M)*

———————————————————— 12 ————————————————————

ABUNDANCE

To dream that you have an abundance of anything is bad. Abundance of money means penury; of food, scarcity of clothing and a shabby appearance; of health, lingering sickness; of beauty, something that will spoil your personal appearance. *(M)*

———— ♦ ————

ABUSE

To be insulted or abused in a dream is a sign that you will be involved in a business dispute. *(GD)*

———— ♦ ————

ABYSS

To dream of an abyss, crevice or cavern, signifies that you will soon enjoy happiness. *(C)*

———— ♦ ————

ACACIA TREE

This signifies good news. *(C)*

———— ♦ ————

ACCEPTED

To dream that you form a romantic relationship with a beautiful young girl, whom you have long desired means trouble ahead. You will have a long and determined opposition to winning your loved one. *(M)*

———— ♦ ————

ACCIDENTS

To dream of having met with an accident foretells that you are about to go through a great trial. A railway accident signifies the loss of money; a road accident, loss of health; an accident on board ship points to loss of friends. *(O)*

Dreams of accidents foretell pleasant surprises, when the dreamer is married. For one of an engaged couple to have such a dream foretells a hasty wedding. *(M)*

To dream that you witness an accident without being involved, signifies that you will profit by a cowardly action. If you give help to the victim you may expect to be betrayed by a friend who will cheat you of some money you expected to receive. *(C)*

———— ♦ ————

ACCORDION

To dream you hear accordion music denotes pleasure and happiness in your home and family. *(M)*

———— ♦ ————

ACCOUNTS

If a young woman dreams of accounts or account books, it indicates that she will soon marry. If the accounts are all paid, her future husband will be successful in business; if they are unpaid, she may experience the problems of debt when married. When a man dreams of account books it means bad luck in business. *(O)*

   To dream that you are keeping accounts, if you are a business man, indicates loss of business by the failure and bankruptcy of those with whom you have had dealings. Unless you are very careful, you will incur other bad debts in the future. *(M)*

———— ◆ ————

ACORNS

Acorns are omens of wealth and happiness to come. If you eat acorns you will get rich very quickly. If a married woman dreams that she is picking acorns she will have a large family, and probably twins. *(M)*

   To dream of acorns do not slight,
   It promises both strength and might. *(N)*

———— ◆ ————

ACQUAINTANCE

   To fight with betokens some evil demand
   And behoves you to husband the money in hand. *(MS)*

   A dispute with an acquaintance signifies failure in some big undertaking. If you fight, a bad illness will follow. *(M)*

   If you fight with an acquaintance, it signifies distraction, especially if the dreamer is ill. *(OM)*

———— ◆ ————

ACQUIESENCE

To comply with a wish, whether your own or somebody else's, denotes that you will shortly be engaged in several love affairs that will give you the greatest pleasure. *(C)*

———— ◆ ————

ACQUISITION

To acquire something signifies profit. If the objects are necessities, it signifies to those that are poor, a return of fortune; to the rich, success in their undertakings. *(C)*

———— ◆ ————

ACROBAT

After dreaming of an acrobatic display you should be on your guard when walking in the street, for a bad accident is likely to happen. *(M)*

———— ◆ ————

ACROSTIC

Working out a puzzle is a sign that your life will be in danger from some unforeseen accident either on the railway, the sea or from a storm. *(M)*

———— ◆ ————

ACTING

To dream that you are acting denotes that you may look forward to a life of ease and comfort, after surmounting considerable difficulty. *(M)*

ACTOR

For a young woman, to dream of an actor means that a great deal of the admiration at present paid to her, which she thinks genuine, is only make-believe. *(O)*

To dream of an actor signifies that you have confidence in your friend; to dream of an actress denotes that you will enjoy great happiness from some design you have in hand. *(C)*

———— ♦ ————

ACTRESS

To dream of seeing an actress on the stage signifies that you will soon get into many difficulties, partly through your own indiscretion and partly from causes over which you have no control. Meeting her in private life in a dream indicates that you are about to discover how 'hand in hand with sorrow love is wont to go'. *(O)*

After dreaming of an actress, either on or off the stage, a single person should guard against jealous quarrels with their partner. A married person may look for temporary discord in domestic affairs. *(M)*

———— ♦ ————

ADAM and EVE

This signifies that you will acknowledge as your own a child by adoption. *(C)*

To dream you see Adam is a happy omen. If he looks pleasant, you will succeed in whatever you undertake. If you are in love, expect your partner to love you. If you are a farmer expect an abundant crop and that your livestock will increase, be top quality and fetch a good price. If you have left home, return if you can, for prosperity is there. If, however, he looks displeased and angry, use great caution in all your dealings; do not travel by sea; do not borrow or lend money for at least a month or two. If he speaks to you, remember his words and observe them as faithfully as you can. *(DSG)*

———— ♦ ————

ADDERS

To fight with adders signifies the overthrow of enemies. *(T)*

You will become rich and marry into money. Adders signify arguments that will benefit you, especially if you dream they bit you. *(D&M2)*

Beware of false friends when you dream of this reptile. *(M)*

———— ♦ ————

ADDRESS

To have lost or be seeking for the address of anyone means that you are about to fall in with an old acquaintance in a place where you least expect to see him. *(O)*

ADHESION
To dream of sticking or sticking to anything is a sign that you should employ prudence in your affairs. *(C)*

◆

ADJUTANT
For a lady to dream that she is in the company of such an officer is a sign that she will meet with an offer of marriage from an officer in the army, but of a lower grade than an adjutant. *(M)*

To dream of this officer denotes approaching cares. *(C)*

◆

ADMIRAL
To dream of an admiral denotes loss of trade; to see one in a naval engagement signifies that you will meet your death by drowning. *(C)*

◆

ADMIRER
To dream that someone is admiring your looks is a sure indication that some wish particularly dear to you will be fulfilled. *(M)*

To dream that you admire someone indicates that someone will lie to you; that you admire yourself and you will be the victim of deceit. *(C)*

◆

ADONIS
To dream of Adonis signifies that you will be subject to the artfulness of your lover; or will employ craft to gain your own ends in love. *(C)*

◆

ADOPTED
For a young person to dream they have become the adopted child of some wealthy person signifies that the death of either father, mother, or some near relative will soon take place. *(M)*

◆

ADOPTION
This signifies wealth and a ripe old age. If you dream of a child related to you by blood, you will shortly benefit from a legacy. If the child is a stranger you may be sure of all that you undertake. *(C)*

◆

ADORNMENT
To receive a present of an article of jewellery is a sign that you will shortly suffer an affliction of a more or less serious nature, according to the value of the present. *(M)*

To dream that you dress yourself up signifies that you have a rival. *(C)*

◆

ADRIFT
If a person in business dreams of being adrift in a boat he may expect to

become a bankrupt. For a young person to dream of drifting is a sign that he or she is about to be married, but will be unhappy, as the other person will be bad tempered and bossy. *(M)*

———— ♦ ————

ADULTERY
To dream that you are tempted to commit this crime and that you resist it is a happy omen, and it is a good time to begin business after such a dream. If you have a law-suit, you will win.

If you are in love, persevere, for your wishes will be gratified. *(GD2)*

To dream you have committed adultery shows you will be involved in arguments. *(D&M2)*

———— ♦ ————

ADVERSARY
If you are continually being thwarted in some undertaking by persistent adversaries it denotes that there is much trouble and worry in store for you, from which you will eventually gain prosperity. *(M)*

To dream that you receive obstruction from an adversary shows that you will complete your business quickly. *(D&M2)*

———— ♦ ————

ADVERSITY
To dream of the adversity of your enemies signifies coming happiness; if you suffer adversity you will require courage in the near future. *(C)*

———— ♦ ————

ADVERTISEMENT
Answering an advertisement foretells that you will shortly experience an alteration in your circumstances. If you were writing on blue paper, it will be for the better; if the paper was white, it will be for the worse. Looking over the advertisement in a newspaper or magazine denotes that you are about to attract considerable public attention by a judicious use of printer's ink. *(O)*

For a young man to dream that he advertises for 'partner for life' is indicative of his shortly becoming the victim of some practical joke or ludicrous hoax, in which his reputation for judicious conduct and wise behaviour will be greatly tarnished. For a young woman to dream she answers such an advertisement is a sign that a young man living near her wants to be introduced to her. To read the same advertisement many times foretells good news coming from abroad. *(M)*

———— ♦ ————

ADVICE
To receive advice, either good or bad, from an alleged friend denotes that enemies are working against you. The friend who is giving the advice, however, is not always a party to the wrong. *(M)*

AFFABILITY
To dream of friendliness signifies madness. *(C)*

———— ♦ ————

AFFECTATION
Seeing people giving themselves airs, for example, a healthy strong woman riding indolently on a horse, or the lover arriving casually to meet his loved one, signifies that the dreamer should avoid all quarrels because he is in danger of a serious fight. *(C)*

———— ♦ ————

AFFECTION
To receive affection from someone signifies that you will be denounced by one you love. *(C)*

———— ♦ ————

AFFIANCED
For a young, unmarried woman to dream that she has suddenly become engaged to a handsome young man is not a favourable dream. Look out for a quarrel with your lover if you have one. If you have not got one you will have to wait a long time before you marry. *(M)*

———— ♦ ————

AFFLICTION
A great affliction to yourself or friends foretells an early wedding, if the dreamer is single. If married, then a change of residence will soon be required by an occurrence which will improve your social standing. *(M)*
    To dream of sorrow denotes beating malicious people. *(C)*

———— ♦ ————

AFFRONTED
If you are affronted at the misconduct of some dear friend, look for a letter full of expressions of good feeling and kindness from a distant acquaintance from whom you have not heard for a very long time, and whom you thought had entirely forgotten you. *(M)*

———— ♦ ————

AFRICA
If you are on the way to Africa, you will soon have to take a journey for the benefit of your health; the doctors will be baffled by sudden and serious illness which will prevent you from working. *(M)*

———— ♦ ————

AGATE
Agates or semi-precious stones signifies sadness, sickness and setbacks. *(C)*

———— ♦ ————

AGE
To see old people is generally a bad sign. *(T)*
    To dream of old people is of great importance to those in business and

who wish to gain credit. *(D&M)*

For a woman to dream she is courted by an old man is a sure sign that she will receive a sum of money, and be successful in her undertakings. For a girl to dream it, shows that she will marry a rich young man, and will have many children by him, who will all become rich. For a man to dream he is courting an old woman, and that she returns his love, is a very good omen. It shows success in worldly affairs, that he will marry a beautiful young woman, have lovely children and be very happy. *(GD)*

To dream that you have lived to an old age denotes that you will shortly hear of the death of a friend. *(M)*

To dream of the old denotes a peaceful and honest life. *(C)*
See also **OLD**.

AGENT or AGENCY
Signifies loss of inheritance. *(C)*

AGGRANDISEMENT
Fairness and magnificence is bad, and shows death to the sick and poor success to lovers. *(D&M)*

Denotes favour and esteem. *(C)*

AGONY
To be in agony, either from mental or physical pain, is a very good dream. You will have general good health, business prosperity, and your domestic happiness will become greater than you have ever known it before. *(M)*

To dream of witnessing a death agony foretells a legacy. If it is the death of an enemy it indicates that you will inherit from your father. The death of a stranger denotes unexpected benefits. *(C)*

AGREEMENT
For a business man to dream that he has made some advantageous agreement is a bad sign. Business will become dull, partly from failure of others, and partly from general depression of trade. Take care how you make your contracts after this dream; many have fallen from a position of prosperity and affluence from neglect of this warning. *(M)*

To dream of an agreement signifies a successful voyage. *(C)*

AGRICULTURE
Signifies unadulterated good fortune. *(C)*

AIR
If the air is clear and serene, you will be loved and respected by everyone, and will make up with your enemies. Your character will be sanguine. If

the air is cloudless, it means you will find something you have lost; overcome your enemies; win a law-suit; make a successful journey. It is generally a very good omen. If the air is cloudy, dark and troubled, that signifies sadness, sickness, melancholy and business problems. A calm air signifies that life will be good and peaceful and that the business and journeys undertaken will succeed. *(T)*

If you dream the sky is clear, of a fine blue, calm and serene, then it is a good omen: you will be successful in your enterprises; if you are seeking promotion you will obtain it; if you are in love, you will marry your lover; if you have a law-suit, you will win; if you are a farmer, you will have good crops, your livestock will increase, you will get good market prices. Those who are married will have many successful children; journeys will fulfil your expectations; sea voyages will be pleasant and prosperous; debts will soon be cleared; prisoners will be freed. To dream the air is full of thick, dark and heavy clouds is unfavourable; you will fall ill and perhaps die; disappointment will attend your business. *(GD)*

To dream the sky is streaked with white, denotes that you will suffer many severe difficulties over which you will eventually triumph. If the sky is fiery red, you will be successful in love, but not in business. It also warns of sickness and trouble coming to your family. *(OM)*

———— ◆ ————

AIRSHIP
To be in a stationary airship denotes that you will have little success in life unless you work hard to get out of the rut into which you have fallen. If the airship is moving very quickly, be wary of investing your money, as it foretells great loss. *(M)*

———— ◆ ————

AISLE
For a young woman to dream that she walks down the aisle of a church or other place of worship in company with a young man indicates that she will be deserted by her male friends. The young man she sees in her dream has never had the least thought of her, but may soon be in her company at a private party or ball. *(M)*

———— ◆ ————

ALBUM
Looking over a photograph album predicts that a close relative will soon die and you will inherit a considerable sum of money. *(O)*

———— ◆ ————

ALDERMAN
Dining with an alderman is a sign of falling into bad company, and you may be led into some bad behaviour unless you are careful. To dream you have been elected alderman means you will be reduced to poverty unless you are exceedingly careful. *(M)*

ALGEBRA
To be working at algebra signifies successful speculation. *(C)*

———— ♦ ————

ALGERIAN
Signifies you will enjoy the pleasures of love. *(C)*

———— ♦ ————

ALMANAC
Reading the almanac foretells that events that took place years ago will make you a richer and wiser person. Some purchase you formerly made in goods or shares will suddenly rise in value, or be sold at a price much above your expectations, and you will find out that you are well repaid for your investments. *(M)*

To dream of an almanac signifies that you have reason to modify the conduct of your life. *(C)*

———— ♦ ————

ALMONDS and ALMOND TREES
To see and eat almonds signifies difficulties and trouble. To see almond trees and eat their fruit signifies riches and content gained with hard work. *(T)*

To dream of eating almonds denotes disappointment and a probable misfortune. If the almonds are bitter, you will be subjected to a great temptation, which will lead to disgrace unless you can fight against it. *(M)*

———— ♦ ————

ALMS
To be asked for alms which you refuse shows want and misery but to dream you give them freely is a sign of great joy. *(GD)*

To give alms to a poor person is a good omen and indicates to a young woman that she is about to receive a most advantageous proposal of marriage, and to a man that he is about to make the acquaintance of an heiress who will fall in love with him and who, independent of her money, will be a wonderful partner. *(O)*

For a person in employment to dream that he or she is bestowing alms is a warning to be careful in business, for the slightest mistake following this dream will lead to dismissal. If the dreamer has been in doubt over any enterprise he should take the advice of his best friend. *(M)*

———— ♦ ————

ALONE
'Tis good to dream thou'rt left alone,
A friend thou hast on highest throne. *(N)*

———— ♦ ————

ALPHABET
To learn letters means a benefit in store for the ignorant, but it will be accompanied by hard work and fear if you want a son. *(A)*

To dream of the alphabet signifies that you will have reason to fear being fatally bitten by a viper whilst in the country. *(C)*

To see all the letters of the alphabet in large characters is a sign that you will make great advancement as a student. You will be proficient in practical studies, and gain eminence as a theologian. If the letters of your name appear in succession before you, it indicates that you will be called to serve your native town or country in some very honourable position. Look out for a well-paid Government situation. *(M)*

> The alphabet coming, or gamut perusing,
> Is the prelude to excellence — time not abusing. *(MS)*

———— ♦ ————

ALTAR

To uncover or discover an altar signifies joy. *(T)*

To be at the altar means joy and gladness. *(GD)*

To stand before an altar is a sign of approaching sorrow and trouble. To be kneeling before an altar indicates that you are about to enter a successful marriage, have many healthy children and great worldly prosperity. *(O)*

> To dream that you're at one is a symbol of gladness,
> But back turned against it is pregnant with sadness. *(MS)*

An altar signifies radiant hope; to erect an altar signifies gladness; to see one overthrown is a very favourable sign to those engaged in scientific, industrial or commercial enterprises. *(C)*

———— ♦ ————

AMBER

To wear rings of amber is good only to women. *(A)*

———— ♦ ————

AMBULANCE

Denotes that you will lose an inheritance. To see one filled with wounded people signifies a violent death. *(C)*

———— ♦ ————

AMERICA

If you have emigrated to America, you will remain in your present position and occupation, and your efforts to improve your present conditions will be successful. You will rise to a reputable and prosperous position through your persistent efforts. To hear good news from relatives in America signifies that you will soon hear bad news of business losses or domestic problems of those relatives who have emigrated. *(M)*

———— ♦ ————

ANCESTORS

A vision of an ancestor means illness in the family, and if the dreamer has arranged a long journey he should abandon it, otherwise an accident is likely to occur to him. *(M)*

———— 22 ————

To dream of your ancestors denotes family law-suits. To see an ancestor arguing or fighting signifies an inheritance. *(C)*

To dream of one's predecessors signifies care which may turn to good or bad depending on the order and circumstance of the dream. *(A)*

◆

ANCHOR

To see an anchor signifies assurance and hope. *(T)*

Seeing an anchor stuck in the sand signifies that someone of whose affections you are doubtful really cares for you and that circumstances will shortly make this fact plain. *(O)*

A ship's anchor is a sign that you will receive a serious setback in business. If it is a large one, then you will come through the ordeal successfully. *(M)*

This emblem of hope denotes some good to the dreamer, possibly very unexpected news. *(OM)*

> To see one implies unexpected success,
> But warns you of persons you're prone to caress;
> Yet beware well of him, who of friendship pretends
> He will clearly deceive you to gain his own ends. *(MS)*

◆

ANCHOVY

To eat anchovies is a sign that some of your teeth will fall out, or that you will have gumboils or inflammation on the roof of your mouth, which will necessitate a liquid diet. *(M)*

This fish denotes good fortune. To eat anchovies signifies pleasant but trifling love affairs. To sell them foretells ruin. *(C)*

◆

ANGELS

An angel or saint is an encouragement to live well and repent of sins; it also denotes good news, increase of reputation and authority. *(T)*

To see an angel or angels is good, to dream you are one is better; but to speak with or call to them is a bad sign. *(GD)*

This is one of the best possible dreams. It is a sure sign of happiness, indicating long life, good health and the fulfilment of all reasonable wishes. *(O)*

This is an omen of wealth and great happiness to those who are married; to the single it is a symbol of a happy and rich marriage. *(M)*

> An angel's form portends a friend,
> Whose love and kindness will not end,
> But angels converse doth imply
> That judgment or reproof is nigh. *(N)*

ANGER

To be angry with anyone denotes that you have many enemies and that some evil plan is afoot against your happiness and security; if you are in love, a rival is slandering you to your sweetheart. *(GD)*

To quarrel with your fiancé denotes love and affection. To be angry with anyone means that person is one of your best friends. If a man dreams of being angry with his partner it signifies many violent scenes with her during the early part of their marriage, arising from rather absurd misunderstanding, but common sense will prevail after a time and they will live peacefully. *(O)*

To be angry denotes success in your undertakings; but if you are in love you must be wary of someone who will try to poison your sweetheart's mind against you. *(M)*

To be provoked to anger shows that you have powerful enemies. *(OM)*

———— ♦ ————

ANGLING

Angling signifies much affliction and trouble caused by something you want to obtain. *(D&M2)*

———— ♦ ————

ANGUISH

Signifies success to the dreamer. *(C)*

———— ♦ ————

ANIMALS

To hear animals signifies gain. *(T)*

If you are attacked by fierce animals and beat them off you will make friends who will help you to rise in the world. If you are bitten by one of the animals, then you must be on guard against a false friend. *(M)*

Animals in herds of different sorts signifies abundance in your business and great prosperity. A few animals signifies news from an absent friend. To feed animals foretells fortune. If they speak to you it denotes illness and suffering. *(C)*

———— ♦ ————

ANISEED

Denotes that there is someone preparing a present for you. To see the plant in flower signifies that you will benefit by a good action. Aniseed sweets signifies that you must exercise the greatest care in your business dealings. *(C)*

———— ♦ ————

ANKLE

If your ankle is put out of joint it means you will soon suffer severe pains in the head, face or shoulders. To break your ankle means that your hair will begin to turn grey. *(M)*

ANOINTED

To be anointed or painted is good to a virtuous woman, but to a promiscuous woman it indicates a speedy marriage.   *(D&M)*

———————— ♦ ————————

ANT

To dream you see ants signifies contention.   *(T)*

To dream of watching ants at work indicates for a young man that he will for a time try to find pleasure in the idle and single life, but that he will at last discover that the truest happiness lies in hard work for the sake of wife and children. The same dream occurring to a young woman foretells that she will soon leave her present way of life to become a housewife and mother.   *(O)*

To see a swarm of ants denotes that, providing you look for it, you will enjoy a large increase in your business.   *(M)*

Good fortune by moving house.   *(OM)*

Dreaming of ants indicates an earthly covetous mind; and as they are subterranean creatures, it also shows the dreamer will not be long-lived. They are good for anyone who works with the public, or to anyone who is sick, if the ants come near them in the dream.   *(D&M2)*

To dream you see ants with wings is not good, for it indicates injury or a dangerous voyage. Common ants are good for they signify fertility, especially to the sick, unless they run across the body of the patient then it nears death, since they are the daughters of the earth and are cold and black.   *(A)*

———————— ♦ ————————

ANTHEM

To hear an anthem played or sung denotes that you will visit a sick friend living some distance away from you. If the music is lively you will profit by the journey.   *(M)*

———————— ♦ ————————

ANVIL

To hear the sound of the anvil is a good dream.
> Tis music of labour and health,
> Brings gladness and joy in its train;
> Prosperity, happiness, wealth,
> Redown to great credit and gain,
> The young may rejoice in the sound—
> The aged long years will attain,
> Young maidens with beauty be crown'd
> And be free from all sorrow and pain.   *(M)*

———————— ♦ ————————

ANXIETY

If you suffer anxiety without being able to find out the cause, be wary if

during the week following someone offers to do you a favour — it will be a
trap.   *(M)*

———— ♦ ————

APES

All sorts of apes and monkeys signify malicious, weak, strange and secret
enemies.   *(T)*

To see an ape denotes that you are in danger from the society you
frequent, of acquiring objectionable habits both of thought and
expression.   *(O)*

To an engaged person this animal denotes a speedy marriage. A married
person will soon be rejoicing over some domestic event.   *(M)*

Strange enemies and deceitfulness.   *(OM)*

See also **MONKEYS.**

———— ♦ ————

APOPLEXY

To be seized with a fit of apoplexy is a sign of inability of the blood to fulfil
its functions. Lowness of spirit and general debility of the system will
follow this dream, unless you strengthen your body with iron and tonics. *(M)*

To suffer or see others suffering from this seizure signifies that your
interests are in danger.   *(C)*

———— ♦ ————

APPAREL

If your apparel is suited to the season of the year it denotes prosperity and
happiness.   *(GD*

Being dressed in fine clothes means that you are in danger of indulging
in extravagance which can have no end but poverty. If you dream of being
in rags, your industry and common sense will in the long run be rewarded
by wealth and reputation.   *(O)*

For a wife or husband to dream of wearing the other's clothes is an
omen that the dreamer will outlive his or her partner. Buying clothes
signifies honour and beauty. Going into company scantily dressed is a sign
of vexation. If you see yourself gaudily dressed, misfortune will follow, but
if you are dressed in rags, then you will have nothing to complain of. If
your clothing is scarlet, it is a warning of an impending calamity; if white,
you will be successful in business and in love. Green predicts a long
journey; black, bad luck in love; blue, happiness; yellow, jealousy and
bickering over love affairs; crimson, that good news is coming to you from
a distance.   *(M)*

To dream you are dressed in white is a sure sign of success in the first
object you undertake. To dream you are dressed in green denotes that you
are about to take a journey to your advantage. To be dressed in black is an
unlucky omen. To be dressed in blue denotes happiness, and scarlet warns
you of some very sad calamity. To dream you are dressed in yellow is

rather lucky than otherwise. Crimson denotes that you will live to a ripe old age. To dream that you are dressed in a variety of colours denotes you will experience a variety of fortunes. *(OM)*

> When decent and proper, propense to the season,
> Propounds all your wishes fulfilled, if in reason,
> If white, your success is most clear and undoubted
> Your lover is constant, your rivals all scouted,
> When 'tis green, you will travel with gain to abroad,
> And reign in your Strephon's affections the lord,
> Black is unlucky and reverts to law-suits
> And beware of a journey, lest you fall in with brutes.
> The person you love is afflicted in spirit,
> And the heart of the object suspicions inherit.
> Blue, purple, or puce, denotes love and esteem,
> And the friends you have lost will your conduct redeem,
> Scarlet portends losses, sickness and quarrels
> Loud and boisterous as gunpowder exploding in barrels,
> Miscarriage to women — death of children, or rage —
> In a word 'tis a colour all troubles presage.
> Yellow is indicative e'er of suspicion,
> If married, beware of your wife's indiscretion.
> Whilst crimson unfolds pleasant news from afar,
> And naught intervenes your affections to mar.
> Varied colours — vicissitudes aptly imply,
> Past, or in prospect, though may hap very nigh
> To dream you're dressed shabby is not a good sign
> But if in high style you've no cause to repine. *(MS)*

See also **CLOTHES, DRESS, GARMENTS.**

———————— ♦ ————————

APPARITION

To see a ghost is very unfortunate. If it is attractive and dressed in white, it shows deceit and temptation to sin; if you are in love it is a sign of unrequited love; someone is about to deceive you, and you are friendly with your worst enemy. Do not undertake a journey at this period for it will be unfortunate. *(GD)*

> To dream a spectre doth appear,
> Portends a fit of sickness near;
> Then pause, and thou may'st break the spell,
> Be thou more temperate and be well. *(NM)*

> These phantoms denote that some mischiefs is nigh,
> Yet should it address you, you will soon tell a lie. *(MS)*

See also **GHOSTS.**

APPETITE
To appease your appetite by eating something you especially like is a sign that you will shortly lose some of your robust and healthy looks; pallid cheeks and gradual weight loss will make your friends concerned at the appearance of decline. *(M)*

To have an appetite indicates the departure of friends; a failing appetite signifies bad news. *(C)*

———— ♦ ————

APPLAUSE
To gain the applause of your friends means that you will become the object of libel or defamation of character in some of the newspapers. Law-suits and quarrels may well follow shortly after this dream. *(M)*

———— ♦ ————

APPLES and APPLE TREES
To see apple trees and eat sweet apples signifies joy, pleasure and recreation, especially to women and girls; sour apples denote contention and sedition. To eat apples signifies anger. To gather apples signifies vexation from some person or other. *(T)*

In contradiction to this the following interpretation is given by *Dreams and Moles and their Significations, 1810*. To dream of gathering apples is a sign of mirth and joy. *(D&M2)*

Long life and success; a boy giving apples to a pregnant woman means faithfulness in your sweetheart, and riches in business. *(GD)*

Seeing an apple tree coming into bloom is an encouraging dream for any who are in low spirits. It is a sign that fortune will shortly shine on them, and that the best of their days are yet to come. *(O)*

To dream that you are eating apples is a good omen promising a long and happy life, although in some cases misfortune will have to be surmounted before the happiness is reached.

> In season this dream is a token most good,
> Tho' perhaps if they're sour, mischief's understood;
> Yet if they are sweet and delicious to taste,
> If about to be married — tarry not but make haste. *(MS)*

———— ♦ ————

APRICOTS
To see or eat apricots in season denotes good health and pleasure; but if you seem to eat them out of season, they signify vain hopes and business failures. *(T)*

To dream of apricots denotes health and prosperity, a speedy marriage, dutiful children and success in love. *(OM)*

———— ♦ ————

APRICOT TREES
This fruit tree denotes pleasure and contentment; if it is loaded with fruits,

———— 28 ————

exercise prudence; while if the fruit has been picked you will enjoy prosperity. To see it loaded with fruit out of season denotes unexpected success; though if the fruit is withered guard against boredom and lassitude. *(C)*

───────── ◆ ─────────

APRIL
This signifies that you will obtain everything you desire and the greatest success will attend all those projects on which you have most set your heart. *(C)*

───────── ◆ ─────────

APRIL FOOL
When a young woman dreams of being made an April Fool, it means that, after having arrived at considerable culture, she will marry one who is a Philistine and so be exposed to unintelligent criticism and interference.

A man dreaming of being made an April Fool may anticipate falling a victim to the false pretences of one in whom he is at present confiding, and may reasonably infer that his only safeguard is a little healthy suspicion. *(O)*

───────── ◆ ─────────

APRON
If a young lady dreams she tears her apron she will meet a young man of wealth, who with skilful handling and encouragement will prove a good husband.

To a married woman the dream promises children who will be her pride in later years. *(M)*

───────── ◆ ─────────

ARAB
For a young woman to dream of seeing an Arab is a sign that she will meet with a young man of orderly and sober demeanour who will speak of marriage but will not have the courage to carry his speech into effect. *(M)*

───────── ◆ ─────────

ARCH
For a young man to dream that he walks with his sweetheart under a railway arch is a sign of opposition from her parents. For a young woman to have this dream is a sign that she will be annoyed by the attentions of her lover's rival, who will come to her home or meet her in the street, and entreat her to listen to his promises. *(M)*

To dream of an arch signifies that you will be flattered. You must take this dream as a warning against the flatterer. *(C)*

───────── ◆ ─────────

ARCHBISHOP
To dream of one, foretells danger in the night. *(C)*

ARCHITECT

To dream that you have business with an architect is a sign that you will incur unexpected expenses, and will have trouble of a character that you have never had before. *(M)*

To dream of one signifies approaching prosperity for the dreamer. *(C)*

———— ◆ ————

ARCHIVES

To dream of archives signifies that an inheritance will be disputed in your family. *(C)*

———— ◆ ————

ARGUING

To dream you argue with intelligent people signifies profit and gain. *(T)*

———— ◆ ————

ARMED MEN

To see armed men is a good sign and denotes a fearless person; to dream you see an armed man run away is a sign of victory; to see armed men attack you signifies sadness. *(OM)*

———— ◆ ————

ARMENIAN

This signifies that you will be pestered by the curiosity of your wife. *(C)*

———— ◆ ————

ARMOUR

A warning to take precautions. *(C)*

———— ◆ ————

ARMS

If any one dreams that his arms have grown bigger and stronger than normal, it signifies that his brothers or his sons will help him gain happiness and profit, and he will become rich. If a woman dreams this, her husband will increase in property and authority. To dream that you have strong arms signifies good fortune, restoration of health, or freedom from imprisonment. To dream your arms or elbows are covered in scabs or ulcers signifies annoyance, sadness and failure in business. If your arms are broken or thin, that is a bad sign, and if you are a powerful person, beware of a loss of authority or an illness attacking your son or brother. This same dream denotes problems, sickness and poverty to the children or brothers of ordinary people. If a woman has this dream, she is in danger of becoming a widow or at least of a separation from her husband. To dream that one of your arms has been cut off signifies the death of your father, son, brother or friend. To dream both arms have been cut off signifies imprisonment or sickness. Some authors attribute the right arm to the father, son, brother and friend; and the left to the mother, daughter, sister, the friend and the loyal employees. *(T)*

To dream you have an arm amputated denotes the death of a relative or faithful servant; male, if it is the right arm; female, if the left. To have both arms amputated means captivity or severe sickness. A broken or thin arm means sickness, affliction, distress in the family; for a married woman, death of her husband, or at least separation from him. If your arm is dirty, it signifies distress, anxiety. A swollen arm indicates riches for a brother or close, affectionate relative. Strong and robust arms signify happiness, recovery from illness or benevolence. Arms larger and more robust than usual indicate joy, profit or unexpected riches. For a woman, it means increase of wealth and power for her husband. Hairy arms foretell increasing wealth. *(M)*

To dream your arms are withered is a sign that your health and fortune will decay. To dream they have grown strong signifies that you will experience an unexpected success. To dream that your right arm is cut off denotes that you will lose some male relation. To dream your left arm is cut off denotes you will lose a close female relation. *(OM)*

─────── ◆ ───────

ARMY
To see an army of soldiers denotes the loss of friends through circumstances over which you have no control. *(M)*

To dream of an army signifies ruin. If it goes into battle, your goods will be wasted by those in whom you have placed the utmost confidence. To dream of a victorious army signifies that you will suffer sadness and grief. A vanquished army signifies the disenchantment of a long courtship. *(C)*

─────── ◆ ───────

ARRESTED
> Ominous always of sadness and trouble,
> Yet e'er when released from care proves but a bubble. *(MS)*

To dream you are arrested signifies lack of wit and determination. *(D&M2)*

─────── ◆ ───────

ARROW
An arrow in flight is a good sign for any love affair that may follow. If, however, the arrow is lying on the ground or is broken, look for sorrow connected with your lover. *(M)*

─────── ◆ ───────

ARSENIC
To dream of arsenic signifies poverty but good health. If you receive arsenic from a friend your virtues will be rewarded. If you give arsenic, you will encounter opposition while trying to perform a good action. *(C)*

─────── ◆ ───────

ARTICHOKES
Vexations and troubles which, however, you will surmount. *(M)*

To dream of this vegetable signifies grief; fried artichokes denote quarrels. *(C)*

ARTIST
This dream means great misfortune; to a lover such a dream indicates that he or she will be jealous because of seeing someone in the company of their partner. *(M)*

———— ♦ ————

ASCEND
To ascend a mountain signifies that your wife will deceive you. *(C)*

———— ♦ ————

ASHES
Misfortune and losses. *(OM)*

———— ♦ ————

ASLEEP
To dream that you are falling asleep is a bad omen for a busy person, unless it proves just a timely hint, because it signifies that he or she is likely to take great pains, but will work in such a drowsy way that the result will be small compared with the work involved. *(O)*

———— ♦ ————

ASPARAGUS
Signifies labour, reward and success. To cultivate asparagus denotes approaching fortune. To eat asparagus is a sign that you and your family will have reason for celebration. To sell asparagus signifies that you will receive money. *(C)*

———— ♦ ————

ASPIC
This signifies money, profitable partnership and an advantageous marriage. *(C)*

———— ♦ ————

ASSAULT
To dream that you are being attacked signifies that your servants have full knowledge of your most private secrets. If you are playfully attacked, it denotes that you will meet with well-earned success. To dream you are assaulted signifies suffering and misery. *(C)*

———— ♦ ————

ASSES
The ass denotes a good servant or slave that is profitable to his master; it signifies also a foolish and ignorant person. To dream you see an ass run signifies misfortune; for a sick person to dream he runs is a very bad sign. To hear an ass bray signifies damage. To see an ass sitting down signifies laboriousness. *(T)*

To dream an ass runs after you, denotes that some slander will be raised against you by a foolish person, who will themselves become the victims of the scandal. *(GD2)*

To dream of seeing an ass denotes that you will spend much valuable time in trying to please everybody, but if the ass is looking away from you, you can take courage, for you will end in being indifferent to the opinion of the others as long as you have the approval of your own common sense. *(O)*

To ride an ass who carries you well is a sign of a good marriage. To dream that an ass has kicked you is a prediction of a serious and perhaps fatal illness. *(M)*

To dream you are riding on an ass is the forerunner of a foolish quarrel. To dream you are driving an ass denotes that you will experience some trouble, but will get the better of it. *(OM)*

ASTER
This flower is an unusually good dream. You will attain proficiency in your occupation, and your judgement and intelligence will become stronger than ever; your love of justice, virtue and honesty will increase. *(M)*

ASTHMA
To dream you are subject to this complaint is a sign that you will be attacked by inflammation of the lungs, and may be so ill that the doctors will fear for your life. You will recover, however, to experience general good health. *(M)*

To dream of this disease signifies that you will discover trickery and combat it. *(C)*

ASTONISHMENT
Signifies recovery from sickness. *(C)*

ASYLUM
To dream that you are in an asylum denotes that you will become famous through some great achievement. *(M)*

To dream of an asylum is a good augury and indicates a way out of all your difficulties. *(C)*

ATHLETE
This signifies adventurous undertakings or business negotiations. *(C)*

ATLAS
To dream that you study an atlas is a sign that you will have commercial transactions, if you are in trade, with some distant parts of the world where you have never traded before. If you are a retailer, foreign produce will be more in demand than before. A workman may have the offer of a situation in a distant part of this country. *(M)*

AUCTION
A warning to be on your guard against being cheated by a plausible acquaintance. Trust only your dearest friends after such a dream. *(M)*

To dream of a sale denotes trials and tribulation in all your affairs. *(C)*

AUTHORITY
It is always good for a rich man to think or dream he is in authority. *(D&M2)*

AUTOMATON
To see an automaton signifies that your child will be as mischievous as a monkey. *(C)*

AUTUMN
This season signifies a legacy and domestic happiness. *(C)*

AVARICE
To dream that you are avaricious or see other people's greed foretells that you will lose your money by foolish speculation. *(C)*

AVENUE
To dream of an avenue signifies an early understanding with the person you most desire. *(C)*

BABY

For a mother to dream that her baby is ill denotes its general good health, and prosperous times in her husband's vocation. To dream that her baby is dead is a sign of the early marriage of her eldest child, who will gain a wealthier position in life than her parents have done. To nurse a strange baby foretells sickness in your family. If the strange baby is ill, look for a death, but not necessarily in your immediate family. *(M)*

———————— ◆ ————————

BACK

To see your back signifies bad luck and old age. To dream a man's back is broken, injured or scabby, signifies that his enemies will get the better of him and that he will be mocked by everyone. *(T)*

———————— ◆ ————————

BACK-BITE

To dream that your character is the subject of scandal by back-biters is a sign that you will be able to gain the object of some of your wishes and have the satisfaction of knowing that others will not ridicule your efforts to do good, and lead an honourable and decent life. Expect to hear someone in authority speak very highly of your character after you have had this dream. *(M)*

———————— ◆ ————————

BACKBONE

To dream of the backbone signifies health and joy, and that the dreamer will take delight in his wife and children. *(D&M2)*

———————— ◆ ————————

BACK DOOR

When a working girl dreams that she meets her lover near the back door of her employer's house, she may feel certain that her boyfriend will desert her for another girl living nearby, or he will get into trouble which will force him to move. *(M)*

———————— ◆ ————————

BACKGAMMON

To play this game is indicative of advancement in theological study. You will become more studious in your habits and, by close application, become proficient in some of the sciences. *(M)*

BACON

To cut bacon signifies the death of someone. To eat bacon signifies gossiping. *(T)*

If you dream of eating bacon you need fear nothing in business; but if you see fat bacon be wary of an attempt to ruin you. *(M)*

Bacon denotes death of a friend or relation. *(OM)*

> Is ominous e'er of the death of a friend,
> And prevalent scandal will gain its full end. *(MS)*

◆

BAG

To dream of carrying a full bag means that you will never have much wealth, but that you will always have as much as you really need. To dream of carrying an empty bag signifies approaching poverty. If the bag is so full that it is impossible to close it, you may expect to receive from somewhere so much money that looking after it will be a constant anxiety. *(O)*

◆

BAGPIPES

Wind instruments such as bagpipes signify trouble, contention and losing a legal battle. *(T)*

To hear the music of bagpipes is a warning of trouble. For a business man, it indicates failure. *(M)*

To play the bagpipes signifies trouble, contention, and losing a legal battle. *(D&M2)*

In contradiction to these last three interpretations, Artemidorous says, 'To dream you play upon bagpipes is good for all, in all ways.' *(A)*

◆

BAILIFF

To dream that the bailiff seizes your household goods for debt is a sign that you will have some unexpected favourable change in your circumstances. It will turn out that you are next of kin to some wealthy person who has died, either in this country or abroad, who has left you a very handsome legacy. You will do well to keep down your domestic expenses, as this dream repeated immediately sometimes has the opposite meaning. *(M)*

◆

BAKER

If you dream of a baker or a baker's shop before applying for a situation or an increase in wages you may be sure that your application will be successful. In other circumstances, such a dream denotes everything that is good. *(M)*

Good fortune is just around the corner. *(OM)*

◆

BAKERY

For a newly-married woman to dream that she is in a bakery signifies that her husband will lose his present employment, and will suffer from scarcity of food and clothing. For a young man to have this dream, his parent or parents, if living, will need social benefits. *(M)*

———— ◆ ————

BAKING
To dream that you are engaged in baking something in an oven is a sure sign that enemies are about to harm you. Be careful of your so-called friends. *(M)*

———— ◆ ————

BAKING and BREWING
To dream of baking and brewing means a bad housewife, who lies in bed when she should be at work. *(OM)*

———— ◆ ————

BALCONY
For an unmarried woman to dream that she is sitting on a balcony with her sweetheart denotes interruption in courtship from a quarter she little expected. Some lingering disease will afflict her lover and keep him in bed for a long time; she will also be afraid that some former sweetheart will gain his affections, but her petty jealousy will soon pass, and she will enjoy his undivided love. *(M)*

———— ◆ ————

BALD
To dream that you are bald or growing bald means that you are about to lose your heart, but it is at the same time a suggestion that that is no reason why you should lose your head. *(O)*

If a young woman dreams that her lover is bald, he will not live to marry her. To dream that one's own head is bald denotes worry. *(M)*

———— ◆ ————

BALL
Dreams of being at balls and dances and such-like festivities are a good omen for lovers:

> Who dream at being at a ball
> No cause have they for fear, .
> For soon they will united be
> To those they hold most dear. *(O)*

To dream you see persons dance at a ball, or that you are at a ball yourself signifies joy, pleasure, recreation or inheritance. *(D&M2)*

———— ◆ ————

BALLET
To see a performance of this kind at the theatre is indicative of your having attacks of gout or rheumatism, sometimes serious. *(M)*

BALLOON

To dream of an ascent of a balloon means that to gain what you want you will have to stoop pretty low, but that, thanks to the lucky star under which you were born, will not stop you from rising up again. *(O)*

To dream that you are in a balloon predicts a perilous journey. *(M)*
Lack of success in business. *(OM)*
To ascend in a balloon foretells difficulties from domestics. *(C)*

———— ♦ ————

BANANA

A good omen; if you dream you are eating a banana it is a sign you will be rich and happy. To dream you see bananas growing denotes success in love. *(M)*

———— ♦ ————

BANDY

To dream that your legs have become crooked or misshapen is a sign that a young man will become tall, straight and good-looking. If an old person has this dream it means that in their old age they will become a good walker, full of vigour and energy, free from nervousness or other physical debility. *(M)*

———— ♦ ————

BANISHMENT

To dream that you are driven from your place of abode, or exiled from your native country, is a good dream.

> A ripe old age your life shall crown,
> And all around you men will own
> Your worth by pedestal and bust,
> Because your virtue they can trust;
> A benefactor you will be
> To those who strive in poverty;
> Your worldly store you'll freely give
> To those who round your dwelling live;
> In future time they'll praise your name,
> For goodness will enhance your fame. *(M)*

———— ♦ ————

BANK

Paying a visit to the bank means, if you are in business, that you are likely to have many bad and doubtful debts, and that unless you adopt a system of prompt cash payment and no credit your ledger will present a long series of accounts balanced by death, 'running away', 'failure' and other similarly unremunerative items. *(O)*

A dream of a bank should be taken as a warning against investment for some time to come. *(M)*

———— 38 ————

BANK BOOK

To see a bank book in a dream is a bad sign, indicating that you will be a heavy loser by someone converting to his own use a cheque with which you have entrusted him. Should a bank book, however, be seen lying on the bank counter or in the hands of a bank teller, it signifies that, however long you live, you will never have any financial worries. *(O)*

———— ♦ ————

BANKER

To dream you have business with a banker is a sign of losing part of your trade through great competition in the type of goods in which you deal. If a person not in business has this dream it means that he will shortly lose part of his wages from slackness of trade or sickness. *(M)*

———— ♦ ————

BANK NOTE

To dream of having a bank note stolen foretells that you are about to lose money and be reduced to comparative poverty, but if you are philosophical about your loss you will be happier with little than you have ever been, or were likely to be, with a great deal. *(O)*

———— ♦ ————

BANNER

A good omen, this signifies a speedy rise to a good position for a man and a wealthy marriage and prosperous life for a woman. *(M)*

———— ♦ ————

BANNS

To dream that you are listening to your own banns is indicative of good and prosperous times for the dreamer, who will become a great favourite in his or her circle of acquaintances. *(M)*

———— ♦ ————

BANQUET

To dream of banquets is a very good sign of prosperity, and promises promotion. *(M)*

To dream that you are at banquets and do not eat, denotes shortage of money. *(P&F)*

———— ♦ ————

BAPTISM

To be present at a baptism is an omen of riches or success in love, according to whether you are married or single. *(M)*

———— ♦ ————

BAR

To dream that you are drinking at the bar of a public house is a good sign. You will avoid the society of those who are loud-mouthed, profligate and disorderly. Your children will grow up virtuous and wise. To dream that you are called to practise at the bar as a lawyer signifies that you will take part in a trial from which you will come away victorious. *(M)*

◆

BARBER

If you dream of a barber or his shop, be careful to follow any advice you may receive from your friends during the following week. If you don't, you may experience loss and even poverty. *(M)*

◆

BAREFOOT

To go on a journey barefoot is a sign of prosperity. You will do well as a merchant, lawyer, artist or in any trade or profesison you may take up. You will also enjoy your travels and meet with good and pleasant company. If you speculate, you will generally be fortunate in your ventures; you will make a fortune by careful trading, and retire in old age with a very handsome pension. *(M)*

◆

BARKING

To dream that you are barking denotes a fundamental improvement in your character. If you hear a dog barking, it is a sign that you will win a lawsuit; if you hear a dog nearby baying at the moon, you will be called upon to help someone. If you are being followed by a pack of barking dogs led by a servant, it signifies approaching danger due to some past folly. *(C)*

To dream of the barking of dogs signifies insulting enemies and detractors who will crow over those who fail to achieve wealth. *(D&M2)*

◆

BARLEY and BARLEY BREAD

Eating barley bread indicates health and comfort. *(M)*
   Eating barley bread signifies health and content. *(D&M2)*
   A good omen; riches await you. *(OM)*

◆

BARLEY FIELD

To dream that you go through a field of ripe barley at an unseasonable time is indicative of great trouble soon coming upon you; either you will lose relatives and friends, or you will be unfortunate in your choice of a partner in life, or sickness and poverty will strike before many months or years are over. *(M)*

◆

BARMAID

For a young man to dream that he has made love to a barmaid is a sign that he will be called upon to leave his present home and occupation, and either emigrate to a foreign country or seek a situation in a distant part of his own country. To dream that you have married a barmaid means that you will fall into an easy situation and that it will not require either much skill or physical energy to do the duties assigned to your new job. *(M)*

BARN

To see a barn stored with corn signifies either that you will marry a rich wife, overthrow your enemy at law, that you will inherit land or grow rich by trading or gifts; it also signifies banqueting or celebrations.   *(T)*

To dream of having a large barn well filled, or of seeing one, means to a young man, marriage to a rich wife. A young woman having a similar dream can expect to meet a wealthy partner.   *(O)*

To dream of a barn is a good or bad omen, according to whether the barn is full or empty. If the latter, be prepared for some calamity involving the loss of your money.   *(M)*

A full barn means marriage and money; an empty one, poverty; a barn on fire means good fortune.   *(OM)*

———— ♦ ————

BASIN

To dream of a basin signifies a nice working girl, and to dream you eat or drink from one shows you are in love with that working girl. For a man to see himself in a basin denotes that he will have children by a working girl.   *(D&M2)*

———— ♦ ————

BASKET

For a man to dream of baskets is bad; it denotes poor business to a merchant, lack of employment to a mechanic and loss of place to a servant; but if a woman dreams she receives a number of baskets, it is good.   *(OM)*

———— ♦ ————

BASSOON

To play this wind instrument is a sign that before very long you will be requested by a friend to take part in an amateur performance for the benefit of a charitable institution.   *(M)*

———— ♦ ————

BASTE

To dream that you are in the act of basting a fowl or joint of meat that is cooking is a sign that you will soon marry. In a mysterious and unplanned way, you will meet someone who will either propose to you or you to them, and you will lead a happy and prosperous life together.   *(M)*

———— ♦ ————

BAT

Bats or night birds of any kind are a bad omen and anyone who dreams of them must undertake no business that day.   *(T)*

To dream that you see a bat flying about in the dusk of the evening signifies that you will meet a person of a deceitful disposition and character. They will propose that you become a business partner, but in fact they are only trying to swindle you out of your hard-earned income, and live at the expense of your forethought.   *(M)*

BATH

To see a bath is a sign of suffering or grief. If a person dreams he goes into, or sees himself in a bath, and that he finds it too hot, he will be troubled and afflicted by members of his family. *(M)*

———————— ♦ ————————

BATHING

Anyone who frequently sees others or themselves bathing naked are of a phlegmatic constitution and subject to delusions. To bathe in a clear fountain signifies joy. *(T)*

To dream of a bath is bad; expect after it to experience many hardships and sorrows; if you are in love, problems await you and your sweetheart. *(GD)*

For anyone in trouble to dream of bathing either in the sea or in a river or lake means that the trouble is about to come to an end, and that a fortunate period will follow. *(O)*

To dream you are washing yourself in clean water denotes happiness, prosperity and success in love; if the water is dirty, it foretells shame, sorrow and a disappointment in love. *(OM)*

To dream you wash or bathe yourself in a hot bath signifies riches and prosperity to the sick, but is bad for a poor man if he washes himself and has many people to help rub him, for it foretells a long sickness. In short, it is evil to the rich if he is alone and has nobody to help him. *(A)*

> If the water be clear, success will elate you,
> But if it be muddy, great troubles await you,
> Yet if in the nude your sweetheart appear,
> Laveing her charms with 'eau' crystal clear,
> It signifies certain, to wed you must hurry,
> Or else in a short time you both will be sorry. *(MS)*

———————— ♦ ————————

BATTALION

For a young woman to dream that she sees a battalion of soldiers on parade is a sign that she will never gain the love of one who wears a service uniform. *(M)*

———————— ♦ ————————

BATTERY

For a young man to dream he stands in front of a battery is a sign that he will be called upon to take the place of a fellow workman who is in the Territorials and on a training exercise in some distant part of the country. *(M)*

———————— ♦ ————————

BATTLE

To see a battle in the street forewarns you against secret enemies; if you are in love your sweetheart is false to you; it is also a sign of war and tumult. *(GD)*

——————————— 42 ———————————

Dreaming of being present at, or engaged in a battle predicts that you will shortly try to be the peacemaker between two friends, and that in consequence you will get yourself into a bad scrape. *(O)*

A battle implies that you will have a quarrel with your sweetheart, although much joy may await you afterwards. *(M)*

To dream of a battle in the streets forewarns you against secret enemies, who will try to harm you. If you are in love, your sweetheart is unfaithful. *(OM)*

———— ♦ ————

BAY TREE

The bay tree denotes a rich and beautiful wife; and also failure of affairs because it is bitter; but it is good for physicians, poets and religious people to dream of this. *(M)*

———— ♦ ————

BAYONET

For a soldier to dream that his bayonet is broken is a bad sign. He will be brought into disgrace by misconduct; if he has obtained promotion he will be degraded to the ranks. If he sees his bayonet shining brightly he will gain the confidence of his superiors, and will soon gain advancement. For a soldier to dream that he uses his bayonet in a battle charge is indicative of his long enjoyment of peace. *(M)*

———— ♦ ————

BAZAAR

To help at a bazaar is a forecast that you will have many lovers; and if you marry early it will prove to be a wealthy match, even though at the time it may not appear to be so. *(M)*

———— ♦ ————

BEAM

If you see a beam break or fall from a height, it is a bad omen, often predicting the death of someone near. *(M)*

———— ♦ ————

BEANS

Seeing the land sown with beans denotes affliction and trouble. To dream of eating beans signifies trouble, arguments and illness. *(T)*

If you are eating beans, you may expect to be invited to a feast. To a person engaged to be married the dream predicts a happy married life and good children; to a person in service it predicts a legacy sufficiently large to make the dreamer independent. *(M)*

To dream you are eating beans signifies trouble and arguments. *(OM)*

———— ♦ ————

BEAR

To see a bear signifies a rich, inexpert, cruel and audacious enemy. *(T)* and *(D&M2)*

If the animal pursues you, then look to your friends — one of them is trying to do you an injury. If, on the other hand, you stroke or pet the beast, you may be sure that your lover will be true to you and bring you much happiness. *(M)*

Persecution; victory over your enemies. *(OM)*

———— ♦ ————

BEARD

Anyone who dreams he has his beard trimmed will be in danger of losing a great part of his property, of being sick, or run the risk of losing his life by some humiliating death. If anyone dreams that his beard has grown bigger than usual, he will grow richer. To dream you have a small beard signifies suits and controversies at law. To have a long beard signifies strength or gain. To see your beard dry signifies joy. To see your beard pulled out by the roots signifies great danger. To dream you wash your beard signifies sadness. *(T)*

For a man to dream he has a long beard denotes good fortune; if he is in trade, he will thrive; if he is in love, he will marry his present lover who will bring him some money; if he is a farmer, it denotes good crops and an addition to his farm. If a married woman dreams of a beard, it is unlucky; it foretells the loss of her husband, and that she will fall into great distress. If a girl dreams of a beard, it denotes that she will soon be married, and that her first child will be a boy. For a woman to dream that she has a beard is a very lucky omen, and denotes that she will speedily attain her greatest desires. *(OM)*

For orators, ambassadors, lawyers or philosophers to dream of a long, rough and thick beard shows success; and for a widow to dream that she has a beard shows that she will remarry and have a loving husband again. To married women it signifies the death of their husband. To dream of your beard falling out or being cut off shows the dreamer will either lose his parents or turn dishonest. *(D&M2)*

For a young child to dream they have a beard signifies death, but to a young man it is a sign he will rise by his own efforts and achieve his greatest ambitions. *(A)*

———— ♦ ————

BEASTS

To dream any furious beast assaults you, such as a bull, bear, lion or dog etc., denotes open enemies plotting against you. *(GFT)*

To dream you have the head of a lion, a wolf, a panther or an elephant instead of your own is good. Anyone who tries something which is apparently beyond his power, if he has had this dream, will attain respect and dignity. To dream you have the head of a dog, horse or ass, etc., means pain and misery. To have a bird's head means you should not stay long in the country. *(A)*

BEATING

If a woman dreams that she beats her husband, that signifies fear, although her husband loves her. If she dreams she strikes her lover, that signifies she is insecure and her lover will get into trouble.   *(T)*

For married people to dream of beating someone shows that they will live a peaceful life; to bachelors, good fortune in their love affairs; if a lover beats his mistress it shows that the match will be broken off.   *(M)*

———————— ◆ ————————

BEAUTY

To dream that you are beautiful generally foretells an illness or disease of the skin, which will detract from your present good looks.   *(M)*

———————— ◆ ————————

BED

To see the bedposts on fire without being destroyed signifies good fortune to male children.   *(T)*

To dream of sitting on a girl's bedside or talking with her is a sign of marriage.   *(GD)*

To dream of buying a bed denotes sickness.   *(M)*

To dream you go to the bedside of your lover foretells a speedy marriage; if you dream you get into bed, you will have a child within twelve months after marriage, who will become rich and support you.   *(D&M2)*

———————— ◆ ————————

BEDCLOTHES

For a wealthy person to dream of bedclothes is very unlucky; it implies a change in circumstances for the worse. But for poor people to dream of bedclothes denotes a change for the better, especially if the bedclothes are clean.   *(M)*

———————— ◆ ————————

BEDLAM

For a young man to dream that he becomes an inmate of a madhouse is a sign that he will shortly be offered a post of responsibility and trust, where he will be required to take on many new responsibilities. He will be well regarded for his sound judgement and good conduct. For a woman to have this dream is a sign that some of her relatives will conduct themselves bravely under trying circumstances, such as saving the life of a person who has accidentally fallen into a river, or rescuing a person from death by fire.   *(M)*

———————— ◆ ————————

BED-MAKING

To all those estranged to this useful employ,
Importeth some sudden and provident joy;
And when you shall turn them, removals appear,
Alteration of station and pregnancy near.   *(MS)*

BEDROOM

For a young woman to dream that she is in a very beautiful bedroom, well furnished with expensive furniture and drapery, is a sign that there will shortly be a very strange change in the circumstances of her life. Be prepared to hear that some wealthy old bachelor asks you to be his housekeeper; and if you refuse he will propose marriage.   *(M)*

———— ♦ ————

BEDSPREAD

To dream that your bedspread is torn means that one of your family will be born disabled, or be disabled by an accident. You will experience good luck if you see a hideous insect or reptile on the bedspread; you, your wife or children will inherit from someone you knew nothing about.   *(M)*

A torn bedspread means an accident to someone in your house.   *(OM)*

———— ♦ ————

BEECH TREES

Signify promiscuous women, and are good for those who are involved in shady business; to others they mean pain and hard work.   *(D&M2)*

———— ♦ ————

BEEF

To dream of eating beef is a sure omen of the death of a friend or relative. *(M)*

———— ♦ ————

BEER

If you are drinking beer you may take it as a prediction that, unless you are careful, you will lose a large sum of money. Above all, avoid horseracing and lotteries. If you only see the beer without drinking it, an accident will follow.   *(M)*

———— ♦ ————

BEES

To see bees signifies profit to country people and trouble to the rich; but if they dream they make their honey in any part of the house that signifies dignity, eloquence and good success in business. If you are stung by a bee that signifies anxiety and trouble caused by envious people.   *(T)*

To dream of bees means general good fortune.

> Happy the man who dreaming sees
> The little humble busy bees
> Fly humming round their hive.   *(O)*

If a swarm of bees hover around you without hurting you, you will be wealthy and respected, but if one stings you, your partner will prove unfaithful. A queen bee alone denotes the same as a swarm, but a bumble bee predicts travel.   *(M)*

To dream they sting you denotes loss of good reputation, and if you are in love, of your sweetheart. To dream you see bees at work is a very lucky dream. To the poor, they denote comfort, affluence and success.   *(OM)*

To dream of these insects denotes profit and gain to your undertakings. If they swarm over you, you will be happy in your love affairs, and if they make their honey in the house, you will achieve success and praise. Should they be angry, be on your guard against receiving an evil account of yourself. If you take them in your hand you will be notoriously lucky; if you kill them you will be overwhelmed by ruin; to dream you give bees away signifies a good marriage. *(C)*

To dream of bees is good if they don't sting you, but bad if they do. To dream that bees fly about your ears shows you are being annoyed by many enemies but if you beat them off without being stung by them, it is a sign of victory and of your overcoming them. To take bees out of a swarm signifies profit and gain. *(D&M2)*

———— ♦ ————

BEESWAX
Dreaming of beeswax is a sure sign that you will receive a sum of money, or that you will become rich through the inheritance of an unexpected legacy. *(M)*

———— ♦ ————

BEETLES
To dream that black beetles creep down your back is a sign that you will be the subject of a foul slander from those you thought were your friends. If they creep over your face it means that you are the subject of praise from people with whom you have not previously had much connection. To dream that you kill beetles means that you will shortly make active efforts to stop the slanderous rumours circulating about a friend or friend of yours. *(M)*

———— ♦ ————

BEETROOT
Eating medicinal herbs such as beetroots signifies freedom from trouble and expedition of business. *(T)*

Dreaming of beetroot indicates that you have an enemy who is trying to do you an injury, but this will turn out advantageously for you. If you dream that you are eating beetroot it implies the existence of a rival who will steal your lover. *(M)*

———— ♦ ————

BEGGARS
To dream of beggars is rather unfavourable especially to lovers and people in business. To dream they beg alms of you and that you refuse denotes misery, want and a prison. If you are in love, some scandalous person will ruin you with your lover. *(GD)*

Predicts a sudden change in your life which may be better or worse, according to how you act. Be very careful, therefore, and avoid confiding in strangers or acquaintances. To a person contemplating marriage, a dream of a beggar denotes there is a rival for his fiancée's affections, and he will have to act firmly to win. *(M)*

To dream that you give beggars alms indicates success in business, and that you will obtain, after much difficulty, the object of your affections. *(OM)*

To dream of poor people or beggars entering into a house and carrying away anything, whether it is given to them or not, denotes very great adversity. *(D&M2)*

———— ◆ ————

BEHEADING

To dream that you are beheaded according to the traditions of the Indians and Persians and that the head is separated from the body, signifies liberty to prisoners, health to the sick, comfort to those in distress and payment of debts to creditors. To anyone in authority, it indicates good fortune, and that their problems and fears will be turned into joy and confidence in their servants and subjects. If anyone dreams that a person he knows beheads him, he will share with him in his pleasure and honour. If anyone dreams that a young child cuts off his head, he will not live long if he is sick, but if he is healthy, he will gain honour. If a pregnant woman dreams this, she will have a boy and her husband will die suddenly; for he is her head. If anyone dreams his head is half cut off, these things will be fulfilled by halves. If anyone dreams that his throat is cut with a knife, he will be injured by someone. If he dreams he cuts the throat of one of his acquaintance, he will do him an injury; if he does not know the person, it will be done to a stranger. If anyone dreams that he is beheaded as a martyr for religion, that man will be elevated to the height of honour, and his soul will be happy in heaven. According to the Egyptian tradition, if anyone dreams he beheads an armed man, he will enter the service of some great person, where he will realize his ambitions. *(T)*

To dream that you are beheaded, whether justly or otherwise, is bad for anyone who has a father, mother and children, for he will lose them, or whatever he treasures most. This dream is good for anyone who has been accused of any crime, but bad for money lenders, merchants or anyone who collects money. It is also good for debtors and anyone in a far country for they will return home. Anyone awaiting an inheritance will receive it, unless he is not entitled to it. To dream that you have your head between your hands and have been careful to trim and comb your hair, is a sign that you will dispose of your business well and see the end of your problems. *(A)*

———— ◆ ————

BELLE

To dream that you are at a ball, and that you dance with the most beautiful girl is indicative of trouble coming to you from some of your female acquaintances. Expect to hear that a beautiful woman is claiming damages against you for breach of promise of marriage; or you will have your reputation tarnished by a report that you have been cruel to women. You will be given leave of absence from work until any unpleasant affairs have been sorted out to the satisfaction of your employers. For a young woman to dream that she is 'the belle of the ball' means that she will meet with an arrogant, conceited fool who will try to engage her affections. If prudent, she will best serve her own interests by avoiding him in every possible way. *(M)*

------ ♦ ------

BELLOWS

To dream that you with bellows blow the fire,
Means that you can never gain the desire
On which your mind is set;
You will be thwarte ev'ry night and morn,
Unlucky was the day when you were born,
Fate will your work beset. *(M)*

------ ♦ ------

BELLS

To hear bells ring signifies an alarm, disturbance and commotions among the people. To play tunes on small bells signifies discord and disunion between employers and employees. *(T)*

To dream of bells shows sickness. *(D&M)*

To hear bells ringing brings good news to some people, but it generally denotes alarms and arguments, especially if the dreamer is married. *(GD)*

Hearing the church bells ringing as if for a wedding indicates that your lover will shortly leave you for another, then another, all which will be your gain, despite the fact that it will not appear so at first. To hear a bell ring in a dream means that you will soon approach an important point in your career when you will have to try to solve the problem of your career direction and whether you will become powerful and wealthy. *(O)*

If you hear bells ringing, it denotes that someone is anxious to be your friend who will be of great help to you. If you are ringing the bells, misery will be almost sure to follow. *(M)*

Denotes a speedy marriage, and very good news. *(OM)*

To hear the rigning of bells, brings good news to anyone of a sanguine disposition, but to others it shows alarms or disturbances and commotions among the people. To play tunes on small bells signifies discord and disunion between employers and employees. *(D&M2)*

In ringing betokens good news to all folk,
Yet in wedlock prognosticate unpleasant jokes. *(MS)*

------ ♦ ------

BELLY

If anyone dreams that his belly is bigger and fatter than usual his family and property will increase proportionately according to the size of his stomach. If your belly has become lean and shrunken, you will avoid a bad accident. If anyone dreams that his belly is swollen but empty, he will become poor, even though he is well-regarded by many. *(T)*

> To dream one's belly's large and great
> Predicts a fair and large estate. *(N)*

— ◆ —

BELLY ACHE

If anyone dreams his belly aches, he will suffer many family problems. *(D&M2)*

— ◆ —

BENEDICTION

An unexpected and unwelcome wedding. *(OM)*

— ◆ —

BEQUEST

To dream that you are bequeathing money or property to friends or relatives is a sure sign that you will soon receive money from an unexpected quarter. *(M)*

— ◆ —

BETTING

To dream that you are betting warns you to be careful of your money for a time. Keep it on you. Do not lend any money, however small the amount may be, otherwise you will lose it all. *(M)*

— ◆ —

BICYCLE

To dream of riding a bicycle means that for some years you will have constant change, always seeking for rest and comfort, but only finding turmoil and problems. *(O)*

— ◆ —

BIER

To see a bier carried from your house denotes the marriage of a member of your family within a short time. If a coffin is on the bier it is a sign that the wedding clothes and rings for both bride and bridegroom have already been bought, ready for the big day. *(M)*

— ◆ —

BIGAMY

For a man to dream that he is guilty of bigamy is a significant dream. He will meet with a partner soon if he is not married; but if he is, he will keep his wife a long time, in fact, she will in all probability outlive him and re-marry after his death. For a woman to dream that she is guilty of this crime denotes great distress in the death of her present husband from a dreadful accident. *(M)*

— ◆ —

BIRDS

To see many birds signifies law-suits. To hear birds sing signifies love, joy and delight. To hear a cock crow signifies prosperity. To see birds fighting signifies misfortune. To see birds fly over your head signifies prejudice by enemies. To see black birds signifies trouble. *(T)*

Birds entering a house foretells approaching losses, sometimes of friends, but most often of money. *(O)*

To hear birds singing foretells news of a wedding. To see several in a cage predicts a happy home life, although a long journey will tear you away from your friends for some time. *(M)*

To dream of a pair of birds or any other animal signifies the birth of a son. *(C)*

To dream of the chirping or singing of birds signifies happy news, but the croaking of ravens or screeching of owls, the contrary, as it signifies the death of friends. *(GFT)*

> To hear warblers sing is a token of health;
> To catch them; of rising to some sudden wealth;
> Of finding a nest without young, tells dismay,
> Disappointment of prospect and hope everyway;
> In a word, singing birds, where so e'er you may see,
> Indicates you prosperity, honour and glee. *(MS)*

————— ♦ —————

BIRD'S NEST

To dream you find a bird's nest is a good sign. *(T)*

To dream you find a nest without eggs or birds signifies great disappointment. *(D&M2)*

————— ♦ —————

BIRTH

For a sick man, this dream signifies death, because the dead are wrapped in linen clothes as children, and laid in the ground. *(A)*

For a woman to dream she is pregnant denotes sorrow and heaviness. *(P&F)*

If a woman dreams she has given birth to a child although she was not pregnant, it is a sign that she will happily accomplish her intentions. A girl who has this dream will quickly lose her virginity if she is not careful. For a man to dream that he sees two or three children born shows that he will have joy and meet with success in his business. When someone who has no children dreams they have many small children, it signifies you will have many anxieties and obstructions in your affairs. To dream of your birth is good for someone who is poor, but to a rich person, it signifies that he will not be in charge in the house but that others will order him about against his will. *(D&M2)*

> Should a female who's not in the family way,
> Dream of having a child, 'tis most lucky they say;
> But if she's a maid, let her prudence advance,
> Or her chastity stands but a very poor chance. *(MS)*

See also **CHILDBIRTH**.

———— ♦ ————

BISCUITS
To eat biscuits denotes that you will suffer from indigestion and will have to follow a very plain diet. Your stomach will have to be treated very carefully, or other complaints will follow. *(M)*

    A fine and prosperous journey. *(OM)*

———— ♦ ————

BISHOP
Sudden death of a friend or relative. *(OM)*

———— ♦ ————

BITE
To dream you are bitten signifies you will suffer the pangs of jealousy. *(M)*

———— ♦ ————

BLACK
This colour is unlucky to dream of. If you are in love, it denotes that your partner is very unhappy and is about to experience some problems. *(GD)*

———— ♦ ————

BLACKBIRD
To see blackbirds signifies tribulation. *(T)*

    Deceit and slander. *(OM)*

    To see blackbirds signifies great trouble. To hear them sing signifies joy and delight. *(D&M2)*

———— ♦ ————

BLACK CLOTHES
To see yourself in black clothes signifies joy. *(T)*

———— ♦ ————

BLACKSMITH
To dream you work in iron and strike on the anvil signifies trouble and law-suits. *(A)*

———— ♦ ————

BLANKETS
To dream that you buy blankets in summer denotes that an affliction from a fever or severe pleurisy will trouble you. To dream that you buy blankets in winter indicates an attack of a very malignant fever. *(M)*

———— ♦ ————

BLASPHEMY
If you dream you are cursing, it foretells bad fortune; if you are cursed, all your expectations will be fulfilled. *(M)*

BLEAT
To dream that you hear the lambs bleat for their ewes in summer is a good sign. If the dreamer is young, it denotes that they will be a dutiful son or daughter, well regarded by all their friends because of their thoughtfulness.

——————— ♦ ———————   *(M)*

BLIND
To dream that you are blind is a sign that you have placed your confidence in someone who is your most inveterate enemy. Be warned to look out for mistakes and avoid them, particularly in love affairs.   *(GD)*

To dream of being blind is a sure sign that you have put your confidence in someone who is your bitter enemy; it also denotes that your lover is unfaithful and prefers someone else; in business, it denotes that you will lose money, and that your employees lack loyalty.   *(OM)*

To dream of being blind is a warning to see your errors and avoid them especially in love affairs.   *(D&M2)*

To dream you are blind signifies loss of children, brothers, father or mother; though it is a good dream to those who are poor or in prison. In the main, though, a bad dream for travellers, soldiers, traders, navigators, astronomers or astrologers. If anyone is searching for something he has lost, and dreams this dream, he will never find it. Only to poets is this dream good, because they need a great deal of sleep if they want to write poetry.   *(A)*

——————— ♦ ———————

BLINDMAN'S BUFF
To play at this game signifies prosperity, joy, pleasure, health and harmony among friends and relations.   *(T)*

——————— ♦ ———————

BLOOD and BLEEDING
To see blood is about as bad an omen as you can receive. If you are engaged, your sweetheart will lose affection for you, and your friends will prove false. To a business man, failure in some big undertaking and robbery will follow.   *(M)*

To dream of bleeding denotes loss of goods and character, and that your lover will not marry you. To dream you see someone else bleeding indicates that someone who pretends to be your friend is about to take advantage of you. To dream you draw the blood of another denotes that you will recover a law-suit, and be successful in love and business. To dream another draws your blood is a certain sign that you will be unsuccessful in love, business and everything you undertake.   *(OM)*

To dream of vomiting a great deal of bright red blood is good for a poor person, for they will get a store of money. It is also very good for anyone who has no children or whose relatives are abroad. The first will have a child of his own and the second will be reunited with his family. To dream of carrying blood is not good for anyone who is trying to hide. To spit a little blood foretells sedition.   *(A)*

To dream of having a nose bleed signifies loss of goods and money to those who are phlegmatic and melancholy; but to the irascible and optimistic, it signifies health and happiness.   *(D&M2)*

BLOSSOMING of TREES

To dream you see all sorts of trees blossoming is a sign of joy, comfort and recreation.   *(OM)*

BLOWS

To dream you strike a blow is a sign of a law-suit. To dream you receive them means a reconciliation with your enemies.   *(M)*

BLUE or PURPLE

Denotes happiness, prosperity and esteem from various people you want to please. To dream you are dressed in a variety of colours denotes a variety of fortunes are in store for you. If you are in love, a quarrel will take place between you and your sweetheart which, after much uneasiness, will be settled by friends.   *(GD)*

To dream of something of this colour predicts that you will soon be receiving a visit from friends.   *(M)*

BOAR

If anyone dreams he has hunted or captured a wild boar he will chase or take some enemy that has the same qualities as the wild boar. If anyone dreams he has the head of a recently killed wild boar brought to him, that predicts that he will soon obtain his desire from his most powerful enemy. *(T)*

To chase a wild boar indicates unsuccessful efforts; to be chased means separation.   *(OM)*

BOAT

To dream that you are in a boat on a river, lake or pond of clear water is very good and signifies joy, prosperity and success. If you are walking in a boat and enjoying yourself without fear, you will have comfort and success in your affairs. To be in a boat in danger of overturning is a sign of danger, unless the dreamer is a prisoner or captive in that case it denotes liberty and freedom.   *(T)*

To dream that you are in a boat on a river or lake of clear water is good and signifies joy, prosperity and good success, but if the water is rough and stormy, it means the opposite.   *(GD)*

To dream of being in a boat is a good omen, and if you are about to embark on a new enterprise you can rest assured that it will be successful.

If, however, the boat is drifting about in all directions, be careful that you do not get into trouble through some illegal transaction. *(M)*

To dream that you are on the water in a boat, provided you are in a company, denotes prosperity and success in your undertakings. If you dream you are in a boat alone, it is a bad omen. To dream the boat overturns is the most fatal of all omens. *(OM)*

———— ♦ ————

BOBBIN

For a dressmaker to dream that her bobbins have no thread indicates business prosperity; if they have plenty of thread on them there will be a lack of both work and money. *(M)*

———— ♦ ————

BOG

For a person to dream that he is in a bog or marshy piece of land, where he sinks deep in the swamp, is a good dream. The dreamer will be eminent as a tradesman, professional man or speculator. Success will attend his efforts; prosperity will crown whatever he puts his hand to. Wealth, advancement and greatness will be the result of all his schemes. *(M)*

———— ♦ ————

BOILED MEAT

Sufferings. *(OM)*

———— ♦ ————

BOLTS

To dream that you are locked in a room with bolts and bars is a sign that your freedom of action in forthcoming legal problems is greater than you at first imagined. You will never suffer imprisonment or detention. The person who has this dream is often a great traveller. *(M)*

———— ♦ ————

BONDSMAN

To dream that you are bond for another person, either in money or criminal matters, is a sign that difficulties are ahead which will launch you into trouble and annoyance on behalf of people who are extravagant in their habits and expenditure. *(M)*

———— ♦ ————

BONES

Signify misfortune which may or may not be overcome by courage. *(M)*

———— ♦ ————

BONFIRE

To dream of helping to build a bonfire indicates that you about to change your mind about many things, when you will burn much that you used to worship, and worship much that you used to burn. *(O)*

BONNET

For a young woman to dream about wearing a new bonnet is a sign that she is about to land in difficulty through love of finery, desire for admiration and envy of the fancy clothes of some of her friends. A young man dreaming of a girl's bonnet, either in a shop window or on her head, may infer that he will marry before many months have passed.   *(O)*

For a girl to dream she gets a new bonnet promises a new lover, but much depends on the colour. If it is green, he will be deceitful; if blue, he will prove affectionate; if pink, his love will not be lasting; if yellow or white, he will quickly propose marriage. But if a woman loses her bonnet, she must guard her reputation; if her bonnet is blown off, she will have something she dearly prizes stolen.   *(OM)*

———— ♦ ————

BOOKS

To dream of reading books, especially if in your dream you are surrounded by a considerable library, denotes that you are not likely to marry, and will in all probability find consolation in literary pursuits. The chances against your marrying can be calculated by the number of books in the surrounding library. To dream of meeting a young lady in a book shop signifies, in the case of a young man, that though he is fond of books he will marry a wife who will care so little for them that when he buys a new book, he will carry it home in his hat and creep in the house by the window.   *(O)*

To dream of many books foretells unhappiness; but should you be reading the Bible, then you will be happy and respected by a large circle of friends. To dream that your book case is almost empty of books is a sign that you will become a scholar of great note, pass many examinations, and ultimately be so proficient in your studies that you will become a certified teacher in a public school if you choose to follow that profession, or that you will either be a good accountant, a proficient astronomer, or else an expert in some physical pursuits. To dream that your book case is full of elegantly-bound books is evidence that you will not have that taste for study which your opportunities offer to you. You will be behind most of your schoolmates in your education.   *(M)*

Books signify the 'life' of the dreamer. Thus to eat them is good for schoolmasters or anyone who earns a living by books or strives to be eloquent. To others it signifies sudden death.   *(A)*

———— ♦ ————

BOOTS

To have good boots or shoes signifies short-lived joy and happiness. The contrary signifies damage, disdain and honour.   *(T)*

Old boots indicate a return to an old love; new ones an entanglement that will bring you a new admirer.   *(M)*

To dream that you are wearing good boots signifies honour and profit through your employees.   *(OM)*

BORAGE
Eating borage signifies freedom from trouble and expedition of business. *(T)*

———————— ◆ ————————

BORROWING
To dream that you borrow anything is a bad dream. You will find the adage true:

> He that goes a borrowing,
> Goes a sorrowing. *(M)*

———————— ◆ ————————

BOTTLES
Foretells bad fortune, bad news, and, if black, the death of a friend. *(M)*
  Empty bottles signify illness; wine bottles, prosperity; upset bottles, domestic troubles. *(OM)*

———————— ◆ ————————

BOUND
To dream that you are bound with rope or cord signifies that you will fall victim to a serious disease. *(M)*

———————— ◆ ————————

BOUQUET
For a young woman to dream that her sweetheart presents her with a beautiful bouquet is a sign that her course in love will be interrupted by many unpleasant transactions on the part of her sweetheart. He will be given to flirting with other girls in her absence, and she will be annoyed by his thoughtlessness or want of consideration with regard to her feelings. For a young man to dream that he gives a splendid bouquet to a bride on her wedding day means that a death will take place among some of his dearest relatives or friends. *(M)*
  To carry a bouquet means marriage; to throw one away, separation. *(OM)*

———————— ◆ ————————

BOW
To dream you shoot with a bow signifies comfort. To carry a bow signifies desire or torment. *(T)*

———————— ◆ ————————

BOX
An empty box predicts unhappiness in love or trouble in marriage. If the box is full of useful articles, then the opposite can be expected. *(M)*

———————— ◆ ————————

BRACELETS
For a lady to dream she is wearing new bracelets is a sign that someone is slandering her. If she allows someone to fasten them for her, she will be ruled by the man she marries. *(M)*

BRAIN
If anyone dreams his brain is well and freed from all delusions he will be an able counsellor to those in authority, will govern himself prudently and will achieve his ambitions with honour and profit. If, on the contrary, he imagines his brain is sick, damaged or painful, he will be unfortunate in his advice and enterprises, will pass for an inexpert and imprudent person and run into many problems. *(T)*

BRANDY
Denotes good news, no matter in what form it appears. *(M)*

BRAY
To dream that you hear the braying of a donkey is a sign that shortly you will hear of the death of some celebrated eccentric local character who has long been noted for oddities in conduct and behaviour. *(M)*
See also **ASS.**

BREAD
To dream of eating white bread made of wheat signifies profit to the rich and damage to the poor. On the contrary, to dream of eating wholemeal bread denotes profit and gain to the poor, losses to the rich. To dream of eating barley bread signifies health and contentment. To dream you carry hot bread signifies accusation. To cut barley bread signifies rejoicing. To eat white bread signifies gain. *(T)*

To dream of your usual bread, and eating it, is good; but if you eat a different sort of bread from usual, that means sickness if you are poor or accusations of false dealing if you are rich. *(D&M)*

To dream that you throw away bread is a prediction that you will suffer from slanderous reports spread abroad by a stranger. If you eat white bread, any particular wish you may make on awaking will be fulfilled; if brown bread, good health will be yours, and a fair amount of riches. *(M)*

To dream you see a great quantity of bread denotes success in life. To dream you are eating good bread denotes that you will be married shortly. *(DSG)*

BREAK
If you break anything in your dream, be prepared for hardships and sadness for some time to come. *(M)*

A bad omen. *(OM)*

BREAKFAST
To dream that you are eating your breakfast shows that you will do something for which you will be sorry. *(M)*

BREASTS
To dream that your breast is beautiful is a good omen. For men, it is also a

good dream if it is hairy as it is a sign of gain, but to a married woman it foretells widowhood. *(A)*

———— ♦ ————

BREATH
If anyone dreams he has bad breath he will be despised by everyone. *(T)*

———— ♦ ————

BRIARS and BRAMBLES
To go through places covered with brambles means troubles ahead. If they prick you, unknown enemies will slander you with your friends, and unfavourable rumours will cause problems with your lover; if you bleed, expect heavy losses in trade. If you dream you pass through them without injury, then you will eventually triumph over all your enemies and be happy.
(OM)

———— ♦ ————

BRIBE
For a man to dream that he receives a bribe at an election contest is indicative of purity and honesty of character of the political parties to whom he is opposed. *(M)*

———— ♦ ————

BRIDE
To see a bride warns you to beware of a rival either in business or love. *(M)*

———— ♦ ————

BRIDGE
To fall on a bridge signifies obstruction. *(T)*

If the bridge is made of wood you may receive some honour; if it is iron, you will encounter many obstacles which will cause you trouble. To stand under a bridge for any length of time is very unlucky. *(M)*

To dream you are crossing over a bridge is a good omen. It denotes prosperity through life and success in love. To dream you are passing under a bridge indicates that you will never be perfectly at ease. To dream a bridge breaks down with you on it denotes sudden death. *(OM)*

———— ♦ ————

BRIGAND
Dangers are in store, but you will surmount them. *(OM)*

———— ♦ ————

BRONCHITIS
To be troubled with this unpleasant disease is a sign that you will, with the proper cultivation of your voice, become a good singer, and if you devote much time and attention to the art you will become eminently popular and successful as a singer. *(M)*

———— ♦ ————

BROOCH
To wear a strange brooch is a good or bad sign, according to the place where you see yourself in the dream. If you are wearing it at home, you will

shortly discover something to your advantage in taking the advice of a friend who has partly succeeded in the construction of a new machine, and who wants you to join him in bringing it before the public as a patent. If you are wearing it before a number of strange people you may expect to be waylaid on your way home, and perhaps robbed. *(M)*

———— ♦ ————

BROOD
For a mother to dream that she sees a brood of chickens gathered under the wing of the hen is a sign that, in spite of her care, earnest prayers and careful education of her children, some of them will go wrong. *(M)*

———— ♦ ————

BROOK
Denotes vexation and sorrow; but if the water is exceptionally clear, wealth will follow the trouble. If the water is muddy, your sorrow will be a long one. *(M)*

A clear brook means constant friends; troubled water signifies family troubles. *(OM)*

———— ♦ ————

BROOM
Beware of a false friend. The broom signifies that someone is seeking to take advantage of you. *(M)*

A proverb of old says a new broom sweeps clean,
Then beware of fresh friends 'til their work shall be seen. *(MS)*

———— ♦ ————

BROTH
A good sign which signifies profit and gain. *(T)*

———— ♦ ————

BROTHER
Talking with your brother signifies vexation. *(T)*

For a girl to dream of a brother is a sign that she will receive a proposal of marriage before very long. For a brother to dream of a brother denotes a coming family quarrel. *(M)*

To dream you see your brother denotes a speedy marriage in your family, and that the dreamer will not be long-lived. *(OM)*

———— ♦ ————

BROW
To dream you have a brow of brass, copper, marble or iron signifies irreconcilable hatred against your enemies. *(T)*

For a young unmarried woman to dream that she is seated on the brow of a hill with her lover is a sign of an unpleasant marriage, if it takes place with the young man she dreams about. The match will be unsuitable because their tastes will be different, their desires will be opposite, their wishes will be contrary, and the conduct of each will be unacceptable to the other. *(M)*

BROWN

To dream of anything brown is a sign that you are putting trust in false people. *(M)*

————— ♦ —————

BUCKET

To dream of a bucket with the bottom knocked out denotes that you will shortly lose heavily by a great mercantile fraud unless you exercise proper precautions. *(O)*

————— ♦ —————

BUCKLE

For a woman to dream that she has lost the buckle of her belt is a sign that some important agreement she has made, or that has been made on her behalf, will be broken, and she will suffer from it. *(M)*

————— ♦ —————

BUILDING

To dream you build or arrange for a house to be built signifies molestation, loss, sickness or death. *(T)*

To dream of a very tall building denotes a long life and happiness. If you dream of being engaged in building any structure it is a sign that some venture dear to your heart will fall through. *(M)*

To dream of being amongst buildings denotes that you will change your present place of residence, and that you will make many friends in life. *(OM)*

————— ♦ —————

BULL

A bull signifies an important person; so if anyone dreams he receives either an injury or something good from a bull, he will receive it from someone in authority. *(T)*

An attack from such a creature is a warning that a supposed friend is slandering you. *(M)*

To be gored means injury from influential people; to kill a bull means suffering; two bulls fighting signifies brotherly love. *(OM)*

————— ♦ —————

BULLDOG

For a person to dream that he or she meets with this faithful animal is a sign that some friends whom you thought had deserted you will again renew your acquaintance and offer their assistance to you by good advice and financial help if necessary. *(M)*

————— ♦ —————

BULLOCK

For a woman to dream that she is frightened by a bullock in the street is a sign that at some future time, when her children are in danger, or her husband is suffering from a serious and infectious disease, she will show great courage, and rush to the place of danger to rescue or help those whom she loves most. *(M)*

————— 61 —————

BULL'S EYE
For a young man to dream that he sees the centre of the target and hits it at the first shot is an unlucky dream, for he will never become a crack shot. To dream that you miss the bull's eye is a good sign. By practice and perseverance you will become a very efficient and successful marksman. *(M)*

———— ♦ ————

BUMPER
To drink or see a large glass of wine indicates a merry meeting.   *(OM)*

———— ♦ ————

BURDEN
Carrying a burden signifies you will depend upon others for help.   *(OM)*

———— ♦ ————

BURGLARS
To dream that you fight with burglars in your own house is a sign that some of your own domestic staff are dishonest.   *(M)*

———— ♦ ————

BURNING
To see a burning light in someone's hands signifies that some mischief done will be discovered and the person punished and that there will be no possibility of excusing or concealing it. When the light is extinguished it means the opposite.

If you dream you see one or more houses burning with fire that is not violent or sparkling and that those houses are neither consumed nor destroyed that signifies goods, riches and inheritances to the poor; to the rich it indicates honours, responsibilities and dignity; but if the fire is burning with a smoky, violent or sparkling fire and the houses fall and are destroyed that denotes the opposite. When a man dreams that his bed is on fire and that he dies, that signifies injury, sickness or death to his wife and if the wife dreams it the same may happen to her husband. If you see the curtains or hall furniture destroyed by fire, that indicates injury or death to the house's owner. If you dream that the kitchen is on fire that denotes death to whoever does the cooking. When a man believes a shop is destroyed by fire that signifies loss of goods and possessions. If the front windows of the house are burning, that signifies the death of a brother; if they are those of the back of the house, it means the death of a sister. If the gates are burning that signifies death to the mistress of the house and sometimes to the dreamer. To see the top of the house on fire denotes loss of goods, law-suits or the death of friends. To kindle a fire which burns immediately signifies that your children will be fortunate and honour their mother. If a woman dreams that she kindles or lights a fire it is a sign she is pregnant and will have a safe delivery of a fortunate child whether it is a boy or a girl. If you kindle a fire with difficulty and it soon goes out, it denotes damage and dishonour to both you and your wife, and you are often the cause of it. To see a castle destroyed by fire signifies injury, sickness or death to the owner and to see a city on fire denotes famine, war or pestilence to that city. To see a man publicly burned signifies loss in merchandise or sickness. If you see your clothes burned, it signifies vexation, injury, reproach, overthrowing at law and loss of friends. Seeing a stack of corn burned and consumed signifies famine and death, but if it is not destroyed, it denotes fertility and great riches to the dreamer. Anyone who sees himself burning and in pain, can expect envy, displeasure, anger and arguments. To hold a burning straw torch in public signifies joy, honour and the good management of affairs. To burn your fingers, signifies envy and sin. To dream you feel burning signifies great danger. To dream you feel burnt denotes a fever. To see a great fire in heaven indicates attacks by enemies, poverty and various misfortunes. A brisk, sparkling fire denotes anger and hasty news but a clear moderate fire is good. *(T)*

To dream of burning an article of value denotes success in love. To see a light burning brightly at a distance signifies prosperity, but if the light is dim you will receive the force of someone's anger before many days have passed. *(M)*

To dream of burning implies a sudden danger. For a man to dream he is burned signifies that he will be rich and respected; but if he imagines that he was burned by a fire that did not quite consume him, he will inevitably perish in the end. To burn yourself means good fortune. *(OM)*

To dream you see burning lights descending from heaven is a very bad sign indeed and portends some dreadful accident to the dreamer. *(GD2)*

See also **FIRE**.

————— ♦ —————

BURY, BURIAL, and BURIED ALIVE
To be buried signifies that you will have as much wealth as you have earth laid on top of you. If anyone dreams he is buried alive he is in danger of being unhappy and unfortunate during his life. *(T)*

To dream that you inter or bury your best friend or nearest relative is a sign that you will hear of good fortune attending some of your friends or relatives who have emigrated, who have prospered in business, and with whom the climate agrees very well indeed. If you see someone you know at a funeral it is a sign that a friend or relative dear to you will die. In most cases it proves to be a rich relative. *(M)*

News of a wedding. Burial-ground means tidings of sorrow. *(OM)*

To dream that you are buried alive is an evil omen and signifies prison and captivity. *(A)*

————— ♦ —————

BUSHES
In verdure apportions protection and favour,
Where least you expect some handsome behaviour;
But stripped of their foliage shows fortune's caprices,
Vicissitudes various and scandal's devices. *(MS)*

BUSINESS

To dream you manage a very important business signifies obstruction. *(T)*

For a working man to dream of business affairs denotes a legacy. To dream of bad business concerns signifies that your ideas will in future turn to religion. *(C)*

---◆---

BUTCHERS

To dream of seeing butchers is in general a very unlucky omen and always foretells some injury to the dreamer. If you are in love, expect disappointments. If you are in trade, someone will defraud you. If you are a farmer, your livestock will fall ill. If you are sick, prepare for death. If you see butchers cutting up meat, some of your friends will die, while you will experience misery and poverty. *(DSG)*

---◆---

BUTTER and BUTTERMILK

Surprises; to make butter signifies a legacy. To drink buttermilk indicates disappointment in love. To the married, it means trouble, sorrow and losses. *(OM)*

---◆---

BUTTERFLY

To dream of a butterfly is a sign you have an inconstant lover or sweetheart. *(M)*

Domestic troubles. *(OM)*

---◆---

BUTTONS

If buttons enter into a girl's dream she will marry a man much older than herself. For a bachelor, such a dream denotes that he will not find the right partner until late in life. *(M)*

To dream of light buttons is always good; if they are fabric-covered, it means sadness. If a man dreams that he has lost all the buttons on his clothes it is a sign that he will not live long. *(OM)*

---◆---

BUYING

To dream that you are making extensive purchases foretells a run of extravagant pleasures which will not be good for you. *(M)*

To dream you are making a purchase is profitable; to witness trading indicates that you should exercise economy. Should you purchase an everyday article, beware of approaching loss. *(C)*

CAB

To dream of riding in a cab promises good fortune in many respects. Generally it predicts travel in a foreign country which will lead to the amassing of great wealth. If married, your children will rise to good positions in life. *(M)*

To ride in a cab means a tendency to great pride; a fall in circumstances; or misery and illness. *(OM)*

———————— ◆ ————————

CABBAGE

To dream of eating cabbage signifies vexation. *(T)*

To dream either of growing or eating a cabbage means that you will shortly receive a proposal which, if accepted, will end in your settling for the rest of your life in the country, and occupying yourself there with agricultural pursuits. *(O)*

For a girl to dream she sees cabbages growing is a sign that she will soon receive a proposal from a man earning his living in the country. *(M)*

To see cabbages signifies riches and happiness; to eat cabbages, unexpected sorrow, loss and illness. *(OM)*

———————— ◆ ————————

CABINET

To dream of a cabinet is a sure sign that you have an enemy in possession of a secret, the divulging of which will do you a deal of harm. To dream that you are hiding something in a cabinet implies that you have a design against some young person not very creditable to yourself, and which will greatly injure your character. *(M)*

———————— ◆ ————————

CABINET MAKER

To dream that you are in love with a cabinet maker indicates that you will marry a man of expensive habits, who will keep you poor and unhappy. *(M)*

———————— ◆ ————————

CACKLE

The married woman who hears ducks cackling in her dream will be blessed with a large family of boys and girls. *(M)*

CAD

To dream that you hear your sweetheart called a cad indicates that he will suffer from much unjust talk and be made the subject of slander. All will come right, however, and you will marry and have a fine family.   *(M)*

———— ♦ ————

CAGE

To dream of seeing a bird in a cage is a sure sign that you will make a happy marriage and live in total harmony.   *(O)*

To dream of a bird's cage denotes that some unforeseen circumstance will cause you to leave home; but if the cage contains a bird, matters will soon be put right, and you will return home at an early date.   *(M)*

If birds are in a cage, it means happiness after trouble. If no birds are in the cage, it signifies disappointment.   *(OM)*

To dream that a girl lets a bird out of a cage is a sign she will not keep her virginity, but as soon as she can will part with her maidenhead.   *(DSG)*

———— ♦ ————

CAKES

A great deal of joy awaits the person who dreams she is making cakes; but if the curious combination of cake, cheese and butter appears she must be careful in her love affairs.   *(M)*

To bake cakes signifies happiness and riches; you will be useful in your life. To dream of cakes twice indicates your own marriage, if you are single.   *(OM)*

To dream you make cakes signifies joy and profit. To dream of cakes without cheese is good, but to dream of both signifies deceit by a Welshman.   *(D&M2)*

To dream that cakes you knead and make,
Thou'lt thrive and many profits take.   *(N)*

———— ♦ ————

CALENDAR

To dream that you are searching the calendar for a date you cannot find signifies that you will soon be making arrangements for getting married. If, however, the dream ends before you find the date, you will very likely have cause to cancel your engagement.   *(M)*

———— ♦ ————

CALF and CALVES

For a young woman to dream that she sees a calf in front of her when out walking with her lover is a sign that her young man after marriage will become a good husband, a faithful and devoted provider for his children and a strict but affectionate father. He will be respected by others for his wisdom and kindness and gain the confidence of his employers by his punctuality and conscientiousness.   *(M)*

Speedy good fortune. You will be tempted to do something unwise and foolish.   *(OM)*

CALLING
To dream of calling on a friend and finding him out means, for a man, that someone with whom he is at present very intimate will be lost to him for ever through his marriage. *(O)*

———— ♦ ————

CALM
The end of trouble and the beginning of happiness. The meeting of old friends. *(OM)*

———— ♦ ————

CALUMNY
You will be respected. *(OM)*

———— ♦ ————

CAMEL
If a girl dreams of a camel, it is a sign that someone who wants to marry her will be lazy and slothful in later life. If, however, she can cure him, he will amass great wealth. *(M)*

You will become rich and live through extraordinary changes and circumstances. *(OM)*

———— ♦ ————

CAMEO BROOCH
For a young woman to dream that she wears a cameo brooch is indicative of success in the art of musical education. She will excel at playing the piano. If she dreams that her cameo brooch is broken, a rupture will take place between her and those she loves at home. *(M)*

———— ♦ ————

CAMERA
To look into one, someone will deceive you. *(OM)*

———— ♦ ————

CAMOMILE
You will attain a fine old age. *(OM)*

———— ♦ ————

CAMP
To dream that you are in a camp of soldiers means, to a young woman, an offer of marriage from a civilian. To a young man it means that he will fall in love with a woman who, either as a soldier's wife or daughter, has seen service in the camp. It also means he will have no taste for service in the army. *(M)*

———— ♦ ————

CAMPAIGN
To dream you enter upon the duties of a campaign means that you will be called upon to do duty at home for a sick wife, if you are married. To an unmarried man it means he will join the Territorials and do garrison duty for a short time. *(M)*

CAN

Good news. To drink out of a can, great joy. *(OM)*

———— ♦ ————

CANAL

To walk beside a muddy canal is a sign that some trouble will shortly afflict you, either at home or in your business relations. If the waters are clear you will have prosperity in your commercial transactions, and peace at home. If you fall into a canal you will shortly be involved in business engagements of an entirely fresh nature from those you have been accustomed to, and all your time and attention will be required to make your new calling successful. *(M)*

———— ♦ ————

CANARY

Through someone who is taking an interest in you, you will rise to a life of luxury and ease. *(M)*

To hear a canary sing indicates a happy marriage to the single. To the married, joy and comfort. *(OM)*

———— ♦ ————

CANCER

This is a good dream. You will feel your bodily health so robust that you will become proficient in athletic or aquatic sports. *(M)*

———— ♦ ————

CANDLE

To see a clear, shining, lighted candle on a table or cabinet is a good sign to the sick, as it denotes recovery and health. If you are unmarried, it signifies that you will soon marry, you will be successful and will gain credit. The same interpretation can be made of a lantern or flaming torch. To see any of these extinguished or darkened signifies sadness, sickness and poverty. *(T)*

Candles burning brightly indicates long continued health and happiness; but should you see them burning dimly you may expect bad luck. *(O)*

Many candles burning brightly foreshadow much merry-making and an important occurrence. If they burn dimly, expect misfortune. If a girl sees a candle being lighted, she will soon receive a proposal of marriage. A bachelor will come into money. *(M)*

To see candles burning clear and bright denotes that you will soon be married. To dream that new candles are brought in, denotes that all your disputes will be amicably resolved. *(OM)*

———— ♦ ————

CANDY

To dream of candy is a sign of domestic tranquillity. *(M)*

———— 68 ————

CANE

Cane is considered a most inauspicious dream, and some authors forbid the dreamer to undertake any business on that day. *(M)*

———————— ◆ ————————

CANNIBALISM

If anyone dreams he has eaten the flesh of a man or women, he will enrich himself by injuries and reproach. If anyone dreams he has eaten the flesh of a man who has been hanged he will be enriched by foul practice and some secret crime. *(T)*

———————— ◆ ————————

CANNON

To hear or see a cannon fired foreshadows a long but not fatal illness. *(M)*
    You will meet with opposition and trouble. *(OM)*

———————— ◆ ————————

CANOE

To paddle down a river in a canoe is a sign that you will make application to a friend to help you financially in your business, but he will refuse. In fact, nearly all your life you will be left to fight your way without the help of any other person, except perhaps your wife. Self-reliance is the principle and practice you must cultivate. *(M)*

———————— ◆ ————————

CANOPY

To sit under a canopy means that you will soon have to move from your present home to another house, for the circumstances of your life will change for the worse. *(M)*

———————— ◆ ————————

CAP

To dream that you put on a cap indicates that you must be careful in your love affairs; to take one down shows that the thing you wish to hide will be discovered; if you receive a cap you will soon get married. *(M)*

———————— ◆ ————————

CAPERS

To dream of capers is not good, unless you dream at the same time of banquets and great feasts. *(D&M2)*

———————— ◆ ————————

CAPONS

To dream that you hear the capon crow signifies sadness and trouble. *(T)*

———————— ◆ ————————

CAPTAIN

For a young woman to dream that she meets with a captain in the army who shows a romantic interest in her is a sign that she will fall in love with one in the army who by good conduct has risen from the ranks. *(M)*

CARCASE of an ANIMAL
Happiness and long life. *(OM)*

———————— ♦ ————————

CARDS
To play cards signifies deceit and craft and that you are in danger of losing your property and money by some wicked person. *(T)*

To dream that you are playing at cards is a sure sign that you will soon fall in love and marry. If you hold a great many picture cards, your marriage will make you rich and happy; if your cards are mostly diamonds, the person you marry will be of a sour and disagreeable temper; if they are mostly hearts, your marriage will be loving, you will be very happy and have many children; if they are mostly clubs, you will get money by your marriage; if they are spades, your marriage will turn out very unhappy and your children will be undutiful and subject to many hardships; if you are hoping for a new job you will get it and if you are in business it will be successful. *(GD)*

To dream of cards is a sign that, although you may be fortunate in other things, your love affairs will not run as smoothly as you might wish. Keep a careful watch on your tongue, and don't trifle with anyone's feelings. *(M)*

To dream of playing at cards, tables or any other game, shows you will be very fortunate. The tables allude to love, so anyone who often dreams of table-playing will be a great gamester. *(D&M2)*

———————— ♦ ————————

CARESS
For a mother to dream that she caresses her child is a sign that the child will soon suffer from a common but serious childhood illness. She will have days of anxiety, and nights of eager watching but it will, with great care, recover. *(M)*

———————— ♦ ————————

CARPENTER
Should a carpenter figure in your dream a calamity is threatening you, although it may not be felt for some years to come. *(M)*

Difficulties will soon be arranged to the satisfaction of everyone. *(OM)*

———————— ♦ ————————

CARPETS
For a lady to dream that she has bought new carpets means that shortly she or her husband will be called upon to pay additional income tax; to dream that your carpets are worn out means success in your employment. To dream you sell carpets is a sign that you will be expected by your relatives to amass a large fortune, which they intend to inherit! *(M)*

———————— ♦ ————————

CARRIAGE
A carriage without horses foretells a calamity, and a long journey should

be avoided during that week. If horses are attached to the carriage, honour awaits you. Should you be sitting in a carriage which is not moving you will suffer from scandal. *(M)*

To dream that you are riding in a carriage indicates that you are never likely to become wealthy. *(OM)*

───────── ♦ ─────────

CARRIERS
Through work and patience you will attain independence. *(OM)*

───────── ♦ ─────────

CARRION CROW
To dream of a carrion crow signifies sadness and sickness. *(DSG)*

───────── ♦ ─────────

CARROTS
To dream of carrots, signifies profit by inheritance. *(OM)*

To dream of carrots signifies profit and strength to anyone awaiting the legal arrangements for an inheritance. *(D&M2)*

───────── ♦ ─────────

CARRYING
To dream that you are carrying someone is better than to dream you are carried; to be carried by a woman, a child or poor person means profit and success; by a rich person the opposite. *(D&M2)*

To dream of carrying a girl means cheerfulness. *(D&M)*

───────── ♦ ─────────

CART
To dream of riding in a cart is a sign that your character is being assaulted, and this will lead to serious trouble unless you can find the guilty party. *(M)*

Your business will not go smoothly. To drive a cart foretells that you will be hard put to it to make ends meet. *(OM)*

To dream of being fixed in a cart to draw it like an ox, an ass or a horse, denotes servitude and pain to everybody. To dream that you are carried in a cart or coach that is drawn by men signifies that you will have might and authority over many or have well-behaved children. *(D&M2)*

───────── ♦ ─────────

CARVINGS
To see a quantity of wood carvings is indicative, if you are a young woman, of your having a husband who has a taste for the arts and sciences. He will be fond of the ornamental part of everything, and pride himself in making his house as beautiful as possible. *(M)*

If you are carving, then expect prosperity. If you are single, expect success in love. *(OM)*

───────── ♦ ─────────

CASHIER
For a young man to dream that he is a cashier means that he will have cares

and annoyances in life on account of others, of which he had no idea before. He will be denounced as dishonest by malicious and evil people. He should make sure he is correct and accurate in all his dealings. *(M)*

———————— ♦ ————————

CASTLE

A castle in a dream foreshadows a good match, but an unhappy married life. *(M)*

A good sign. You will rise in life. *(OM)*

———————— ♦ ————————

CASTOR OIL

For a young woman to dream of taking castor oil is a sign of increasing good looks. *(M)*

———————— ♦ ————————

CAT

The cat signifies a cunning thief so that if anyone dreams he has met or killed a cat, he will commit a thief to prison and the thief will die. If he thinks he eats cat's flesh he will have the goods of the thief that robbed him. If he dreams he has the skin, then he will enjoy all the thief's goods. If anyone dreams he fought with a cat that badly scratched him, that signifies sickness or affliction. *(T)*

To dream of cats means that you are about to suffer from the treachery of one you have trusted for a long time. The cats in this case must appear to be alive and active. Should you kill a cat in a dream it denotes that you are shortly to have an opportunity of being revenged on a person who has done you an injury. *(O)*

A cat washing itself signifies that you will command respect and love where your affections are placed. If the cat is restless, be wary of treacherous friends. *(M)*

To dream of these domestic animals is indicative of much trouble and vexation; it denotes to the lover that their sweetheart is treacherous. If you keep servants, they are unfaithful, and will rob you. *(OM)*

To dream of a cat signifies that you will have dealings with an adulterer or harlot. *(A)*

> Of these emblems of trouble no one is a stranger,
> They amplify poverty, sickness and danger. *(MS)*

> To dream a cat doth fiercely cling
> And blood and anguish from thee bring,
> Denotes a foe both dread and dire,
> That would against thy life conspire. *(N)*

———————— ♦ ————————

CATARACT

To dream that you see a cataract is a sign that you will, if you see the waters clear and bright, have good success in your domestic affairs. You and your children will have sound health and good looks. You may also expect to receive birthday gifts for your children from a quarter where you do not expect them. If the water of the cataract is muddy and dirty-looking, expect trouble and sickness to overtake some of the members of your household. *(M)*

────────── ♦ ──────────

CATECHISM
To study the catechism is a sign that you have a retentive memory. You will be a good scholar in mental arithmetic and adding up accounts. *(M)*

────────── ♦ ──────────

CATERPILLARS
To dream you see caterpillars signifies bad luck and misfortune caused by unknown enemies. *(T)*

────────── ♦ ──────────

CATHEDRAL
To attend a service in a cathedral predicts an early marriage to a person of title. *(M)*

You will be protected from everything bad if you see a cathedral. If you enter the cathedral and pray, expect happiness, joy and success in everything. *(OM)*

────────── ♦ ──────────

CATTLE
Cattle signify wealth and plenty. *(T)*

To dream you are keeping cattle denotes disgrace. *(GD)*

Fat cattle denote prosperity, then misfortune. To dream of buying cattle is a sign that some project which you have in hand will not prove successful. If you are about to be married when such a dream comes you will be wise to postpone the ceremony until you have made sure you have really chosen the right partner. If you are married, beware of gossiping tongues which try to make domestic trouble for you. *(M)*

To see cattle denotes prosperity and unexpected success; to a lover, it foretells a happy marriage with many children; and to the man, it shows that his wife will receive some unexpected legacy. *(OM)*
See also **OXEN.**

────────── ♦ ──────────

CAULIFLOWER
To dream that you are eating cauliflower is a very good dream. You will have joy and peace in all aspects of life. You will abandon any bad habits and replace them with domestic happiness and contentment. *(M)*

Illness and inconstancy. *(OM)*

────────── ♦ ──────────

CAVALIERS
Indicate restlessness and much trouble. You are likely to go into rowdy company. *(OM)*

CAVALRY

To dream that you see a regiment of horse soldiers on parade is a sign that, if you are unmarried, you will meet with a partner for life who will be able to keep you well by his own industry and thrift, and that you will have children who will at some future period of their lives what to lead a soldier's life. For a young man to have this dream means that he will meet with a young woman of a staid, peaceful and affable disposition.   *(M)*

CAVES

To be in a cave indicates many and considerable changes in your happiness.   *(OM)*

CEILING

To dream of sitting in a room where the ceiling collapses is a sign of the sudden loss of a friend or relative.   *(M)*

CELERY

To dream that you are eating celery is a sign that the dreamer is a person of very robust constitution, full of vigour up to an old age.   *(M)*

Be careful in your choice of companions.   *(OM)*

CELLAR

To dream of being in a cellar denotes that you will travel and make many new friends. If the cellar is full of wine, however, be careful of these friends, for one, at least, will prove unfaithful. If there is coal in the cellar you may expect to hear good news.   *(M)*

To be in a cellar, you are threatened with illness.   *(OM)*

CEMETERY

You will overcome all problems.   *(OM)*

CENTIPEDE

To see centipedes signifies ill luck and misfortune by unknown enemies. *(T)*

CERBERUS

To dream you see the dog Cerberus, the porter of Hell, signifies sin and arrest.   *(T)*

CHAFF

To dream of chaff signifies that your plans will not succeed.   *(OM)*

CHAIN

To dream of a chain with long links of which you see both the beginning and the end foretells that you will carry on a long correspondence with someone beginning formally, becoming very friendly, but eventually ending on a cold and formal note. *(O)*

If you dream of a broken chain you may reasonably look forward to a change of business which will be good for you. If unbroken, the reverse, while if you are married your love affairs will not run smoothly until you have experienced some disappointments. *(M)*

Chains of pearls, precious stones, etc, and all jewellery of the hands and necks of women are good dreams for women; to girls they signify marriage; to those that have husbands and children, purchases and riches. *(DSG)*

To dream of a chain signifies that your wife is preventing all success in your affairs and is a hindrance to you instead of a help. *(A)*

CHAIR

To sit beside an empty chair signifies that you are about to meet and talk with one who for several years has been on your mind a great deal. *(O)*

An empty chair in a dream denotes that you will soon be meeting one who is dear to you, but who has been absent for many years. *(M)*

CHALK

A dream of vast quantities of chalk foreshadows disappointment in business or matrimony. To a farmer it is a sign that his cattle will die of disease. *(M)*

CHAMBERMAID

For a young, unmarried man to dream of courting a chambermaid means that he will either marry a cook, housemaid or nurse. He will cause a rupture in the family he visits, for no one can tell which of the girls he professes to be engaged to. *(M)*

CHAMBER POT

To dream of seeing a fish in a chamber pot is bad for those in authority or the sick. *(A)*

CHAMPAGNE

For a young woman to dream that she is drinking champagne means that she will, in spite of the warnings and entreaties of her parents, keep company with a young man who, though he promises well, will turn out to be worthless; he will be deficient in education, loose in his moral character, and profligate in his habits. *(M)*

CHAMPION

To dream that you are the winner in any kind of competition is a sign that despite study and practice on your part, you will not gain the efficiency and success you desire. Try some physical employment rather than a mental one. *(M)*

———— ♦ ————

CHANGE

To dream of changing anything — changing sides, or changing clothes, or changing books at a library, or changing money (but not changing houses, for which see Removal) — means that you are about to enter on a period of unrest. It will turn out for the best if in your dream you gained by the change you made. *(O)*

———— ♦ ————

CHAPEL

If you see the outside of a chapel, then you will become rich. If you are inside and see the priest, be careful of your actions. It indicates that a trap is set for you, and if you fall into it you will regret your mistake all your life. *(M)*

———— ♦ ————

CHAPPED HANDS

To dream that your hands have become chapped is a bad sign. There will be a great deal of problems in your family from one of your children. He will be troubled with a desire to take other people's goods, for no other reason than that he has an unaccountable desire to possess them. He suffers from that curious problem known as kleptomania, which will continually recur to disturb your peace of mind. *(M)*

———— ♦ ————

CHARADE

To act in a charade at a private party is a sign that your friends will fight shy of your society, and not extend their invitations to you as they have done before. This will cause you trouble, but you will soon find out the cause and put matters right. *(M)*

———— ♦ ————

CHARCOAL

If you dream that you are sitting beside a fire of charcoal you will soon hear news of an exciting character from friends abroad. *(M)*

———— ♦ ————

CHARIOT

For a woman to dream that she rides in a chariot means poverty from sickness and lack of employment. For a young man to have this dream means that he will soon have to move, because he will lose his job due to fierce competition. *(M)*

CHARITY

For a rich person to dream that he is charitable signifies loss of fortune; if a lady dreams it she will fall in love with an unworthy person.   *(M)*

―――――― ♦ ――――――

CHART

For a rich person to dream that he is studying a chart signifies loss of fortune; if a lady dreams it she will fall in love with an unworthy person. *(M)*

―――――― ♦ ――――――

CHASTISE

For a father to dream that he scolds his children for disobedience means that they will be good tempered and obedient.   *(M)*

―――――― ♦ ――――――

CHEATED

To be cheated at any game of chance, or in any purchase, is a sign that you will become more circumspect in your trading, and will therefore make very few, if any, bad debts.   *(M)*

―――――― ♦ ――――――

CHEEKS

To dream you have fat cheeks is good; if thin, bad.   *(D&M)*

To dream of your cheeks is a good omen. To a person employed in business it denotes that he will be successful in surmounting all his difficulties, and will rise to the top of a large business. To an unmarried lady the dream promises much pleasure and a happy marriage.   *(M)*

To dream that you have plump, rosy cheeks, is a good sign, especially to a women; but to dream that you are lean, pale and full of wrinkles signifies grief and heaviness.   *(D&M2)*

―――――― ♦ ――――――

CHEER

If the sound of cheering enters your dream, you will soon have cause to shed many tears.   *(M)*

―――――― ♦ ――――――

CHEESE

To eat cheese signifies profit and gain.   *(T)*

A girl who dreams of cheese should be careful not to give too much credence to any tale she may hear about her lover. The dream foreshadows a small loss for a man.   *(M)*

This dream is important whate'er is thought of it,
And always precedes great and unlooked for profit.   *(MS)*

―――――― ♦ ――――――

CHEESE CAKE

If a young woman dreams of eating cheese cakes, she will soon meet a witty, humorous, intelligent, fair young man who will invite her to take a walk in the moonlight. Act discreetly, judge his character, think of his promises, and see how you can sum up his worth. If he is good at heart, good will come of your moonlit walks. *(M)*

———————— ♦ ————————

CHEMIST

For a person of a sharp temper to dream of a chemist's shop is a sure sign that, unless that person takes care to improve the fault, married life will be a failure, and much sorrow will be brought about by a sudden death. To a person of milder temperament the dream gives warning of sickness and the failure of some long-cherished scheme. *(M)*

———————— ♦ ————————

CHEQUE

Dreaming of receiving a cheque means that you are in danger of being victimised by a plausible and garrulous imposter who will get money out of you on the strength of his great expectations. *(O)*

To dream that you have received a payment of money by cheque is not so pleasant as it may at first appear. Be wary of an imposter, who will be so plausible that you will be tempted to advance him money which will never be returned. *(M)*

———————— ♦ ————————

CHERRIES

Indicate disappointment and rejection in love and vexation in the marriage. *(GM)*

To see the fruit growing is a disappointment in love or marriage. To dream that you are eating cherries foreshadows a great disappointment of a series of petty worries. *(M)*

To eat cherries signifies deceitful pleasure; if they are out of season, they signify travel and fruitless labour. *(D&M2)*

> To dream of cherries doth declare
> That thou wilt many pleasures share,
> But from excess thou must refrain,
> Or e'en your pleasures will bring pain. *(N)*

———————— ♦ ————————

CHESS

The game of chess and tables is the representative of a field prepared for battle, the two players are the two generals of the armies and the tables and the chess men are the soldiers that make up the two armies. If anyone dreams he plays chess with an acquaintance, it is a sign that he will fall out with somebody that he knows, and if he imagines in his dream that he wins, he will be victorious over his enemies; or vice versa. If the dreamer imagines he has taken many men in play, that foretells he will take many of his enemies prisoner. If a ruler or general of an army dreams he has lost his chess board or that it is broken or stolen from him he will lose his army, either by the enemies' assault or else by plague or famine.   *(T)*

To dream that you play chess signifies gain by lying and deceit. To dream that you see others play chess signifies loss by craft.   *(A)*

———————— ♦ ————————

CHESTNUTS and CHESTNUT TREES

To dream that you are eating chestnuts is a sign that wisdom will be one of the most prominent features in the character of your partner. For an unmarried women to have this dream means that she will meet with a very bashful young man who is deeply in love with her, but has not the courage to talk to her on the subject.   *(M)*

Domestic affliction. Profitable undertakings.   *(OM)*

———————— ♦ ————————

CHICKENS

To dream of chickens is unlucky. If they are roosting, then the bad luck will affect your domestic affairs, and will not be very serious; if they are strutting about, the trouble will be more severe, and will extend even to your own or your partner's business.   *(M)*

To dream of a hen and chickens is the forerunner of bad luck; your sweetheart will betray you and marry another. If you are a farmer, you will have a bad crop, and lose many of your poultry. If you are in trade, some con man will defraud you. If you go to sea, you will lose your goods and narrowly escape shipwreck.   *(OM)*

———————— ♦ ————————

CHILDBIRTH

If a woman dreams she gives birth to a child without being pregnant it is a sign that she will happily accomplish her intentions. To dream that a woman is in labour and the child is stillborn, after a difficult and painful labour, shows that she will work hard for something which will never be accomplished. If the child is alive, she will achieve her ambitions — through hard work.   *(DSG)*
See also **BIRTH**.

———————— ♦ ————————

CHILDREN

Male children bring good success; daughters signify that you will be put to a good deal of expense, if they are your own. To see other men's children is good when they are fair and attractive, for this signifies that a good and happy time is at hand. If anyone dreams that he sees himself wrapped in children's clothes it signifies a long sickness unless his wife is pregnant for then he should have a son born like himself. If his wife has such a dream she shall have a daughter, but if anyone in prison has such a dream, the accusations against him will be such that he will not be freed.   *(A)*

To see children born signifies damage. If someone with no children dreams that he has many small children and that they seem to him to run

———————— 79 ————————

about the house, that signifies that it will be very difficult for him to have any, and that he will have many cares and obstructions in his affairs. Anyone who dreams he sees an infant wrapped in swaddling clothes and suckling at his mother, that signifies a chronic and dangerous illness unless his wife is pregnant; if so it signifies that the child will be short-lived. If a woman dreams this it is a sign that she is or will shortly be pregnant and have a daughter, unless she is sick or her husband dies.   *(T)*

To see a beautiful fair naked child denotes joy. If you see many children playing innocently together you will become wealthy. If the dream is the opposite and the child is ugly or deformed, especially about the genitals, then you will know shame and reproach. To dream of anything happening to small children which is not relevant to their age, such as boys having beards and grey hair or little girls married with children, signifies death to the dreamer.   *(D&M2)*

If you dream of many children together be prepared for good news, wealth and much happiness later in life.   *(M)*

To dream you see children denotes success in your undertakings. To dream you see a child born denotes a speedy marriage and that you will be very happy with your family. To dream you see a child die imports that you will experience some heavy misfortune.   *(OM)*

------- ♦ -------

CHINA

To dream of china is a sign that, providing you persevere in your occupation, you will make a big success and die rich.   *(M)*

------- ♦ -------

CHINAMAN

To see a Chinaman in a dream is a warning that someone who you have trusted will prove false and cause you trouble.   *(M)*

------- ♦ -------

CHOCOLATE

To dream of buying chocolate is a prediction that you will bring sorrow on yourself by a foolish action unless you keep a firm hold on yourself during the following nine days. If you are eating chocolate, however, you will receive a gift from someone you despise.   *(M)*

------- ♦ -------

CHOIR

The singing of a choir means that you will soon be speaking to an old sweetheart. If the music is solemn, however, you must be wary of any advances he may make, for he does not mean half he says.   *(M)*

------- ♦ -------

CHOKING

To dream that you are choking is significant. You will be praised by some of your friends for your proficiency in the studies of science and intellectual culture. In physical health you may be troubled with indigestion from time to time, but careful diet will help you through the most painful part of this disease and give you vigour in your old age. *(M)*

———————— ◆ ————————

CHOLERA

To dream that you are the subject of this disease is indicative of some accident happening to you before long. If you are about to start on a journey it will be prudent for you, after having this dream, to remain at home for a while, especially if the weather is foggy, windy or stormy with a heavy downpour and thunder and lightning. *(M)*

———————— ◆ ————————

CHORISTER

To dream that you are a chorister in a church choir is indicative of success in the art of public speaking if you cultivate your abilities. You may be able to enter, through the influence of friends, into a college and become a student for the ministry. For a young woman to dream that her lover is a chorister means that she will meet with one who has a desire for singing, but not for sacred songs; sentimental and comic songs will occupy his attention more than oratories and sacred music. *(M)*

———————— ◆ ————————

CHRIST

To talk with Jesus Christ signifies consolation. To see the body of our Lord signifies honour. *(T)*

———————— ◆ ————————

CHRISTENING

For a young woman to dream that she is at a christening ceremony is indicative of sudden illness of some of her nephews or nieces. Perhaps before very long some of those who are peculiar favourites in her family will be seized with croup or bronchitis. For a young man to have this dream is indicative of trouble on account of his religious beliefs. He will be the cause of anxiety to his parents because he will imbibe new theological doctrines. *(M)*

———————— ◆ ————————

CHRISTMAS

A dream connected with this season denotes a reconciliation between two old-time friends who have quarrelled, with much jubilation as a result; or, if you have not had a disagreement of this kind, you may expect to hear from a friend or relative of whom you have lost all trace for some time. *(M)*

———————— ◆ ————————

CHRISTMAS TREE

To dream that you see a beautifully decorated Christmas tree is a sign that the festivities of the Christmas season will be remembered for a long time, because you will meet with someone under the holly who has never spoken to you before, but who will seek your company, first as a friend, afterwards as a lover, and lastly as a marriage partner. Your marriage will be long and happy. *(M)*

———— ♦ ————

CHURCH

To dream you are in church and praying devoutly to God signifies joy and comfort. To build a church signifies that one of your relations will receive a present. To see yourself sitting or lying in a church signifies change of clothes. *(T)*

To dream that you do nothing but talk and sing idly at church signifies envy or sin; and the persons dreaming this, if wicked, should alter their way of life. To dream of seeing the sacrament administered in church is a good dream. *(GD)*

If you see a church in your sleep, you should make inquiries into the character of your sweetheart's or spouse's companions. The chances are that they will not be pleasant. *(M)*

To dream of church is portentous of evil. If in church during divine service, you will be engaged in a law-suit, or some other quarrel that will come very close to ruining you. If you are in love, your sweetheart is unfaithful. *(OM)*

———— ♦ ————

CHURCHYARD

To dream of walking in a churchyard is an omen of a pleasant surprise, with a probability of wealth to come. *(M)*

———— ♦ ————

CHURNING

To dream that you are churning milk is good. You will gain the respect of social, jolly company because of your powers of reciting some of the best pieces of favourite authors. Your company will be much sought after and enjoyed by both young and old. But to attain greater proficiency you must practise regularly. *(M)*

———— ♦ ————

CIDER

Good fortune follows a dream of cider, and if you drink it the luck will be even better. For a student it signifies honours in an examination. *(M)*

———— ♦ ————

CIGAR

To dream that you are enjoying the luxury of a first-class cigar is a significant dream. You will have much to be thankful for; and even if you do have problems, the fumes and flavour of your finest brands will help to lighten the load of trouble that would otherwise weigh you down. *(M)*

CINDERS

To sweep up cinders is a sign that you will have trouble with some of your relatives. Some of them even decide to tramp the country; in all probability they will become vagabonds and be a disgrace to their family.
(M)

◆

CIRCUS

Examine yourself well after dreaming of a circus, for it proves that you are developing some bad habit, probably selfishness, which, if not checked, will make you unhappy.
(M)

◆

CLARET

To dream that you are drinking this favourite wine is a sign that there is a pretty handsome fortune in store for you, if only you have the means to redeem it from those who have heavy mortgages upon it. Some of your relatives have been too extravagant and have not lived within their means, and the consequence is you may lose your inheritance through their extravagance.
(M)

◆

CLARINET

To dream that you hear music from this kind of reed instrument is a sign that you will have a taste for piano music, and could become adept at playing this instrument is you practise carefully. But if you allow your energies to remain unused, they will be of no use to you at all. Your ideas of harmony and time will be very correct.
(M)

◆

CLARIONS

To play or hear playing on wind instruments such as clarions, signifies trouble, contention and losing a court case.
(T)

◆

CLAVICHORD

To dream you play, or see someone else play a clavichord, signifies the death of relations or funeral obsequies.
(T)

◆

CLEAN SHAVEN

If your face is clean shaven, it signifies sudden shame and problems. To see the back of the head shaven signifies poverty and bad luck in old age; although it is good for anyone appealing to the legal profession, or anyone who is afraid about something; it also signifies to a prisoner that he will escape.
(A)

CLERGYMAN

For a young unmarried woman to dream that a clergyman wants to meet with her is a sign that she will be disappointed; the man she most desires as a husband is engaged to someone else, and she will marry someone she loves less. She will, in the end, marry a craftsman, a mechanic or an unskilled worker. She will never rise to a position of affluence.   *(M)*

———————— ♦ ————————

CLIMBING

If someone dreams that he climbs a great tree, he will be promoted to some honour or dignity, and will have authority over others. To ascend a ladder signifies honour. To ascend a very high mountain, the same thing. To ascend up to heaven signifies grandeur.   *(T)*

To dream of attaining the summit of a hill signifies that the dreamer will get his desires, but if you fall before you gain the top you will not attain your ends.   *(D&M)*

To dream you are climbing up a very steep hill or place foretells many difficulties in life and much sickness. If you reach the top, you will get over all your difficulties and recover from your illness, but if you awake before you have reached the top you will be disappointed in love and all other projects in life and may die in your next illness.   *(GD)*

If you dream of climbing it is a sign you will have some dignity conferred upon you, or that your circumstances in life will improve. To unmarried people it predicts that they will marry above their station.   *(M)*

To dream that you are climbing a tree denotes that you will be successful in life.   *(OM)*

To dream that you are climbing up a tree denotes that you will arrive at a position of honour, and that you will be successful in life. If you are in love you will marry your partner after a long courtship. To dream that you are climbing up a very steep hill or place foretells many difficulties in life and much sickness. If you reach the top you will overcome all your difficulties and recover from your illness but if you awake before you have attained the summit you will be disappointed in love and in all projects and die during your next illness.   *(DSG)*

———————— ♦ ————————

CLOCK

To hear clocks strike signifies infamy.   *(T)*

To dream of a clock breaking is dangerous, especially to the sick, although it is better if the hour is before noon than afterwards.   *(D&M)*

To dream of a clock, especially when it is the chief clock in the house, having stopped means that you are in danger of a serious illness, but if the clock is wound up and set going again in your dream it is a sign that the illness may be averted by the strictest attention to the rules of health.   *(O)*

To dream of a clock that has stopped working indicates that you will be mixed up in sickness and a business loss. To hear a clock striking foretells a wedding at an early date.   *(M)*

To dream you hear the clock strike denotes that you will be speedily married, and that you will be moderately successful in life.   *(OM)*

To dream of a clock signifies attempts to improve your affairs. If you dream that a clock fails or breaks, it signifies problems and great dangers, especially to the sick.   *(A)*

> Times telescope e'er should advocate to youth,
> A steady adherence to wisdom and truth;
> For as a mere trifle, its movements unhinge,
> So intemperance in life many years will infringe;
> To age it behoves to pass well the hours remaining
> And so life's closing scenes with firmness sustaining.   *(MS)*

------------- ♦ -------------

CLOTHES

If someone sees his clothes destroyed by fire it signifies vexation, injury, reproach, legal problems and loss of friends. If anyone dreams he has a suit on, which he likes, it signifies joy, profit and good success in business. If a woman dreams she is dressed in a hood, that indicates damage and dishonour. If someone dreams she is dressed very expensively, it signifies honour to her and her husband. If a man or woman dreams they are poorly dressed, it signifies trouble and sadness. If anyone dreams his clothes are filthy, or that he has tattered clothes that signifies sin, blame and shame in the world. To dream your clothes are embroidered signifies joy and honour.   *(T)*

For a girl to dream of putting on new clothes means that she will soon marry.   *(D&M)*

For a wife or husband to dream of wearing the other's clothes is an omen that the dreamer will outlive his or her partner. A dream of buying clothes signifies honour and beauty.   *(M)*

To dream of white garments is good only to priests, to others it signifies trouble. To dream of a black garment signifies good luck and good health. To dream you are wearing clothes of many colours or scarlet, for priests or actors is good; to others it signifies troubles and dangers resulting from the revealing of secrets, and to the sick, that they will become seriously ill. To dream you see a woman in a fine dress is good only to those who are unmarried or to actors. To the married this dream sometimes foretells the illness or loss of their wife. To dream that you have a dress in the fashion of a foreign country signifies good luck to someone who is about to travel there or live there; to others it signifies sickness or problems. To dream you have a delicate and sumptuous dress is good for everyone, as it indicates increased prosperity. To dream of a coat, short cloak or skirt of woollen cloth signifies anger, but it is better to dream you lose them than that you find or have them; but the loss of any other garment is evil, for a garment lost signifies loss of evils that are associated with them. It is always better to dream of having good, attractive and clean clothes than old and dirty ones. *(A)*

See also **Apparel, Dress, Garments.**

———— ◆ ————

CLOUDS

To see a cloud coming for a short while over the sun denotes that the friends of your partner will place barriers in the way of your relationship. For a time these will seem insurmountable. However, the tide of fortune will eventually begin to flow in your favour, and you will be welcomed by those who formerly would have nothing to say to you. *(O)*

If the clouds are thick and heavy, you will shortly be mixed up in a quarrel which will leave you with fewer friends, and the dispute will not end satisfactorily for you. If, however, the clouds disperse, you may look for happiness after the trouble is settled. *(M)*

To dream of white clouds signifies prosperity; clouds mounting high denotes voyages, the return of the absent and revealing of secrets. *(OM)*

———— ◆ ————

CLOVER

Health, wealth and happiness await the person who dreams of walking in a field of clover. *(M)*

Look forward to the future with hope, for it will be bright and happy. To the young and the lover it foretells a happy marriage *(OM)*

———— ◆ ————

CLOVES

Your offspring will be a source of great pleasure to you. *(OM)*

———— ◆ ————

CLOWN

Others think you stupid. *(OM)*

———— ◆ ————

COACH

To dream you get out of a coach signifies being degraded from great honour, and disgrace for criminal actions. *(T)*

To dream you are riding in a coach denotes that you love idleness, are proud and will die poor. *(GD)*

To see a coach drawn by black horses means that you will be present at a funeral. If, however, you are riding in a coach, you may look forward to a spell of luxury and idleness. Be on your guard against some disgraceful act, if you dream of alighting from a coach. *(M)*

To dream you are riding in a coach is a very unlucky omen. It foretells poverty and disgrace. If you are in love, your sweetheart will be idle and bad-tempered. If you are in trade, you will become bankrupt, and if you are a farmer, your goods will be seized. It also denotes that the dreamer will shortly be put in prison. *(OM)*

------------------------------- ♦ -------------------------------

COALS, COAL-PIT, COAL-MINE and COLLIERY

To see burning coals signifies humiliation and reproach. *(T)*

To dream of putting coals on the fire means that in, at most, a few days you will meet with a stranger who will have much to do with your future life. A young man dreaming of taking coals off the fire can assume that he will change his mind about his current sweetheart, and from thinking her perfect will come to find no end of faults in her. *(O)*

To dream that you are shovelling coals foretells a gift of money, and if you are putting the coals on the fire and they burn brightly, other people will chase you for the money. *(M)*

If you dream of walking in or looking down the shaft of a coal-mine, be careful that your partner in life is not a widower or widow. Unhappiness will follow such an alliance if you ignore the warning. For a young woman to dream that she is wandering in a colliery means that she cannot obtain all her desires. In love, her imagined perfect partner is far above what the reality will be; he will be a faithful lover, but not wealthy, and she will be compelled to moderate her ambition. She will also be disappointed in other things, but not as badly off as many. She will have a comfortable home, though it will not be as elegant as she wishes, but it will be contented and peaceful. *(M)*

To see coals burning brightly foretells success in love. To dream of coals is a very unlucky omen. It denotes many problems. To dream you see coals burning is a good sign if they are clear and bright. To dream you see the coals extinguished and reduced to cinders denotes death, either to yourself or some near relation or friend. To dream of being in the bottom of a coal-pit signifies marrying a widow; but whoever marries her will never fully understand her intentions. To be in or near a coal-pit warns you of danger. *(OM)*

To dream you see dead coals signifies expedition in business. To dream you see burning coals threatens you with humiliation and reproach. *(D&M2)*

These always infer a fair signal of honour. *(MS)*

------------------------------- ♦ -------------------------------

COAT

To dream that you have torn your coat is a sign that your mature years will not be happy. Your children will desert you and offer no financial support when you need it. To dream you tear the sleeve of your coat is a sign that you will commence a new business and work hard to be successful; but it will not live up to your expectations and desires. To dream that you are wearing a beautiful and fashionable coat is a sign that financial problems will shortly overtake you. *(M)*

To dream of a coat of mail warns you to be careful in all your dealings. *(OM)*

————— ♦ —————

COBBLER

You will cope with your problems and experience good fortune to follow.
(OM)

————— ♦ —————

COCK

To dream you see or hear a cock crow signifies joy and prosperity. To see two cocks fighting denotes quarrels and fighting. *(T)*

To dream of the crowing of a cock is the forerunner of good news. *(M)*

You will be loved by the opposite sex if you see a cock. To see cocks fighting indicates disagreements and trouble in your home. *(OM)*

To dream of a cock signifies that you will become a father, or the master in your house. *(A)*

To dream you see a cock in the house is a good sign for anyone about to marry. It also signifies that you will earn enough money to live comfortably. It is a bad omen for the sick since it indicates feverishness. It also foretells that secrets will be revealed. *(A)*

To hear a rooster crowing in the morning means that you will soon receive a letter containing news which will cause you considerable and lasting uneasiness. *(O)*

————— ♦ —————

COCKLES

Expect bad news from abroad. *(OM)*

————— ♦ —————

COCOA

To dream that you are drinking cocoa is very good. You will live a contented life. The things that once troubled your mind will not affect it now. *(M)*

————— ♦ —————

COFFEE

To see or roast coffee indicates unhappiness and persecution. *(OM)*

————— ♦ —————

COFFEE HOUSE

To eat your meal in a coffee house is a sign that you will have pretty general good health; you will also be popular among your work colleagues; and, even when some trifling difficulties arise in the conduct of those you work with, you will not be blamed, because you will be of a very peaceful turn of mind and disposition. *(M)*

You will hear of misfortune concerning a relative or acquaintance. *(OM)*

————— ♦ —————

COFFIN

To dream of seeing a coffin is a very bad omen, suggesting a downward turn in all your affairs. *(O)*

A coffin in a dream denotes a wedding invitation and sickness for the bride or bridegroom during the first year of married life.   *(M)*
   Disagreements and losses.   *(OM)*
   To dream of coffins and black shrouds means sudden death.   *(P&F)*
            No dependance can well on this ever be placed,
            Tho' in it I conclude a surprise may well be placed.   *(MS)*

——————— ♦ ———————

COINS

To dream of coins is a very significant dream. If you dream of a large number of copper coins it is indicative of plenty. To dream you see a large quantity of silver coins means an average crop, trade or business, and fair weather. There will not be many independencies made for some time; want of confidence in the money market and on the Stock Exchange will prevent much business being done. But to dream that you see a great quantity of gold coins is indicative of commercial depression; for some time the scarcity of work and wages will be so great that want will be felt pretty keenly in some families.   *(M)*

——————— ♦ ———————

COKE

To dream that you see a bright fire of coke is a sign that either your father or mother are about to fall ill or there will be slackness of work and you will be short of money and need to borrow to obtain the necessities of life. *(M)*

——————— ♦ ———————

COLD

To dream that you are suffering from a chill denotes a falling-off in affection, either of a friend or a sweetheart.   *(M)*
   Comfort and good friends. Though you may have many problems, in the end you will be happy.   *(OM)*

——————— ♦ ———————

COLLAR

For a young woman to dream that she is putting on her collar before a mirror is a sign that there is a young man in her neighbourhood who wants to marry her. He may meet her when she doesn't expect him; she has never met him before, but he has wanted to meet her for some time and has been calculating the best way to approach her.   *(M)*

——————— ♦ ———————

COLLAR BONE

To dream that your collar bone is broken in an accident means that some unpleasant affair will happen in the circle of your friends or acquaintances and some of your friends will break a limb.   *(M)*

——————— ♦ ———————

COLLEGE

For a young man to dream that he is a student in a college is a sign that he needs to further his education before he will rise to a position of eminence and trust. *(M)*

------------- ◆ -------------

COLONEL
For a young woman to dream that she is in the company of the first officer of a regiment is a sign that her husband will never be of the first rank in any profession. She need not look so high for a partner for life. Her husband will be a good man, but not a leader in authority. *(M)*

------------- ◆ -------------

COMBING
To dream of combing the hair is a sign of prosperity following grief. If you are combing another person's hair, you will be obliged to accept a low situation, but unless the comb breaks you will rise to higher things. *(M)*

For any person to dream of combing his own or someone else's hair is good, both for a man or a woman, because it signifies getting out of difficult times. *(D&M2)*

Your work will be heavy and profitless, especially if you find difficulty in combing your hair; but if easy and the hair is beautiful, it means gain and a new friendship. *(OM)*

------------- ◆ -------------

COMEDIAN
For a young girl to dream that a comedian has fallen in love with her is a sign that she will have a desire to go on the stage as a professional actress. It would be best to stifle the desire, as there will not be that success attending her efforts that she should wish. *(M)*

------------- ◆ -------------

COMEDY or FARCE
To dream you see a comedy, farce or some other recreation, signifies good success in business. *(T)*

You are not well thought of by others and will meet with trouble and loss of reputation. *(M)*

------------- ◆ -------------

COMETS
To see several comets, or other stars with streaming tails, signifies future evils such as war, epidemics and famine. *(T)*

A comet in a dream is a forerunner of evil, and often forebodes shattered hopes and wrecked affections. *(M)*

To dream you see a comet is ominous of war, plague, famine and death. This dream warns you to avoid all changes; do not travel or walk on an unmade road. *(OM)*

------------- ◆ -------------

COMFORT
To dream you comfort anyone means injury and mishap to the rich and

happy; but to the poor and suffering, aid and comfort. *(OM)*

———— ◆ ————

COMMANDING

To command anyone signifies trouble. To see someone in command signifies anger and authority. *(T)*

———— ◆ ————

COMMUNION

Happy love, enjoyment. *(OM)*

———— ◆ ————

COMPASSES

For a young man to dream that he is working with this instrument is a sign that some of those who are studying with him will be far ahead of him in the branches of study in which he is spending his time. More close application is required before he will be able to pass examinations with flying colours. *(M)*

———— ◆ ————

COMPETITOR

For a young man to dream that he is a competitor in either racing, jumping, swimming or rowing races is a sign that he will soon lose his physical strength by an accident. *(M)*

———— ◆ ————

COMPLIMENT

To dream that you are receiving compliments from a stranger is a sign that you will arouse the jealousy of your sweetheart through appearing to appreciate the attentions of a third party. *(M)*

———— ◆ ————

CONCERT

To dream of taking part in a concert as a member of the chorus denotes, if the concert is going off successfully, that you will play an important part in society, and work harmoniously with your friends and colleagues. Should the concert of your dream, however, be remarkable for bad tune and bad time, this predicts that you take more pleasure in spiting your enemies than in pleasing your friends, and that you will soon discover this to be a mistaken policy. *(O)*

For a young man to dream he is at a concert is a sign that he will never become proficient in the art of public speaking or reciting. He will have an ear for time and tune, but will not want to cultivate the art of singing. *(M)*

———— ◆ ————

CONCERTINA

For a young man to dream that he hears one of these instruments played means that he will become fond of dancing, in which he will become adept by practice. *(M)*

CONFECTIONERY

To dream you make pies, cakes, tarts or sweets signifies joy and profit. To taste sweet things signifies subtlety. *(T)*

   To dream that you make confections or sweets means pleasure. To eat them, you will meet with advantages and success. *(OM)*

———— ♦ ————

CONFIRMATION

For a young woman to dream that she attends the confirmation service and is a candidate of that ceremony is a good sign. She will become a scholar in theology and able to defend the doctrines of the church of which she is a member. *(M)*

———— ♦ ————

CONFRONT

To dream that you confront someone who has deceived you is a sign that you will not have courage to speak in your own defence when opposed by someone who does not believe or practise some of the principles which you adopt. *(M)*

———— ♦ ————

CONFUSION

Dreaming of things about you being in confusion is a sign that the many plans on which you are at present engaged require weeding out, for some of them are worthless and wasting your time and energy. *(O)*

———— ♦ ————

CONGREGATION

To dream that you see a large congregation of people assembled in a chapel or other place of worship is a sign that you will be left alone when you are ill. Very few of your friends will call on you as they did before, probably because someone has been spreading lies about you. *(M)*

———— ♦ ————

CONJURER

To dream you see a conjurer perform is a sign that you will be deceived by the words of a deep, designing woman, who uses great cunning and coaxing to get what she wants. *(M)*

———— ♦ ————

CONSUMPTION

To dream that you are subject to this lingering disease is a sign that you will have a strong voice, healthy look, sound body and fair complexion. If you work at a desk job you had better have a change, one that will be for the better preservation of your health. *(M)*

———— ♦ ————

CONUNDRUM

To dream that you compose a conundrum is a sign that you will never become adept at solving intricacies or explaining mysteries. You will feel your want of suitable language when trying to tell a story. *(M)*

————— ♦ —————

CONVICTED
To be convicted of fraud, theft or murder is a sign that all your life you will be a law-abiding citizen, highly respected, well regarded and much loved. Your integrity, virtue and love of justice will raise your character very much in the minds of those of your friends who know you better than any strangers possibly can do. *(OM)*

————— ♦ —————

COOK
To dream you see a cook in the house is good to those who want to marry and also to the poor, but it also signifies the revealing of secrets, for the cook's apparel is white and is seen by many. *(DSG)*

————— ♦ —————

COOKING
Either roasting or frying, stewing or boiling. Represents the approach of evil turmoiling. *(MS)*

————— ♦ —————

CORKSCREW
To dream of using a corkscrew is indicative of a long illness, but not necessarily of the dreamer. Probably a near relation will fall ill and cause anxiety. To dream that in using this article you break it, is a sign that you will suddenly lose a dear friend through some infectious disease. *(M)*

————— ♦ —————

CORN, CORN STACKS and CORNS on the FEET
If anyone dreams his flesh is covered with corns he will grow rich proportionately to the number of corns. To see a stack of corn destroyed by fire signifies famine and death, but if it is not destroyed it denotes fertility and great riches to the dreamer. To dream that you gather ripe corn signifies profit and riches. To dream that you see stacks of corn signifies profit and abundance to the dreamer. On the contrary, to see a small quantity, signifies famine and need. *(T)*

To dream you see corn fields denotes success in business, joy to the lover or a prosperous voyage to a sailor. To dream of peas and all sorts of grain is good as they indicate abundance. *(GD)*

A field of corn denotes plenty, with poverty to follow, unless you are careful to put by for a rainy day when you are prosperous. To dream of a corn on the foot is a warning that your friends talk about you behind your back. *(M)*

To dream that you see fields of corn, or that you are among unthreshed corn, is a very favourable omen; it denotes success in business. To the lover it announces that you will marry and become rich and happy. *(OM)*

To dream you are in a field of standing corn, denotes prosperity and great joy. *(P&F)*

To dream of seeing a barn full of corn indicates marrying a good wife or overcoming enemies. *(D&M2)*

———— ◆ ————

CORNER

For a young woman to dream that she stands in a corner with her sweetheart is a sign that her marriage is not to take place yet; perhaps years may intervene before she is asked to become a bride. For a young man this means that he is too slow in courtship for the young women he is dating. She does not think it is necessary for them to start out with their own house and new furniture before they marry. Unless he sets a wedding date, she will go off with someone else if she gets a chance. *(M)*

———— ◆ ————

CORNET

To hear a cornet being played foretells strife and family quarrels. If you like the music, you will be involved in the unpleasantness. *(M)*

———— ◆ ————

CORPSE

If you see the corpse of a near relative, do not enter into a hasty marriage, for unhappiness will follow. A little thought will probably show you that your prospective partner differs from you in so many things that such a relationship would be foolish. To see your own corpse signifies that you will soon find much happiness in ministering to the wants of others. If the corpse is that of a complete stranger, someone will take an interest in your welfare and bring much happiness into your life. *(M)*

News of the sick; a drowned corpse means estrangement. *(OM)*

———— ◆ ————

COTTAGE

For a young unmarried woman to dream that she is sitting with her husband in a newly-furnished cottage is indicative of an argument and unpleasant problems in their relationship because of their different tastes and because they are unaware of each other's failings. She has to learn that give and take is vital in any relationship. *(M)*

———— ◆ ————

COTTON

To dream that you see great quantities of cotton is a sign that the manufacture and demand will be scarce. Those who work in the production will have short time and poor wages. *(M)*

———— ◆ ————

COUGH

To dream that you are troubled with a violent cough is a sign that you will have great strength of lungs and chest. You may well be attacked with a bout of gout or rheumatism, however. *(M)*

COUNTENANCE
To dream you see a very handsome face signifies joy, content and health. To see a beautiful face, unlike your own, signifies honour. *(T)*

———— ♦ ————

COUNTING the HOURS
To dream that you are counting the hours, if it is in the morning, indicates happiness and that your partner is true to you, but if it is in the afternoon, that you will suffer problems and that your mistress is unfaithful. *(DSG)*

———— ♦ ————

COUNTRY
To dream of the country promises success to some project you have in mind, if only you apply yourself seriously to it. *(M)*

———— ♦ ————

COUNTRY TOWN
To dream of having moved to a country town is a sign that by your present pursuits and general course of life you are liable to fall intellectually asleep, and that prudence suggests your taking steps to counteract that danger. *(O)*

———— ♦ ————

COURT of LAW
To dream you are giving evidence in a court of law foretells that you are about to incur a heavy bill for legal expenses. Should the counsel examining you have a piece of paper in his hand, you may infer that you are to get into trouble through writing a letter of importance and neglecting the wise rule of going over it afterwards and striking out all the adjectives. *(O)*

———— ♦ ————

COURTSHIP
For a young woman to dream that she has started courting is a sign that she will have many followers, but she will not like any of them. Through being too particular as to appearance, she will not marry until late in life. For a young man to dream that he has started courting is a sign that the grand ideas he has always had of the pleasures of being single will remain unchanged. He will be afraid of getting involved with a charming girl, and avoid the idea of marriage as an expensive and unwanted tie. He will long remain a bachelor. *(M)*

———— ♦ ————

COUSIN
To dream that your cousin writes to you is indicative of news from an old lover, who wants to renew a loving relationship. *(M)*

———— ♦ ————

COWS
To dream you see or have many cows signifies wealth and plenty. *(T)*
One cow means good luck; a herd means prosperity. *(OM)*

COWSLIPS

If in your dream you see cowslips in full bloom, there will be a sudden and unexpected change in your circumstances. A young wife may become pregnant, a young man may find a new lover, although he will not marry her. *(M)*

———— ♦ ————

CRAB

Beware of the law. *(OM)*

———— ♦ ————

CRADLE

For a mother to dream that her child's cradle is broken means the illness and possible death of her youngest child. She will have nights of watching and days of anxiety over the sick bed of one of her favourite children, but by care and attention the child may recover. To dream that the cradle rocks itself, the mother may expect twins to be her next charges. *(M)*

> From this symbol of infancy some apprehend
> The death of a dearly beloved absent friend;
> But I must conclude—to believe me you're bound—
> That it shortly to you will most useful be found. *(MS)*

———— ♦ ————

CRANES

To dream you see a flock of cranes on the wing foretells the approach of enemies and thieves. In winter it signifies bad weather. *(T)*

———— ♦ ————

CRAWL

To dream you are crawling on the floor is bad; but to dream you are crawling on the roof of a house is good. *(OM)*

———— ♦ ————

CREAM

To dream you see cream spilt on you signifies the infusion of some grace by the Holy Ghost. *(T)*

———— ♦ ————

CREPE

To dream that you wear this emblem of mourning is a sign that you will soon receive a piece of wedding cake from an old schoolmate or some other dear friend of your youth. *(M)*

———— ♦ ————

CREW

To dream that you see the crew of a vessel hard at work, reefing their sails and doing other duties on board, is a sign that storms at sea will be frequent, in some of which your friend or friends will be exposed to shipwreck or loss of goods. *(M)*

CRICKET

If you see a cricket or hear it chirp, beware of a stranger who will attempt to flatter you. To dream that you take part in a game of cricket is a sign that you will suffer from an injury to your legs either from ulcers, gout or rheumatism.
(M)

━━━━━ ◆ ━━━━━

CRIES

If in your dream you hear a cry of distress, expect glad news; some of your relatives who have been married for some time and are childless, will soon be expecting a baby. If the cry is one of joy you must look out for someone bringing or sending you news of the death of a close friend. If the cry is one of despair, as in the case of shipwreck or fire at sea, either you or your wife will in due course gain a great deal by speculation.
(M)

━━━━━ ◆ ━━━━━

CRINOLINE

For a woman to dream that she is wearing a large, old-fashioned crinoline means that she will be forced to save money at home, both on clothes and household expenses, because money will be short.
(M)

━━━━━ ◆ ━━━━━

CROCHET WORK

For a young woman to dream that she is crocheting is a sign that her hobbies are carried on at the expense of her more important jobs.
(M)

━━━━━ ◆ ━━━━━

CROCODILE

Dreaming of seeing a crocodile indicates that your good nature is at present imposed upon by one who enjoys the triumph of gaining sympathy by telling lies to people.
(O)

Denotes false friendship. Probably someone is imposing on your good nature.
(M)

Great dangers.
(OM)

To dream of crocodiles signifies pirates and robbers at sea or murderers and wicked people.
(A)

━━━━━ ◆ ━━━━━

CROCUS

To dream that you see a number of these early flowers of spring is a sign that peace and domestic happiness will be yours.
(M)

━━━━━ ◆ ━━━━━

CROSS

To dream you see a cross carried along signifies sadness.
(T)

To see a cross of gold is an indication that you will marry well and be happy; or, if you are already married, your marriage will continue to be a happy one. If the cross is of wood, however, and you are single, your marriage will not be a wealthy one, but it will be happy all the same. If married, you will have your share of petty worries, but nothing serious will spoil your domestic bliss. *(M)*

━━━━━ ◆ ━━━━━

CROSS BONES

To married or single, a moral prediction,
Of health in decay and wants malediction. *(MS)*

━━━━━ ◆ ━━━━━

CROSS PURPOSE

To dream you play at cross purposes signifies prosperity, joy, pleasure, health and harmony among friends and relations. *(OM)*

━━━━━ ◆ ━━━━━

CROW

To dream you see a crow signifies completion of successful business. *(T)*

To dream of a crow and other birds of prey flying in cloudy weather denotes anger, loss and misery. *(D&M)*

To dream you see a crow flying is bad luck; and if it is croaking unpleasantly, so much the worse. *(OM)*

━━━━━ ◆ ━━━━━

CROWING

To dream you are crowing, or that you hear others crowing, denotes bad luck, especially to lovers; but to dream that you hear pigeons cooing is good, especially to those who are newly married, as it denotes happiness. *(OM)*

━━━━━ ◆ ━━━━━

CROWN

To dream you are wearing a gold crown signifies that you are appreciated by those in authority and will receive many presents. To carry a gold crown in your hand signifies honour and dignity. *(T)*

A crown of precious stones predicts that you will shortly receive an invitation to a wedding which will give you great pleasure. A crown of gold or silver denotes enemies, of whom you must be wary; of brass or iron signifies illness and distress. *(M)*

To dream you see these emblems of royalty portends success and elevation to dignities, either in the church or state. For a girl to dream of a crown shows she will marry a very industrious man, or one who is rich. *(OM)*

━━━━━ ◆ ━━━━━

CRUCIFIED

To dream you are crucified in a town signifies that you will obtain property or a job in that town. *(A)*

━━━━━ ◆ ━━━━━

CRUST

To dream that you are forced to beg for a crust of bread is a good dream.

Though your parents may not have been well off, you will rise to be a wealthy and respected member of society. *(M)*

————————— ♦ —————————

CRUTCHES

To dream you are walking on crutches is a very unfavourable omen. To dream you see someone else walking on crutches denotes that these things will happen to some friend. If you are a married man, then your wife is unfaithful. *(OM)*

For a married woman to dream of crutches signifies that her husband is ruining himself with a mistress. *(DSG)*

————————— ♦ —————————

CRYING

If you weep in your sleep you will have reason to smile when you are awake. *(M)*

————————— ♦ —————————

CRYSTAL

To dream that you see a crystal substance is a sign that those whom you have respected will lose their good character and prospects by succumbing to some temptation that is presented to them. *(M)*

————————— ♦ —————————

CUCKOO

If a girl dreams of hearing the cuckoo, she can tell how many years will elapse before she marries. The number of years will be the same as the number of times the bird is heard calling in the dream. A young man's dream in which he listens to the cuckoo means that he is at present in danger of making a wrong choice; be warned that when choosing a marriage partner, it is most important to take a bird out of a good nest. *(O)*

After hearing a cuckoo sing, be on your guard. It is a warning against the evil designs of a supposed friend. *(M)*

Misfortune; to hear one indicates mourning. *(OM)*

————————— ♦ —————————

CUCUMBER

To dream of eating cucumber denotes vain hope. Some are of the opinion that when sick people dream of melons and cucumbers, that means they will recover. *(T)*

To dream of cucumbers denotes recovery to the sick, and that you will soon fall in love, or that you are in love and you will marry. *(OM)*

> To the sick always augurs health's restoration,
> And always preludes a removal of station. *(MS)*

————————— ♦ —————————

CUP

An empty cup is a sign of troubled times ahead. A full one tells of good opportunities coming your way, which you must grasp without hesitation if you want to make a success of life. *(M)*

CUPBOARDS or CABINET

If you dream you see a cabinet or cupboard burning, that signifies sickness or death to the owner. *(T)*

To dream that your cupboard doors open by themselves means that there will be plenty of the essentials in your home, but you can expect the bread-winner to fall ill before long. *(M)*

———— ♦ ————

CURATE

For a young woman to dream that she marries a curate is a sign that a lawyer will seek her company and want to marry her. It may, however, prove a very long engagement, if in fact they do marry. *(M)*

———— ♦ ————

CURRANTS

Blackcurrants are forerunners of good fortune, and if you are eating them your married life will be happy, and you will have a large family. Redcurrants are not such good omens, for false friends and sickness follow in their wake. *(M)*

Whitecurrants indicate success. *(OM)*

———— ♦ ————

CURTAIN

To dream of seeing a curtain and hearing a noise behind it means that on the following night you will dream another dream which will make a surprising revelation to you in the future. *(O)*

To dream of a curtain means that someone is hiding something from you which, if you knew of it, would make for good fortune. If you touch the curtain, the thing will be revealed to you at an early date. *(M)*

———— ♦ ————

CUSHION

To dream that the cushion of your chair is torn is a sign that you will have sciatica, or severe pains in the back. It will be best for you to consult a skilful doctor. *(M)*

———— ♦ ————

CUSTARD

To dream that you eat custard is a sign that you will have severe dental problems in a few months or years, and will require the skills of a good dentist. *(M)*

———— ♦ ————

CYPRESS TREE

To dream you see a cypress tree denotes death, affliction and obstruction in business. *(T)*

Dreaming of a cypress tree denotes bad news is about to come to someone who is dear to you. *(OM)*

DAGGERS

To dream of seeing a dagger, either held by yourself or anyone else, portends that you are about to have a serious argument with a close acquaintance which will end in your becoming enemies for life.   *(O)*

These weapons denote evil influences which, however, will make for your good in the end.   *(M)*

———————— ◆ ————————

DAHLIA

To dream of these flowers is a sign of thrift. If a lady dreams of them it foretells that her husband will make money rapidly. To a young girl it predicts the same of her lover.   *(M)*

———————— ◆ ————————

DAIRY

If you are helping in the work of a dairy you will marry someone in the same station of life, but you will have plenty all your life. If you are already married your social position will improve. If you are skimming milk and taste the cream, you will have a windfall of money from an unexpected quarter. *(M)*

Happiness, a fortunate marriage.   *(OM)*

———————— ◆ ————————

DAIRYMAID

For a young man to dream of seeing a dairymaid busy at work denotes that he will fall in love with an industrious seamstress or dressmaker, whose business will be a great help to him, and aid him in his prosperity in financial affairs.   *(M)*

———————— ◆ ————————

DAISIES

To dream about gathering daisies is exceedingly fortunate. It foretells that you will obtain your wishes whatever they may be.   *(O)*

Your dearest wish will be fulfilled. But beware of trusting strangers; you will be deceived unless you are very careful.   *(M)*

It is good to dream of daisies in the spring and summer, but bad in autumn or winter.   *(OM)*

———————— ◆ ————————

DAMSONS

If you dream of eating this kind of plum when it is out of season expect great trouble, annoyance and vexation. Some of the affairs of your life will be very complicated and difficult. *(M)*

———————— ♦ ————————

DANCING

To dream you see yourself or other people dance at a ball signifies joy, pleasure, recreation and inheritance. *(T)*

To dream you are dancing at a ball foretells that you will shortly receive some joyful news from a long-absent friend and that you are about to inherit some unexpected fortune; it foretells success and happiness. *(GD)*

To dream of watching dancing means that before long a death will occur in your family of one regarded with great affection by you all. *(O)*

To dream that you are at a dance is a good omen. Pleasant news is travelling towards you, and someone loves you dearly. If you merely look on at the dance you will receive a big disappointment, but something will happen to recompense you. *(M)*

To dream you are leaping and running in a dance signifies prosperity in affairs; but to dance without music foretells want of money. *(A)*

———————— ♦ ————————

DANDELION

If you dream that you see these flowers in profusion it is a sign that news will shortly come to you of the marriage of one of your closest male friends. *(M)*

To dream of gathering dandelions is ominous. To dream you see a large bed of them denotes that you have many new enemies forming, who will injure you behind your back. If one in love dreams of dandelions, it denotes that their sweetheart is or soon will be unfaithful to them. *(OM)*

———————— ♦ ————————

DANGER

To dream of being in danger shows success in life; to shun it, misfortune. *(M)*

———————— ♦ ————————

DARKNESS

To dream you see darkness signifies sin. *(T)*

To dream of being in the dark is a sign of disappointment. *(D&M2)*

To dream of groping about a strange place in darkness denotes that you will receive an urgent message calling you to an unfamiliar location where sorrow awaits you. *(M)*

To dream you are in a very dark place, or that you are in the dark, is a very unfavourable omen. To dream you get out of darkness denotes good to the dreamer. Expect good news from a distant country. *(OM)*

———————— ♦ ————————

DATES

You are likely to be admired by some member of the opposite sex. *(OM)*

DAUGHTER

For a newly-married woman to dream that her first child will be a daughter denotes that her husband will be presented by her with a fine, healthy chubby-faced boy. *(M)*

------- ♦ -------

DAWN

To see the dawn, days of storm and stress lie before you. *(OM)*

------- ♦ -------

DEAD MARCH

To hear this played is a good sign for your dearest friend. He or she will have reason to rejoice at an early date. *(M)*

------- ♦ -------

DEAFNESS

To dream that you are afflicted with deafness denotes that, through the kind actions of a stranger, you will miss hearing something which would cause you unhappiness. *(M)*

------- ♦ -------

DEATH

If anyone dreams he is dead, he will work for someone in authority, will grow rich and live a long time, although not without much envy. If it seems that he is put into a grave and buried, that indicates he will die poor, although some people believe that to dream you are dead and buried means that you will inherit property, the size of which will be in relation to the amount of earth under which you are buried. If a person dreams he sees someone who is dead and he believes him to be alive, that signifies that he is bringing God's message and should be listened to. If anyone dreams that a dead man takes away his clothes, robs him of his money or food, it is a sign of death to him or to some of his nearest relations and friends. To dream you see a man who is already dead die a second time signifies the death of your nearest relations of the same name and surname. If anyone dreams he was involved with a dead woman he will be loved and maintained by some great lady. To dream that you give anything to someone who is dead signifies loss. *(T)*

To dream of a dead friend and talking with him denotes prosperity. To dream of death or seeing a friend dead denotes that they are at ease. *(D&M)*

To dream you are dead denotes a speedy marriage and that you will be successful in all your undertakings; to those who are married it foretells young children and that they will be dutiful and give you great comfort. To dream you see another person dead denotes friends will abuse you; if you are in love your sweetheart will prove false; if you are in a trade, you will be conned; if you are a farmer, you will lose money and may be robbed. If anyone dreams of seeing a friend who is dead it is a sign of hearing of some friend or person whom you have not seen for a long time. *(GD)*

To dream of seeing the spirits of the dead, whether relations or friends, means long life to the living, combined with good health and easy circumstances. Should you see a dead body in a dream it signifies a speedy marriage, either for yourself or for a friend. *(O)*

To see a friend dead means that person is in good health. *(P&F)*

If you dream of a death you will hear of a birth. If the person who is supposed to be dead is someone you know who has been ill for some time, he or she will recover. To dream that you stand beside the death bed of one of your friends or relations is indicative of marriage. *(M)*

To dream of talking with dead people is a good, auspicious dream, and signifies a boldness of courage and a very clear conscience. To dream that you are dead denotes a speedy marriage. *(OM)*

To dream of death is a good dream for fathers, poets, orators and also philosophers, for the first will have children who will live and prosper, and the others will compose works worth remembering. It is also a good dream for anyone expecting an inheritance, or who wants to buy land. *(A)*

To dream that you see death denotes happiness and long life; though if you are a farmer you will lose money by horses and may be robbed. *(GD2)*

> To dream of death a marriage means;
> So variegated are life's scenes. *(N)*
> To dream you are dead foretells speedy marriage,
> In pregnancy ever a fatal miscarriage. *(MS)*

DEATH'S HEAD

You may discover some hidden secret. *(OM)*

> This awful phenomenon inculcates to all,
> The fate that to man must infallibly fall.
> Then remember to die is the bold way to face it,
> Not care you how soon then is sculptured 'Hic jacet'. *(MS)*

DEATH TICK

To dream that you hear the approach of death means that you will commit the error of marrying in haste, and will repent at your leisure. *(M)*

DEBT

To pay a debt in a dream denotes a loss of money through carelessness. If you dream that a debtor is paying you, be on your guard against lending to a friend. His or her story of woe will be false. *(M)*

DECAPITATE

To see someone decapitated, you will overcome enemies. It also indicates the return of a long-lost friend. *(OM)*

DECORATE

To decorate a room means poverty either of yourself or your friends. Some unfortunate circumstance will shortly happen to reduce your style of living. To dream you decorate yourself in beautiful clothes means want of neat clothing. You will have difficulty in obtaining fashionable clothes. *(M)*

————— ♦ —————

DEER

If anyone dreams he has killed a deer, and that he has the head or skin, that signifies that he will inherit the estate of some old man, or that he will overcome deceitful, cowardly and irresolute enemies. To dream you see a deer running signifies great wealth gained by application and subtlety at sport. *(T)*

If you see a deer in a forest and attempt to pursue it, you are wasting your time over some project which will never be brought to a successful conclusion. If the animal is dead, you will be the innocent cause of pain to your dearest friend. *(M)*

This is always a bad dream, indicating loss of money and trouble. *(OM)*

————— ♦ —————

DEFORMED

To dream that you are deformed, you have to fear shame, humiliation and sadness. *(OM)*

————— ♦ —————

DELICATE

For anyone to dream their health is delicate, if they are ill, means that recovery is at hand. For a healthy person to have this dream it means a greater robustness and strength will be enjoyed. *(M)*

————— ♦ —————

DELIGHT

To dream that you are really delighted with some event in your life means sorrow and trouble will shortly cross your path from some unexpected source. *(M)*

————— ♦ —————

DELUGE

Business loss. *(OM)*

————— ♦ —————

DENTIST

To dream you visit a dentist is indicative of indigestion becoming a source of illness to you. You had better take care of your health. *(M)*

————— ♦ —————

DESCENDING

To dream you descend a ladder signifies damage. *(T)*
Sickness and ill health. *(OM)*

DESERT

To travel in the desert indicates difficulties and dangers. *(OM)*

————— ♦ —————

DESK

To dream of sitting at a desk means that you are about to receive news that will be important or not, according to how near to or far away from the window you are. A closed desk signifies that a frequent correspondent is about to have a serious illness which is likely to prove fatal. *(O)*

If you are sitting at the desk, you will shortly be the recipient of a letter which will bring both good and bad news. If the desk is shut, you will lose a friend or relative who has corresponded with you regularly for some time. If a stranger is sitting at the desk, you will have dealings with a lawyer before you are many years older. *(M)*

————— ♦ —————

DESPAIR

To dream that you are thrown into a state of despair by some sad event means that you will soon have cause for joy and rejoicing. Your children will show great success in their education, or some of your friends will become more devoted to you by some act of great kindness towards you. Expect some very favourable turn of fortune from this dream. *(M)*

————— ♦ —————

DESSERT

To dream that you eat dessert of unripe or unseasonable fruit is a very bad dream. You will have trouble and sorrow on all counts. You will soon learn that troubles come in troops, or quickly follow in succession. To dream that you eat dessert of ripe and seasonable fruits is a good dream; no event will happen that will trouble or annoy you, but a succession of happy and prosperous things will take place in your life. *(M)*

————— ♦ —————

DESTROY

To dream of destroying something of worth denotes that an acquaintance will shock you by performing a mean act, and will try to drag you into the trouble which will follow. Keep a guard on your tongue and avoid scandal. *(M)*

————— ♦ —————

DESTRUCTION

To dream you destroy any place signifies deceit. *(T)*

————— ♦ —————

DETECTIVE

To dream of having dealings with a detective is a sure sign that you will never find yourself in a court of law or have reason to apply to the law for protection. *(M)*

DETEST

To dream that you detest a person means that you will shortly lose a valuable friend through some wicked slander which will be started by an enemy.   *(M)*

———————— ♦ ————————

DEVIL

If you dream you have seen the devil, and that he was tormented or frightened, that signifies that the dreamer is in danger of being rebuked or punished by a magistrate. If you dream you strike the devil, or someone you believe to be possessed and that you beat them, it is a sign that you will beat your real enemies. If anyone dreams he is possessed by some evil spirit, he will receive benefits from the government and be long-lived. If anyone dreams that he sees the devil, it is a very bad sign; for such a vision cannot bring along with it any good tidings; to the sick it foretells death and to the healthy it signifies melancholy, anger and violent sickness. If anyone dreams that the devil speaks to him, that signifies temptation, deceit, treachery, despair and often the ruin and death of the dreamer. To dream you are carried away by the devil is a worse dream; yet often this is a delightful dream to the dreamer, because when he wakes up, he feels delighted that he has been freed from so great an evil. To dream you see the devil as he is drawn by painters and poets—black and hideous, with horns, claws and a great tail—signifies torment and despair. To see yourself fight with the devil signifies gain.   *(T)*

To dream of the devil denotes many dangers will threaten you, all of which you will overcome.   *(GD)*

If in love, it forebodes that someone is endeavouring to alienate the affection of your sweetheart, but will be unsuccessful.   *(OM)*

For a sailor to dream of the devil signifies that he will marry a rich wife, while to those who are poor it signifies that they will find a good job. *(GD2)*

———————— ♦ ————————

DEW

To dream of the dew glittering in the morning sun is a very lucky omen. It means to the lover encouragement, to the husband and wife happiness in the home, to the businessman wealth, to the literary man reputation, to the musician applause—in short, to everyone his heart's desire and the reasonable reward of all his hard work.   *(O)*

Dewdrops predict happiness for the lover and success for the business man or woman. If domestic problems have arisen they will be resolved. *(M)*

———————— ♦ ————————

DIADEM

For a person to dream that he wears a crown is a sign of degradation. He will not have a happy life but will be dogged with failure and difficulties.
                                                                              (M)

DIAMONDS

If diamonds are seen in a dream they have a different meaning, depending on whether they belong to you or to someone else. If they are owned by someone else they mean for you wealth and success in all your endeavours. Should they, however, be your own, then you may infer that you are in danger of getting into severe problems caused by debts.   *(O)*

To see diamonds sparkling with great brilliance means happiness. To dream that you wear one or more predicts that you will be mixed up in some gossip that will lead you into serious trouble, and may even lose your job if you have one.   *(M)*

This is a dream of contrary indicating misfortune. To pick up diamonds means loss and sorrow; to eat them, much profit, wealth, success and happiness.   *(OM)*

———————— ♦ ————————

DIARRHOEA

Illness, loss and sorrow.   *(OM)*

———————— ♦ ————————

DICE

To dream you play at dice signifies deceit and craft and that you are in danger of losing your money to some wicked person.   *(T)*

Good fortune in marriage or business should follow a game of dice if you lose the game. If you have good fortune in the dream, however, look out for the contrary.   *(M)*

To dream that you are playing at dice or backgammon, denotes much good to the dreamer, in either love, marriage or business.   *(OM)*

———————— ♦ ————————

DIFFICULTY

If you imagine in your dream that you are in great difficulty, or in personal danger of any kind, it is a favourable sign, as such dreams always go by contrary.   *(M)*

———————— ♦ ————————

DIGGING

Much depends upon what you dig. If it is a grave, you may look for good fortune for yourself in some small affair, and the reverse for a friend. To dig up treasure of any kind signifies that you will soon have need for all your spare money. To dig a ditch or trench means illness.   *(M)*

Good fortune if the ground is good and dry; finding money means good fortune if you discover a lot.   *(OM)*

———————— ♦ ————————

DINNER

Being present at a dinner party indicates that you are about to be an innocent sufferer from the actions of someone in whom you have placed confidence. If you see any guest referring to a piece of paper, the probability is that you will be taken in through accepting a valueless cheque which will bounce. *(O)*

To dream that you are dining alone at a table laid for several people and that your meal is a frugal one denotes that after trouble there will be reason to celebrate. If you are a guest at a dinner party someone is playing you false, and you should look to your friends. If someone present is making a speech beware of flattery, which will lead you astray unless you keep a guard on your actions. *(M)*

If alone, avarice and poverty. In company, dissipation and prodigality. *(OM)*

———— ◆ ————

DIPLOMA

For a young man to dream that he has obtained a diploma for the practice of medicine, it is a sign that he will become skilled in surgery, if he studies it. Anatomy will be the most valuable study for him to follow. *(M)*

———— ◆ ————

DIRT

To dream of filth and dirt denotes dishonour and sickness. *(D&M)*

To dream of falling in the dirt shows disgrace and malice. *(GFT)*

To walk through dirt indicates misfortune. If your clothes are dirty, it shows sickness and trouble. *(OM)*

———— ◆ ————

DISCUSSION

If the discussion is between yourself and a number of people you will make a success of life by your own individual efforts rather than from anyone's help. To have a friendly discussion with an acquaintance means rapid promotion in your business, or an improvement in the affairs of your husband or sweetheart. *(M)*

———— ◆ ————

DISEASE

To dream you are stricken with a serious disease foretells that you will develop a liking for drink, which will lead to your ruin unless a friend keeps a watchful eye on you. *(M)*

———— ◆ ————

DISGRACE

To dream that you fall into disgrace by some thoughtless act is a sign that in most of your affairs you will display prudence of a kind that will bring you into the favour and reputation of your friends and acquaintances. *(M)*

———— ◆ ————

DISGUISE

If your friends appear to you disguised for a fancy dress party it means that you will have a visit from some old schoolfriends, whose altered personal appearance will prevent you from recognising them. *(M)*

DISH

For a woman to dream she has broken a pewter dish means that she will have a greater loss in a short time; some of her relatives will lose one of the faculties of the five senses. *(M)*

———— ♦ ————

DISPUTE

To dream that a dispute happens between you and some person with whom you have business is a sign of bad luck. After such a dream you should be careful of yourself, and be as gentle and reasonable as possible so that you do not give anyone any advantage over you. If you are in love, someone has attempted to injure you with your partner, and that they have in some degree succeeded; you should, therefore, after such a dream, be particularly thoughtful and attentive. *(M)*

———— ♦ ————

DISTRESS

Great distress in a dream is a sure omen that some person will make you indebted to him or her all your life. Probably they will help you make advances in life. *(M)*

———— ♦ ————

DISTRUST

To dream that you have reason to distrust a person generally means bad luck for a friend, or illness for a relative of whom you are very fond. If someone distrusts you, your friends have been talking about you, and you will have cause to regret ever having known one or more of them. *(M)*

———— ♦ ————

DITCH

To see great ditches or precipices and that you fall into them signifies that the dreamer will suffer a great deal of injury, hazard himself and his property by fire. To fall into a ditch signifies the loss of a cause or suit at law. To go over a ditch on a small plank signifies deceit by lawyers. *(T)*

To dream of a ditch containing muddy water is a sign that you will narrowly escape from a bad accident. If you fall into a ditch, whether dry or otherwise, you may look for serious trouble through an accident caused by your own carelessness. To dream of leaping over ditches indicates troublesome children, of which you will have a good share. *(M)*

To dream of deep ditches, steep mountains, rocks and other eminences, foretells danger and misfortune. *(OM)*

———— ♦ ————

DIVING

If you dive into water, some speculation in which you are involved will turn out unfavourably, or you are placing trust and confidence in someone unworthy of it, who will let you down. The young may infer from this dream that their lover is deceiving them. *(M)*

DIVORCE
Fidelity and love. (OM)

———————— ♦ ————————

DOCKS
To visit the docks of a seaport town is indicative of being confined at home to your room from gout, rheumatism or some other painful and severe illness. (M)

Good news from a distance. (OM)

———————— ♦ ————————

DOCTOR
To become a physician signifies cheerfulness. (T)

To open the door to a doctor portends good news, which you will receive by word of mouth. If, however, you see the doctor tending a sick friend or relative you will meet a friend whom you have not seen for many years, and will renew the old friendship. (M)

A good omen; fortune and health; a rise in life. (OM)

———————— ♦ ————————

DOGS
Dogs denote fidelity, courage and affection, if they belong to you; but those that belong to strangers signify infamous enemies. To dream that a dog barks and tears your clothes signifies an enemy is slandering you or trying to deprive you of your livelihood. To be disturbed by dogs barking signifies success over adversaries. (T)

To dream of dogs barking and pursuing you denotes lust, but if you pursue them it means the opposite. (D&M)

To dream of dogs has very different significations, according to how you see them. If they are friendly it is a lucky omen; if you have had a quarrel with a friend or sweetheart, you will make up to your advantage; if you are in love, your sweetheart will marry you and make you very happy; it denotes health, riches and honour. If they are barking and snarling at you, then your enemies are secretly endeavouring to destroy your reputation and happiness; if you are in love, be careful of your present sweetheart; if you marry him or her you will be unhappy and poor. If you dream they bite you, then you will experience some loss, if you are in love, your sweetheart will deceive you, and make you very unhappy. (GD)

To dream of seeing a dog begging means that you will experience the misery of waiting and watching for favours from those who are farther advanced in life than you:

> To speed to-day, to be put to-morrow;
> To feed on hope, to pine with fear and sorrow. (O)

Dogs are good omens. Your sweetheart will remain faithful to you, and you will have no cause to complain of lack of money or friends. Should the dog snarl at you, or be vicious in any other way, you will score over your enemies before long. (M)

DOLPHINS

To dream you see dolphins playing in the water denotes the loss of your sweetheart and the death of some near relation or friend. It is an unfavourable dream and signifies that your present pursuits will not be to your advantage. You would do well to move. *(DSG)*

———— ♦ ————

DOOR

To dream of a door opening unexpectedly is an intimation that you ought to be saving as much as possible, because if you accumulate a certain amount of capital a chance will occur which will enable you to make a lot of money. *(O)*

To see many doors indicates a visit from a person whom you distrust. If you are knocking at a door of a strange house and gain admittance you will make a new friend shortly; but if the door is not opened you will be disappointed in an engagement. *(M)*

———— ♦ ————

DOVES

These birds are omens of good fortune to come. If married, your partner in life and your children will make you happy, and never cause you a moment's anxiety by reckless behaviour. For the business man, the birds bring promise of increase in trade. If the birds are feeding out of your hand it denotes a removal to the country, where you will be greatly respected. *(M)*

Happiness in domestic affairs. *(OM)*

———— ♦ ————

DOWRY

For a man to dream that he has received a dowry with his wife is a sign that she will keep him poor all his life by her extravagant ways. *(M)*

———— ♦ ————

DRAGON

To see a dragon is a sign that you will see a person in authority and power. It also signifies riches and treasures. *(T)*

To see one, illusive happiness. By some authors it indicates great riches. *(OM)*

———— ♦ ————

DRAMA

To dream you see tragedies played signifies travel, fighting, injury and a thousand other evils; but to see a drama with a happy ending means that you will also experience a happy ending to your affairs. *(A)*

———— ♦ ————

DRAUGHTS

Playing draughts means your affections are being trifled with; beware. *(OM)*

DRAWBRIDGE
You will undertake an unexpected journey.   *(OM)*

————— ◆ —————

DRAWER
To find your drawer open is a sign of the security of your property, if you have any; if not of the security of your character from scandal.   *(M)*

————— ◆ —————

DRAWING
To draw pictures signifies joy without profit.   *(T)*
   To see drawings, expect good business increase.   *(OM)*

————— ◆ —————

DREAMS
To dream you relate your dreams to anyone shows that something unexpected will take place.   *(M)*

————— ◆ —————

DRESS
To dream of a new dress predicts that you will live to want; of an old one, that you will be comfortable all your life, but never really rich.   *(M)*
   White dresses mean good and kind friends; black ones indicate the death of a friend or relative; a torn dress shows misfortune.   *(OM)*
See also **APPAREL, CLOTHES, GARMENTS**

————— ◆ —————

DRINK
To dream you are drunk indicates an increase of money and recovery of health; but when you dream that you are drunk without drinking any alcohol, it is a bad omen, and you run the risk of being disgraced by some criminal action. If a man dreams he is drunk from a sweet and pleasant drink, it is a sign he will be respected by powerful people and they will make him rich. If a man dreams he is drunk with pure water, he will boast of his wealth without reason, and praise another person's strength. If anyone dreams he is drunk and vomits, he will run the risk of losing his money because he is forced to account for any illegally acquired money or because he loses everything through betting. To dream you are drunk signifies sickness. To dream you drink clear water is a good sign. To drink hot water signifies sickness. To drink stinking water signifies violent illness.   *(T)*
   To dream of drunkenness shows you will find a serviceable friend.   *(GD)*
   To dream of drinking unreasonably signifies that you will fall into some violent disease.   *(P&F)*
   To dream that you are suffering from thirst and somebody gives you a glass of wine, you will make a discovery through a friend which will bring you happiness. If instead of wine you receive water from a man, you will be married within the year if you are not engaged; and, if married, your

husband will introduce you to a friend of whom you will become very fond. *(M)*

To dream you drink wine with moderation is good. To dream that you are drinking from a stream or fountain, is a sign of sickness. To see a drunkard, opposition and worry. To dream you are drunk denotes that some person whom you do not yet know will become a very good friend. To a woman, it denotes that she will be loved by an excellent man whom she has not yet seen. *(OM)*

To dream you drink cold water is good, but hot water signifies sickness and problems. To dream you drink wine with reason but not to get drunk is good. To dream you drink sweet wine and see fair women and sleep under shady trees means success in love to anyone who wants to marry. To dream that you drink cocktails is only good if you are accustomed to drinking them. To dream you drink oil signifies sickness from poison. To drink from vessels or tankards of gold, silver or earthenware is good because it signifies tranquillity. All vessels of horn are good because they are unbreakable, but vessels of glass are evil. *(A)*

———— ◆ ————

DRIVING

To dream of driving is a sign that a habit you have acquired will lead you into serious trouble. To a business man or woman it denotes a falling-off of customers or clients, and to a lover disappointments brought about by his or her own foolishness. *(M)*

Expect to hear of a wedding or a christening. Honour and power will be yours. *(OM)*

To drive, lead or guide chariots through woods or deserts signifies death to all at hand. *(A)*

———— ◆ ————

DROPSY

To dream that you have dropsy is indicative of decline of health from diabetes. You will have good health for a long period, and then this complaint will set in. *(M)*

———— ◆ ————

DROUGHT

For a farmer to dream of seeing his crops or grass drying up for want of rain denotes that an accident will happen to him or his property during a storm, or that some of his livestock will die or meet with an accident. *(M)*

———— ◆ ————

DROWNING

To dream you are drowning or see another person drowning is good to the dreamer and denotes that he will be preserved through many strange difficulties. If you are a lover it denotes that your sweetheart is good-tempered and wants to marry you; if you are a sailor, it foretells a favourable and pleasant voyage. *(GD)*

To dream of being drowned denotes loss to the merchant and tradesman, and to young women signifies that they are about to discover that their affections are being trifled with. *(O)*

Great difficulties will beset the path of the person who dreams of drowning. If the scene takes place at sea, then the trouble will not arrive for some time; if on a river, the first signs may be looked for almost immediately. *(M)*

To be drowned through the fault of others, great difficulty and loss. To see a drowned person, joy and gain. *(OM)*

Of seeing another or drowning yourself
Manifests preservation and increase of wealth. *(MS)*

DROWSINESS
To dream of having a feeling of drowsiness is a sign of bad luck, and may be interpreted as meaning that in your anxiety to make progress you are working too hard, and that you will accomplish more by frequently doing nothing. *(O)*

DRUM
To hear the beat of a drum or drums foretells fame and popularity. *(M)*

To hear drums indicates a slight but not substantial loss. *(OM)*

DRUMMER
For a young man to dream he is a drummer in an instrumental band is a sign that he will become a musician of another kind. *(M)*

DRUNKENNESS
To dream you are drunk is one of those dreams by which the dreamer is forewarned of things he knows nothing about. It denotes that someone you have not met will become a very good friend, and promote your welfare; through his means you will acquire money and reputation. *(DSG)*

To dream you are drunk is good only to those who are afraid, for it signifies they will lose their fear. *(A)*
See also **DRINK.**

DUCKS
To dream of a flock of ducks walking or flying is an omen of good news coming by post. If the birds are swimming, good health and a contented mind will be yours for some time. *(M)*

If you see ducks swim, you will overcome all evil spoken about you and all problems. *(OM)*

DUET

To dream you sing a duet with a lady shows that you can win her if you want. To dream you sing with a man shows you have a secret but powerful enemy, and is a sign that you will never marry. To hear a duet sung denotes business troubles. *(M)*

Trouble from friends and relatives. You have treacherous enemies. *(OM)*

———— ♦ ————

DUMB

For a man who is married to dream that his wife is dumb is a bad sign. He will have many doctors' bills to pay both for her and his children and, later in life, his wife's gossiping will cause him some serious problems. For a married woman to dream that her husband is dumb is a sign that he will become a public speaker or lecturer. He will be fond of showing off his abilities, and may be successful at it. *(M)*

To see a dumb person, mildness and gentleness will bring you many blessings. *(OM)*

———— ♦ ————

DUNGEON

To see a dungeon means difficulties and doubts in connection with love or home life. If you dream of being a prisoner in a dungeon, you will be hampered all through life by a weakness of will which will give other people the advantage over you. *(M)*

This is a good dream and indicates respect. You will rise in life and enjoy good health. *(OM)*

———— ♦ ————

DUNG HILL

For a poor man to dream he sleeps on a dung hill signifies that he will accumulate considerable wealth. To the rich it signifies public estate, office and honour. *(A)*

———— ♦ ————

DUSK

For a young woman to dream that she walks with her lover in the dusk of the evening means that the fact of her courtship will soon be made public among friends and acquaintances. *(M)*

———— ♦ ————

DUST

For a girl to dream of being in a dusty house signifies that she will soon marry. A young man, however, dreaming of dusty surroundings is warned that he is in danger of contracting a life-long alliance with a girl who is too vain ever to be a good housekeeper. *(O)*

For an unmarried girl to dream of dusting a room predicts a short engagement. For a married woman to dream of dust in any form is an omen that she will have to neglect her home through being called upon to nurse a sick friend. *(M)*

Blinded by dust indicates business difficulties and losses in the family
circle.
(OM)

———————— ♦ ————————

DYE

To dream you dye fabric signifies joy without profit.   (T)

For a person to dream that he or she dyes their hair is indicative of a vain
and conceited character, fond of appearing in company to the best
advantage, determined to be fashionable at all costs. Affected and conceited
in deportment, they will become the laughing-stock of the prudent friends
and companions they meet.
(M)

To dye clothes indicates slight pleasure. To see clothes being dyed, your
confidence will be abused.
(OM)

EAGLE

To dream you see an eagle in a high place is a good sign to those who are in business and especially soldiers. If you dream that an eagle lands on your head or carries you into the air, it signifies death to the dreamer. If a woman dreams that she gives birth to an eagle, that foretells that the child she is pregant with will be a great person, and that he will have many under his command. If anyone dreams he sees a dead eagle, that signifies death to a powerful man, and profit to the poor. To see an eagle fly over your head signifies honour. *(T)*

If eagles are seen flying overhead in a dream you may infer that you are entering on a period of unusual prosperity, in which you will not only obtain much personal advantage but be the cause of many benefits falling to others. *(O)*

To see an eagle in its nest is a sign that laziness, not necessarily your own, will cause you trouble. If, however, the bird is flying, you will have success in life, and the higher the bird soars the greater your triumph will be. *(M)*

To dream you see an eagle soaring very high in the air denotes prosperity, riches and honour; to the lover, it foretells success in love and a happy marriage. To dream you see an eagle perched on the steeple of a church, or on any high eminence, is a very good omen. *(OM)*

---------- ♦ ----------

EAR

To dream a man has many ears signifies that he will gain the love of his employees and they will work well for him. To dream that a man picks his ears signifies that same thing. To dream his ears are full of corn signifies he will inherit money from his parents. To dream you have asses ears signifies servitude. To dream you have the ears of a lion or of any other wild beast signifies treachery or deceit by your enemies and those who envy you. If you dream that your ears have become larger than usual, you will prosper with the person to whom you communicate your secrets. If anyone dreams their ear is hurt or cut, they will be offended by a friend to whom they have entrusted their secrets. If it seems that the ear is completely cut off, their friendship will be destroyed. If anyone dreams their ears are stopped, it is a sign they will alter their resolutions and will deceive those who confide in them. *(T)*

To dream you have many ears is good to someone who has many people working for him. *(D&M)*

Dreaming of having a pain in one of your ears is a sure sign that you are about to be made the subject of a false charge, your innocence of which it will be exceedingly difficult to prove. *(O)*

For a young man to dream that he has lost his ears denotes some misfortune about to come upon him; but to dream that his ears are washed shows he will hear good news. *(D&M2)*

To dream that you are suffering from a disease of the ears indicates that you will hear of a death that will bring you a legacy. To dream that your ears have been cut off, or that you have lost them through any accident or unusual occurrence, is a sign that you will offend one of your relations by disclosing a secret affecting that person. To dream of a singing in the ears portends false news. *(M)*

If a man dreams his ears are quite attractive and well shaped, it shows he will become well known, but if he dreams his ears are ugly and deformed, it shows the opposite. To dream you pick or clean your ears indicates that you will hear good news. *(OM)*

To dream you wash your ears is a sign of good news; but to have your ears beaten foretells bad news. To dream you have ants crawling into your ears is good only to philosophers and school masters, for the ants represent children who are forced to listen to such pedants. To others it foretells death, for they are daughters of the earth and return to the earth. *(A)*

EARACHE
For a person to dream that he or she is suffering from earache is indicative of some part of the body being affected with scurvy, or a swelling will paralyse the leg or arm. *(M)*

EARRINGS
For a young woman to dream that she has had a pair of earrings presented to her means that she is going to have a new lover, although she will not care for him. *(O)*

If a young man dreams of buying earrings, he will shortly quarrel with his sweetheart. For a girl to dream of receiving a present of earrings is a sign that she will fall in love with a man who does not return her affection. *(M)*

EARTHQUAKE
To dream you see an earthquake signifies that your affairs and life are in danger. To dream that the whole earth quakes signifies a Government announcement will shock everyone. If you dream that the house shakes, then the announcement will affect your property; it indicates the loss of

goods and legal problems. If the walls and top of the house fall in because of the earthquake, that denotes the destruction and death of the chief persons in the house. To hear a shaking signifies deceit which will happen to the dreamer. *(T)*

To dream of a house falling on you shows the dreamer to be oppressed by some superior hand, but if the weight seems removed you will regain your former station. *(D&M)*

To dream of being in an earthquake means that for a long time everything will appear to stand still, and then suddenly there will come a time when everything will be turned topsy-turvy. *(O)*

An earthquake in a dream foreshadows rejoicing to a married woman, or one not engaged in business. To a person in employment it gives forewarning that someone is trying to usurp his or her place. To one about to undertake a long journey it gives promise of a safe return. *(M)*

To dream of an earthquake warns that your affairs are about to take a very great change. If you see many houses tumble into ruins, then it will be a great deal for the better. *(OM)*

To dream of great ditches or precipices or the land split by the violence of the earthquake and you falling in them signifies that you are in danger from fire. *(A)*

––––––––––– ♦ –––––––––––

EARTHWORMS
To dream of earthworms signifies enemies that try to ruin and destroy you.
(T)

––––––––––– ♦ –––––––––––

EARWIG
To dream of having an earwig in one of your ears means much the same as that of having a pain there. Both suggest that you are to be the victim of slander and ill will. *(O)*

To dream of seeing a swarm of these insects is a sign that you will be pestered by gossips concerning your love affair or domestic life. But you need take no steps to find out the mischievous party, for she will bring about her own punishment. *(M)*

Beware of enemies. You have one who will cause you trouble. *(OM)*

––––––––––– ♦ –––––––––––

EASEL
To dream of purchasing an artist's easel is a good dream for women; to widows and girls it signifies marriage; to those who have no children it indicates that they will have children; and to those that have husbands and children, it means purchases and riches. *(M)*

––––––––––– ♦ –––––––––––

EASTER
To dream of this season is a prediction that someone with whom you are only slightly acquainted will cause you happiness by introducing you to a stranger. *(M)*

EATING

To dream you eat a variety of meats signifies loss. To see silver eaten signifies great advantage. *(T)*

To dream you are eating is unlucky; it denotes disunion among your family, losses in your trade, disappointments in love, and is a sure sign of quarrelling. To dream you see others eating means the opposite; and foretells success in all your present enterprises; if you marry the present object of your affections, you will grow rich, be happy and have dutiful children. *(GD)*

To dream of eating signifies that you will hear good news. *(D&M2)*

To dream of eating is a bad dream. In business it means that you are about to lose money through carelessness in not taking a receipt, the amount being in proportion to the quantity of food you have in front of you. In love affairs it signifies separation, coldness and quarrels. *(O)*

If you dream you are eating a heavy meal, you may rest assured that you will be blessed with good things during the remainder of your life. If you see another person eating, you will miss something good by not taking advantage of an opportunity that will come to you in disguise. *(M)*

To dream of eating human flesh signifies labour and distress; to eat lard or salt signifies gossiping; to eat cheese signifies gain and profit; to eat apples signifies anger. *(OM)*

━━━━━ ◆ ━━━━━

EATING HOUSE

To dream that you are having a meal in an eating house is a sign of inducement being given to you to become a commercial traveller for an insurance company, or for the sale of books or other merchandise. *(M)*

━━━━━ ◆ ━━━━━

EAVESDROPPER

To dream that you are playing eavesdropper to some private conversation is a sign of approaching trouble. You will be assailed by unscrupulous enemies, and be hard put to it to defend your home and reputation. *(M)*

━━━━━ ◆ ━━━━━

ECHO

To dream of listening to an echo means for a young woman that she will marry a man who thinks himself particularly clever, and for a young man that he will marry a girl of the old-fashioned sort who will have no mind but his. *(O)*

To hear an echo in your sleep is a sign that you will hear of a secret concerning a person of some importance. *(M)*

━━━━━ ◆ ━━━━━

ECLIPSE of the MOON

To dream you see an eclipse of the moon, denotes that you will lose some female friends—your mother, if she is alive. *(M)*

EGGS

To dream of eggs signifies gain and profit, but if there are a number of them, it denotes care and legal problems. To see broken eggs is a bad sign. *(T)*

To dream of eggs, either collecting, buying or eating them, foretells anger, and is a sign that you will shortly be involved in violent arguments between relatives and friends. *(O)*

If you see a number of eggs, keep a guard on your tongue, for you will be in danger or trouble through over-plain speaking. To dream that you are carrying eggs and break some or all of them indicates unfaithfulness and sorrows. To dream of eating eggs is a sign that you will be spared a great evil which is threatening you. *(M)*

To dream you are buying or selling eggs is a very favourable omen. To dream that you are eating eggs denotes that you will shortly have a child. To dream that your eggs are broken denotes loss of goods, quarrels and poverty. *(OM)*

To dream that you are eating eggs foretells that you will shortly have a child. *(DSG)*

———— ♦ ————

ELBOW

To dream of a pain in, or any trouble with, your elbow may be taken as a sign that you will have need of all your strength in an emergency which will soon arise. *(M)*

———— ♦ ————

ELDERBERRIES

For a lover to dream of this fruit is a warning that he or she must be on her guard in dealings with the opposite sex, otherwise much trouble will ensue. For a married person the fruit is an omen of sickness in the house. *(M)*

To dream of elderberries signifies trouble in love, and illness. *(OM)*

———— ♦ ————

ELEPHANT

If someone sees an elephant, it signifies fear and danger. *(A)*

If someone dreams that he gives an elephant anything to eat or drink, it is a sign that he shall work for some powerful person, to his advantage. *(T)*

A herd of these animals indicates a big surprise. One elephant may be taken as a sign of stability in love and domestic happiness. *(M)*

To dream of an elephant is very fortunate indeed. *(OM)*

———— ♦ ————

ELM

To dream of a tall elm tree is an omen that your partner in life will rise to distinction through his intelligence. To a man it denotes a long life of luxury. *(M)*

ELOPEMENT

To dream of eloping with your sweetheart is a sign that your honeymoon will be marred by some unforeseen happening. To elope with a stranger is an omen of a happy marriage. *(M)*

Signifies an unexpected and early marriage. *(OM)*

———— ◆ ————

EMBARKING

To dream you embark in a small vessel signifies sickness. *(T)*

———— ◆ ————

EMBRACE

To dream of embracing anyone does not have a good meaning, the interpretation being that death will shortly claim either that particular person or one of his or her close relations. *(O)*

Beware of the friend or lover who embraces you in your dream; he or she is deceiving you. But should you see your sweetheart embrace another be content that you are well loved. *(M)*

———— ◆ ————

EMBROIDERY

To dream of embroidery signifies an affection that is returned. *(OM)*

———— ◆ ————

EMERALD

To an engaged person, a dream of an emerald is a warning against a rival. To one who is married it tells of petty annoyance from an enemy. *(M)*

———— ◆ ————

EMPEROR

To dream of an emperor signifies disquietude. To see kings and emperors together denotes much success in life. *(OM)*

———— ◆ ————

EMPLOYMENT

To dream that you are seeking employment and cannot obtain any is a sign that you will not change your place of occupation many times during your life. If you obtain lucrative employment it is a bad sign, and you will probably be seen looking for a situation. *(M)*

———— ◆ ————

ENCHANTMENT

To dream you are enchanted signifies secrets and sorrows. *(T)*

———— ◆ ————

ENEMIES

To dream you are obstructed by an adversary signifies success in business. To talk with your enemy signifies you must look out for him. *(T)*

To dream of meeting an enemy is an omen of success for you and trouble for him. *(M)*

ENGAGEMENT

To dream you enter into an engagement is a good or bad sign, according to the kind of engagement you make. To dream of a matrimonial engagement is a sign that you will not be married for many months or years. If you have a lover, look out for a quarrel. A trade engagement is a sign of difficulties besetting your career as a business man. An engagement to meet a friend means an unfortunate encounter with a creditor of yours, in which you will quarrel; coldness, if not absolute hatred, will follow, and you will become alienated from the intimacy of your friend. *(M)*

———— ◆ ————

ENGINE

To stand beside a steam engine at work is a sign that you will lose your physical strength through illness. To dream you are riding on a railway engine is indicative of your having an offer of railway shares at a very cheap rate, or of a disagreement with someone engaged on the railway. *(M)*

Beware of thieves after dreaming of an engine; although according to some writers it indicates riches or a present of money. *(OM)*

———— ◆ ————

ENGRAVE

To dream that you are engraving your name on metal denotes that you will have an offer of good, regular work at a new company. Someone connected with you will marry a wealthy man, but will be left at home while he is engaged abroad. *(M)*

———— ◆ ————

ENJOYMENT

When a married woman dreams that she is enjoying herself, it is a sign that she will soon have to undertake a disagreeable journey, but that she will eventually profit by it. To a single woman it predicts a quarrel over her love affair, but not with her sweetheart. On the contrary, he will stand by her and defend her from the malicious attacks of others. To a business man or woman the dream predicts worry. *(M)*

———— ◆ ————

ENLIST

For a girl to dream that her lover or someone for whom she has a great regard has enlisted is a sign that she will marry, but will lose her husband early in life. If a man dreams that he has enlisted, he will do well to look out for a new job. He will soon be in need of one. *(M)*

———— ◆ ————

ENTERTAINMENT

When a girl dreams that she is enjoying herself at a place of entertainment, she will do well to take a ticket for a concert or some such entertainment and use it, for there she will meet the man who will eventually become her husband. For a married woman the dream foretells a happy family and a contented mind, especially if at the time of the dream, things are not as comfortable as they might be. *(M)*

———————— ♦ ————————

ENTRAILS

If anyone dreams he has excreted his entrails, some of his family will be engaged abroad in a quarrel which will cause him damage and suffering. If anyone thinks that he has eaten his entrails, he will gain by the death of someone who works for him; if he dreams he has eaten the intestines of someone else, he will enrich himself by the estate of another. *(T)*

If you dream you are dead and see your innards, it is good if you are poor, for you will have a child and gain financially. But to a rich man, it means shame and dishonour. For a man to dream that he is cut open but cannot see his entrails, it signifies that he will leave his house and lose his children; it also indicates death by sickness. This dream can, however, be a comfort to anyone suffering from problems because he will lose those things which are causing pain and grief. For example: the heart or lungs signifies man; the liver signifies a son; the gall bladder indicates melancholy, money, women and wives; the spleen signifies pleasure and laughter; the belly and guts signify children. *(A)*

———————— ♦ ————————

ENVELOPES

To dream of seeing a packet of envelopes signifies that you may expect to receive many Valentines on the next 14th of February. If you see many directed envelopes you will have problems collecting money owed to you. *(M)*

———————— ♦ ————————

ENVY

If you are envied in a dream you will be admired. *(OM)*

———————— ♦ ————————

EPAULETS

To a man a dream in which epaulets figure denotes early promotion. To a girl it is a sign that she will fall in love with a soldier or sailor who will rise in the service of his country. *(M)*

———————— ♦ ————————

ERRAND

To dream that you are out on an errand and have forgotten your mission is a sure sign that someone in authority will cause you grief through a thoughtless act or speech. If the errand is a difficult one and you accomplish it to your own satisfaction you may look for a present of money from a quarter in which you least expect it. *(M)*

ERUPTION

To dream that an eruption breaks out in some part of your body is a sign of illness from exposure to cold; bronchitis or inflammation of the lungs will attack the dreamer, but the illness will not be very severe. *(M)*

————— ♦ —————

ESCAPE

Inability to escape indicates trouble will overtake you; a successful escape means you will overcome your present difficulties. *(OM)*

————— ♦ —————

ESTATES

If anyone dreams that he owns considerable fenced lands, he will have a beautiful wife, and her beauty will compare with the goodness of the land in the dream. But if the land seemed spacious and not enclosed, that denotes pleasure, joy and riches, comparable with the extent of the land. If it seems that the enclosed lands have lovely gardens, fountains, fields, pleasant groves and orchards adjoining them, that signifies that the dreamer will marry a discreet, chaste and beautiful wife and they will have very handsome children. If he saw the land sown with wheat, that signifies money and profit with hard work. If he saw it sown with any kind of pulse that denotes affliction and trouble. If he saw it sown with millet, that signifies vast riches to be gained with ease and much delight.

(T) and (A)

See also **FIELDS.**

————— ♦ —————

EVERGREENS

Evergreens in profusion, either plants or branches cut for decoration, portend good fortune throughout the year. *(M)*

To see or pick them, you will have the true friendship of some person. This is a most favourable dream indicating happiness, honour and success. *(OM)*

————— ♦ —————

EWER

For a woman to dream that she breaks a water jug is a sign of unpleasant interruption to her correspondence with her young man; some mischievous local busybodies will contrive to obtain possession of the love-letters that pass between them. The secrets of their conversation may become a source of gossip among the neighbours where she lives. *(M)*

————— ♦ —————

EXAMINATION

The student who dreams that he or she is sitting an examination, and is in difficulty over the problems set, will come through the course of study with flying colours. To dream of passing an examination with ease is a bad omen. *(M)*

EXCHANGE
For a business man to dream of success in exchanging goods is a sign that someone will try their best to swindle him out of his property by trading with him in inferior goods. Much care and forethought is needed by the dreamer after the revelation of this dream. *(M)*

✦

EXCISEMAN
If a woman dreams of an exciseman she must expect a brother or close male relative to gain a financially rewarding civil service post. *(M)*

✦

EXCREMENT
For a man to dream that he puts excrement in his bedroom signifies great sickness or divorce of his wife, but probably a change of lodging. It is very bad to dream that you relieve yourself in a church, market or greenhouse as it signifies that you will suffer humiliation and pain by the revelation of unfortunate secrets. *(A)*

✦

EXCUSE
For a young woman to dream that she puts off with a paltry excuse a young man who asks her to take a walk, is a sign that she will shortly meet with a fair-haired, light-complexioned young man who will desire her company and take no denial. *(M)*

✦

EXECUTOR
To dream that you are the executor of some person recently deceased is a sign that you will be called upon to pay money on another person's account. Either you will be bondsman in a money club or surety for a person who has committed a breach of the peace, and will have to forfeit the bond; or you will give your word of honour for the payment of goods they wish to possess, and they will fail. *(M)*

✦

EXECUTION
To dream of execution signifies that you will be asked a favour. *(D&M)*

To imagine yourself present at the execution of a criminal is a good omen. You will get on in life, and will soon be in a position to administer charity, which will make you well-regarded by many. *(M)*

The success of your undertakings will be doubtful. *(OM)*

✦

EXERCISE
To dream that you are taking vigorous exercise is a sign of hard work to follow. *(M)*

EXHAUSTED

To dream you are exhausted from some violent exercise or passion is indicative that a change in your disposition will shortly take place. You will become more accustomed to hard work, and become used to a great deal of worry. *(M)*

◆

EXHIBITION

To dream you visit an exhibition is a sign that you will form a liking for some indoor amusement. Cards, dominoes, draughts or chess will be the game that will keep you in your home each evening after work. *(M)*

◆

EXILE

To dream you become an exile in a foreign country is a sign that you will be more in love with your native land than ever. At the first public or private convivial or social party you will be called upon to give the loyal toast, which you will perform to the satisfaction of everyone and make a speech that will surpass any you have ever delivered before. You may be offered a job working for someone who is about to become a foreign ambassador. *(M)*

◆

EXPEDITION

To go on a dreary expedition or a voyage of discovery is a sign of removal to some other locality through fear of a house being badly drained, or because of unpleasant or unhealthy smells continually coming from various parts of the lower rooms. *(M)*

◆

EXPRESSION

To dream of a cloudy look denotes want of money; or being blind in both eyes denotes the loss of both children or parents; but for anyone who is poor or in prison, it is a good dream; for soldiers or merchants, the opposite. *(D&M2)*

◆

EXTRAVAGANT

To dream that you are spending extravagantly is a sign of success in your domestic arrangements. You will have many home comforts which will make you enjoy your home more than ever. For a woman to have this dream means that you will be a good financier, and your husband or those dependent upon your management will be pleased to stay beneath your roof. *(M)*

◆

EYEBROWS and EYELIDS

If anyone dreams his eyebrows and eyelids are more attractive and larger than they usually are, it is a sign he will be honoured and well regarded by everyone, that he will prosper in love, and grow rich. If someone dreams that he loses the hair of his eyebrows, or his eyelashes the opposite will happen. *(T)*

If a woman dreams her eyebrows are hairy and beautiful, it means good fortune, but naked brows declare her unfortunate. *(D&M2)*

If you dream that you are losing or have lost your eyebrows, you will be surprised at something which will occur to please you during the following day or two. If your eyebrows are growing rapidly, you will lose some of your friends; but you will make others in a better social position. To dream of any trouble to your eyelids is a sign that someone you know is in distress, but hesitates to ask your help, although you would freely give it if you knew it was wanted. *(M)*

———————— ♦ ————————

EYES

The eyes are the windows of the soul and the Ancients represent by them faith, the will and the light of understanding. If anyone dreams he has lost his sight, he will violate his word, or else he or some of his children are in danger of death, or he will never see his friends again. If anyone dreams that he has grown bleary-eyed, he will commit a dreadful crime and afterwards repent of it; he is also in danger of losing his property. To dream you have a good and quick sight is an extraordinarily good dream; it means that you will succeed in your enterprises. But a troubled and weak sight signifies want of money and failure in business. *(T)*

To dream you lose your eyes denotes change of circumstance for the worse, loss of friends and disappointments in love. If a pregnant woman dreams of it, it denotes that the child she is carrying will be very unhappy, and will be imprisoned before it arrives at years of maturity. *(GD)*

To dream you have a sharp sight is good; but a dull vision shows sorrow. To lose an eye shows the sudden death of a near relative and to have troubled sight denotes a vast want of money and sickness to anyone with children. *(D&M)*

To dream of the loss of an eye is bad for soldiers and merchants. To dream of having three or four eyes is good for those that are married; but to dream of having another man's eyes denotes the loss of one's own. *(D&M2)*

To dream of failing eyesight means that you are in danger of wasting your best years and your choicest thoughts on someone who is quite unworthy of you. *(O)*

To dream of an injury to the eyes or a disease affecting them is a sign that you have enemies seeking to take away your good character and many problems will fall on you, ending in the death of a dear friend. To be haunted by a pair of staring eyes is an omen of good fortune. *(M)*

To dream that you have three or four eyes is good for those who do not have children, but who would like a family. *(A)*

FABLE

If a young woman dreams that she is reading a fable it is a sign that she will become attached to an unfit young man, with whom she will only keep company for a short time. Some of her friends will advise her to drop his acquaintance because of his failing health. *(M)*

———————— ◆ ————————

FACE

To dream you see a black face signifies long life. To see a beautiful face, unlike your own, signifies honour. To dream you wash your face signifies repentance of your sin. *(T)*

To see a strange face is an indication that you will soon be changing where you live, either permanently or otherwise. To see your own face reflected in a mirror is a promise of a long life to yourself and your sweetheart or spouse. A number of faces familiar to you is a sign that you will soon receive an invitation to a party or a wedding. *(M)*

To see a beautiful face in the water indicates a long and happy life. *(OM)*

———————— ◆ ————————

FACTORY

For a young woman to dream that she is in a factory denotes some change in her health. She will be surprised by the news of a son, daughter or other near relative suffering some accident from machinery, or some unforeseen calamity from fire and water. *(M)*

———————— ◆ ————————

FAGGOTS

To dream of faggots signifies that you will receive bad news. *(OM)*

———————— ◆ ————————

FAILURE

To dream that you fail in anything indicates success by your own efforts. *(OM)*

———————— ◆ ————————

FAINTING

To dream that you are fainting is a very sad omen. It foreshadows family arguments and disgrace for someone in whom you have trusted. If you faint in a crowded street, beware of some infectious disease, and if in a place of entertainment look to your sweetheart's or partner's health. They will have a serious breakdown unless you take great care of them. To dream that you are tending someone else who has fainted is a sign that you will lose money through robbery. *(M)*

FAIR
To dream you are at the fair denotes that some pretended friend is about to do you an injury. *(GD)*

To dream of being at a fair in company with your sweetheart indicates a separation caused by jealousy. If you are alone, you will grow dissatisfied with your sweetheart's attentions and find someone more thoughtful. *(M)*

To be at a fair you will come into contact with many people through whom you will gain. *(OM)*

Should a fair and its pastime obtrude in your sleep
Some friend will deceive you and cause you to weep. *(MS)*

FAIRIES
Whatever happens in a dream about fairies, the opposite will take place. If the fairies are helping you, look out for the evil tongue of an enemy who will try to do you harm. *(M)*

For a girl to dream she sees a fairy shows she will soon marry. *(OM)*

FAITHLESS
For a young woman to dream that her sweetheart is unfaithful is a good dream. She will find that he is true to her, even though a richer woman tries to tempt him away. *(M)*

FALCONS
To see birds of prey or falconry signifies increase, riches and honour to the rich, and to the poor, the opposite. To dream you carry a falcon on your fist and walk with it signifies honour. *(T)*

If you dream of a falcon it signifies that you are surrounded by enemies who envy you. *(OM)*

FALLING
If anyone dreams he has fallen from a tree, and been scratched by thorns, or otherwise injured, it signifies that he will lose his job. To fall in the dirt signifies treachery, or disturbance by some person or other. To fall into the water signifies death or personal danger. To fall into a clear fountain signifies honour and gain. To fall into a pit or ditch signifies the loss of a cause or law-suit. To fall into a troubled fountain signifies accusation. To fall on the ground signifies dishonour and scandal. To fall from a bridge signifies obstruction. *(T)*

To dream you fall from a high place, or from a tree, denotes many troubles will follow. If you are in love, it indicates that you will never marry your present partner. To the tradesman it denotes decline of business; and to the sailor, storms and shipwreck. *(GD)*

To dream you fall into a pit denotes sudden surprise and danger. *(P&F)*

To dream of falling means that you will shortly become very depressed, imagining that the whole world is going wrong, but will after a time rediscover your equilibrium, perhaps after a course of medicine. *(O)*

The person who dreams of falling from a height will be overwhelmed with problems, but will surmount them after a breakdown in health, if they are faced with courage. A fall from a stool or chair is indicative of loss of dignity through some thoughtless action. *(M)*

> To fall from high places, or even a tree,
> Imperviously warns you much trouble you'll see. *(MS)*

———— ♦ ————

FALSEHOOD

To dream that you have told a serious lie is an indication of an upright nature. If you hear someone else tell a lie, you will be the recipient of good news concerning someone dear to you. *(M)*

———— ♦ ————

FAME

To dream of sudden fame is a sign that you will have to strive your utmost to make ends meet for some time to come, and you would do well to start saving while your affairs are prosperous. To dream that a friend or lover has achieved fame is an indication that you will be disappointed by an action of that person. *(M)*

———— ♦ ————

FAMINE

A dream of famine is the reverse of fame. You will have no cause to complain of the successes which will come to you in life. *(M)*

Prosperity, health and happiness. *(OM)*

———— ♦ ————

FAN

To dream of a fan indicates a flirtation which will lead to trouble unless you keep a grip on your good sense and nip the affair in the bud. *(M)*

If a girl dreams she has been fanned by a man, she will soon make a new conquest, or marry the present object of her affection. *(OM)*

———— ♦ ————

FAREWELL

To dream of saying farewell to a friend about to leave you for good is a sign that you will never have cause to doubt the fidelity of your acquaintances. If you should be the one who is leaving, you will make new friends. *(M)*

FARM

To dream that you are staying as a guest at a farm denotes quarrels and bickering in your family. To dream of working on a farm is a sign of steady improvement in your affairs, but nothing wonderful. *(M)*

This dream indicates unhappiness. *(OM)*

————— ♦ —————

FARMER

For a young woman to dream that a farmer wants to take her out is good; she will meet with a young clerk, who, though he is not particularly well paid, knows how to use the means at his command. He will be a faithful and devoted sweetheart to her. *(M)*

To dream you become a farmer signifies hard work. *(T)*

————— ♦ —————

FARMING

To manure and cultivate the earth signifies melancholy to those who are usually cheerful, and to labourers it signifies gain and a plentiful crop. To dream you are in woods or in meadows and looking after animals signifies disgrace and loss to the rich; and to the less well-off, it signifies profit. To dream you do business in the fields signifies joy, profit and health. *(T)*

————— ♦ —————

FAST

If you dream that you observe a fast day you will inherit wealth although it will come late in life. *(M)*

————— ♦ —————

FAT

To dream you are stout is a sure indication of riches. To see fat children, many happy years are in store for you. *(OM)*

————— ♦ —————

FATES

To dream that the fates are against you is indicative of prosperity in whatever you may put your hand to. *(OM)*

————— ♦ —————

FATHER

To dream of your father is a sure sign of his love for you. *(OM)*

————— ♦ —————

FATHER-IN-LAW

To see your father-in-law, either dead or alive, is bad luck especially if you dream that he uses violence or is threatening since it signifies vain hopes and deceits. *(A)*

————— ♦ —————

FATIGUE

To feel tired in a dream is a sign that you should try to put up with present difficulties and inconveniences because there is fame and profit in store for you, and not in a very distant future either. *(O)*

To dream that something you have done has left you fatigued is an omen of good fortune to come after many hard knocks. *(M)*

Success in business. *(OM)*

───────── ♦ ─────────

FAULT

To dream that you commit some fault and receive censure for it from your friends is a sign that you will become more loved by those who know you best. You will be esteemed and respected for your wisdom and integrity. Some of those who would criticise you will be compelled to admit your good character and honesty. *(M)*

───────── ♦ ─────────

FAWN

If the creature is running, be on your guard against a danger threatening you. If it is standing still, things will go well with you. *(M)*

Disappointment in love and inconstancy. *(OM)*

───────── ♦ ─────────

FEAR

If you are afraid of a mysterious event, it is a sign that you will feel great joy. You will receive news from a lawyer some way away that a wealthy relative has left you a legacy of a large amount of money. Your children who have left your home have obtained good positions in their different employments, and are making money in speculations of various kinds. *(M)*

To be afraid or in terror, you will receive good news. *(OM)*

───────── ♦ ─────────

FEASTING

To dream you are at a feast denotes that you will meet with many disappointments, particularly concerning the thing which you are most anxious about. In love it forbodes much uneasiness, and to those who are married, it foretells problems with children, with many heavy losses. *(GD)*

To dream of feasting is not a lucky omen; it indicates the same as EATING, but the evil is even more pronounced. *(O)*

If in company with many friends, bad fortune will follow. If the feast is a solemn one, then happiness will follow. *(M)*

───────── ♦ ─────────

FEATHERS

To dream of seeing feathers floating in the air is a sign that you will have cause to be anxious over some matter concerning yourself or someone immediately connected with you. If you are wearing the feathers, dishonour will come your way through a member of your family. *(M)*

To see white feathers is a good dream and indicates that your credit and honour will never be called into question. *(OM)*

FEEBLE

To dream that you are feeble and weak in your health means that you will soon become noted in your neighbourhood for your physical strength and powerful body. Great exertion will develop your powers; and by exercise you will become an expert in a field of gymnastics or physical skill. *(M)*

----------- ♦ -----------

FEEDING

To dream you feed or bring a lamb to the slaughter signifies torment. To dream you feed cattle is a good sign. *(T)*

   To dream that you are feeding cattle, horses, poultry or pigs means that you will have success in your work, whatever it may be, and that, providing you are thrifty, your old age will be financially secure, with your children also well provided for. *(M)*

----------- ♦ -----------

FEET

If anyone dreams he has three or four feet he is in danger of being crippled in the legs or feet by an illness or accident; nevertheless this dream is advantageous to merchants, and those that work on the sea. To dream a man has fire at his feet is a bad sign. To dream that a man is nimble-footed, and that he dances well signifies joy and friendship. To dream your feet or legs have been cut off signifies pain and damage. To dream you see the feet of your little children signifies joy and profit, good health and pleasure. To dream that you have an ulcer on your foot signifies assurance in business. To dream you are near a river or fountain and that you wash your feet signifies humility and success. To dream you kiss the feet of someone signifies repentance, contrition and humility. To dream you see a serpent or some other creature that will bite your feet signifies envy; and if the creature bites you that signifies sadness and discontent. To dream that anyone scratches the soles of your feet signifies loss or flattery. To dream that anyone bathes your feet with herbs, or perfumes them with beautiful scents, signifies honour and joy from employees. If anyone dreams that his leg or foot is dislocated, it signifies that an employee will receive loss and damage, or die, or that he will be prevented from making a journey. To dream you wash your feet signifies molestation and disturbance. *(T)*

   To dream of having many feet is good for merchants and masters of ships, for they will command many men; though other men who have had this dream have lost their sight, and criminals have been imprisoned. To dream you put your feet in the fire is bad and signifies loss of goods to children and employees. *(A)*

----------- ♦ -----------

FENCE

To dream of building a fence is an omen of good fortune provided you have no difficulty with the work. If part of the fence falls down, misfortune will mar the good fortune at one part of your life, but it will not banish it for ever. *(M)*

   Climbing a fence indicates a sudden rise in life; creeping under a fence is a warning to avoid shady transactions. *(OM)*

— ♦ —

FENCING

To dream you are fencing is a sign that you will be fond of dancing, and do your utmost to get into the company of those who are about to have a ball or private party. *(M)*

— ♦ —

FERRET

If in your dream you see one of these little animals it is a sign that you will have a desire to search out difficult things, explain problems, unravel mysteries and understand puzzles. *(M)*

— ♦ —

FERNS

To dream that you see a large number of ferns growing luxuriantly is a very good dream. You will have great cause for joy; if you are married you will have children, some of whom will grow up to fill good positions in life. Your second son will show a quickness of intelligence that will put him at the head of his profession. If in your dream you see ferns which are stunted in their growth it is a sign that you will meet with nothing but misfortune; your children will not rise above mediocrity, and gloomy prospects will blight your life. *(M)*

— ♦ —

FERRY BOAT

To dream you ride a ferry boat is a sign that if you are single, you will marry a woman who is afraid of going in a boat. But if you are married and have children, one of them will have a great desire to go to sea, and when you give your consent and he is employed on a merchant ship, he will desert and go on a long voyage on another vessel; eventually he will beg to be taken home again. *(M)*

— ♦ —

FESTIVAL

To dream that you are at an annual celebration of a society is a sign that you will soon have to remain at home because of the illness of one of your children. You will suffer considerably from the loss of a respected friend; or you will yourself suffer from headaches. *(M)*

— ♦ —

FETTERS

To dream that you have fetters placed on your legs as a criminal is a sign that your liberty will be curtailed by some complaint such as gout or rheumatism. Someone will claim that you owe them money, but when you produce your settled account, the difficulties will be sorted out. *(M)*

FEVER

To dream that you are suffering from fever is a sign that you will have no serious illness for some time to come. Should you be nursing a person suffering from a fever, however, you will lose a close relation. *(M)*

———— ♦ ————

FIDDLER

To dream you hear a fiddler play is a sign that one of your children, if you have any, will be attending a dancing school without your knowledge. It also means that you had better get a musical instrument into your home, or some games for evening amusement, to keep those whom you love from bad company. *(M)*

———— ♦ ————

FIELD

To dream of wandering in a field is a token that your life will have no great events to relieve the monotony. If the field is ploughed, however, your own exertion will bring you success, while if it is planted with corn you will have either children or a legacy late in life. *(M)*

To dream you are in green fields is a very favourable omen. To dream you are in ploughed fields forebodes some severe disputes that will be brought against you by someone who has no children. To the lover, it denotes disappointment; to the married, unhappiness and problems with your children. *(OM)*

To dream of fields sown with wheat signifies that you will work hard for money and profit. If it is sown with any kind of clover it denotes affection and trouble; if sown with millet it signifies vast wealth which can be achieved easily. *(A)*

See also **ESTATES.**

———— ♦ ————

FIEND

If you see a friend or evil spirit it is a sign that one of your family will have a strong desire to become either a clergyman or dissenting minister. Cultivate their powers of public speaking and give them as good an education as possible so that they can go on to theological college. *(M)*

———— ♦ ————

FIFE

If you hear music from a fife you can make preparations for going on a long journey; for either son or brother has enlisted, or a sister has married a soldier, and you will want to see them before they join their regiment. *(M)*

———— ♦ ————

FIG

To dream you see figs in season signifies joy and pleasure; out of season, the opposite. *(T)*

Figs are the forerunners of prosperity and happiness; to the lover they denote the accomplishment of their wishes; to the tradesman, increase of trade; they are all indicative of a legacy. *(GD)*

This fruit denotes plenty, and you will never be short of the good things of this world, even though you have ups and downs in the early part of your life. *(M)*

Dried figs indicate rejoicing; green figs signify hope; to eat figs means you can expect bad luck. *(OM)*

To dream of figs is the forerunner of prosperity and happiness. To the lover they denote accomplishment of their wishes. *(GD2)*

──────── ♦ ────────

FIGHTING

To dream you are fighting forebodes much opposition to your wishes, with loss of character and property; to the sailor it denotes storms and shipwreck, with disappointment in love. *(GD)*

To dream you win a fight shows you will get the better in law-suits. *(P&F)*

To dream that you are fighting indicates that someone abroad is thinking of you, and will leave you money at a future date. To see a fight is a warning to you not to be envious. If you are experiencing bad luck, better times are on the way. *(M)*

To dream that you are fighting denotes that a lover will lose their partner through a foolish quarrel. *(OM)*

To dream of fighting is bad for anyone except butchers, surgeons and cooks or anyone whose job involves blood. *(A)*

──────── ♦ ────────

FIGURES

To dream of any number above one and below seventy-eight means good fortune to the dreamer, but forty-nine is the most lucky. All numbers above seventy-eight are uncertain except three hundred and forty-three, and that is a very lucky number. *(M)*

──────── ♦ ────────

FILBERTS

To dream of filberts forebodes much trouble and anger from friends. *(OM)*
See also **NUTS.**

──────── ♦ ────────

FILE

To see a file is a sign that one of your sons will express a desire to become a mechanic; if you help him to achieve this, he will become an excellent workman. If a young unmarried woman has this dream she will marry a man who is a mechanic. *(M)*

To dream of dealing in files indicates a busy life. *(OM)*

FIND

For a young man to dream of finding property, either accidentally or after a search, is both lucky and unlucky. It means he is sure to get on in business, but he is by no means sure of winning the woman he loves.

(O)

If you dream of finding a purse, see that your savings are in a safe place, otherwise you will lose them. To pick up an article of jewellery, such as a brooch or a ring, means success in love but disappointment in business.

(M)

———————— ◆ ————————

FINGER

To burn your finger signifies envy and fun. If anyone dreams his hands or fingers have grown slimmer than usual, he will find that his employees cheat him and do not like him. To dream the fingers have been cut off signifies loss of friends or employees. To dream that one has six or seven fingers on each hand signifies friendship, new acquaintances, good fortune and inheritance or benefits. If anyone dreams that his fingertips or nails have been cut off, that signifies loss, disgrace and arguments with his relations and friends. To cut your fingers, or see them cut by someone else, signifies damage.

(T)

To dream of losing your fingers denotes loss, perhaps loss of a job. To debtors it indicates that they will pay a great deal of interest on their loan. If you have more fingers than usual it indicates the opposite. *(D&M)*

To dream of cutting a finger is a warning that, unless you interfere less with other people's affairs, you will be led into a quarrel which will have serious consequences, and perhaps bring you into a law-suit. *(M)*

To dream you cut your fingers and make them bleed is a very good omen. You will be successful in love, and your sweetheart will prove kind and true.

(OM)

———————— ◆ ————————

FINGER NAILS

To dream of long nails signifies pain; and to dream of having your nails pulled off indicates great misfortunes. *(D&M2)*

———————— ◆ ————————

FIRE

People who dream of fire often have a fiery temper. To dream you have been burnt indicates a violent fever. To see a moderate fire in your grate without smoke or sparks signifies that you are in perfect health, and if a sensible person dreams that a fire is put out, it means his death. When someone dreams their bed is on fire and that they are killed, it signifies damage, sickness or death to their spouse. To dream you have handled a fire without hurting yourself signifies that you will not be harmed by your enemies and you will achieve your ambitions. To see fire burning signifies a deluge or change of place.

(T)

To dream of fire signifies health and happiness to the lover, marriage with your lover and many children; it also denotes that you will be very angry with someone on trifling occasions. To dream you see burning lights descending from the sky is a very bad sign indeed, as it portends some dreadful accident to the dreamer, such as losing your head, having your brains dashed out, breaking your legs, getting into prison or other strange accidents. *(GD)*

To dream you quench a fire signifies overcoming anger and recovery from sickness. *(P&F)*

If a man dreams he sees a cabinet on fire, it denotes the death of its owner. If a woman dreams that she kindles a fire, it shows she will have a male child. To dream of seeing a stack of corn burnt down is a sign of death and famine. *(D&M2)*

Flashes of fire show sudden death. *(D&M)*

To dream of a house on fire or of a chimney on fire means that you will shortly be saddened by the death of a close relative. Dreaming of a fire burning in the grate is to young people a sign of approaching marriage. *(O)*

To dream of lighting a fire in a grate is an indication that you will hear important news in an unexpected manner. If you see your own house burning, you will have reason for happiness at an early date. To dream that you witness a big conflagration, such as the burning of a factory, is an omen of a big improvement in your affairs if you are married, and an advantageous engagement if you are single. *(M)*

To dream you see a clean, pure and clear fire is threatening to people in powerful positions because it indicates the approach of enemies, poverty and famine. It is an even worse dream to carry fire. *(A)*

See also BURNING.

———— ◆ ————

FIREARMS
To dream of using firearms indicates a quarrel of a long-standing nature. To see another person using them means slander. *(M)*

———— ◆ ————

FIRE ENGINE
To dream that you see a fire engine is a warning for you to insure your property against fire and take every sensible fire precaution. *(M)*

———— ◆ ————

FIRESIDE
To dream of sitting by the fireside with someone you love means, to the young, a speedy happy marriage, and to the old and middle-aged it foretells that what remains of life will be contented and happy, although neither splendid nor brilliant. *(O)*

If you imagine yourself sitting by the fireside talking to a close companion you will have no cause to complain of lack of comforts when

married, and your partner will always love you. For an elderly person it
signifies a peaceful death at an advanced age. *(M)*

FIREWORKS

To dream of taking part in an exhibition of fireworks denotes that before
long you will be in great danger of losing your temper with an
acquaintance, and that you will be tempted to assault him to ease your
anger and frustrations. *(O)*

To dream that you witness a display of fireworks is a sign that you will be
deceived by appearances. Someone will offer to sell something to you
which will turn out to be worthless. Be careful if you are buying cheap
articles at auction sales. *(M)*

FIRMAMENT

To dream that you see the heavens red is a sign of fair weather; if the
heavens are murky or dusky, do not take a journey at present, as there will
be very severe storms; if there are mackerel clouds, the weather will be
reasonable, but there will be no sunshine, and the nights will be cold. If
you see the sun rise blood-red, there will be storms; or if you see the moon
shining silvery bright, there will be some days of continued fine weather. *(M)*

FISH

If anyone dreams he sees or catches large fish, it signifies gain and profit,
according to the quantity he takes; if the fish are small, it signifies sadness.
To dream you see fish of many different colours signifies poison to the
sick, and to those in health, injuries, arguments and grief. To dream you
eat large fish signifies poor health. To dream you find dead fish in the sea
signifies vain hope. A pregnant woman who dreams she gives birth to fish
instead of a child, will have a stillborn child, or one who does not live long.
To catch sea fish is a bad sign. *(T)*

To see many large fish is a sign of good health and good fortune; small
fish mean good health and a fairly easy life. An unmarried person who
dreams of eating fish will marry well; a married person will have a large
family. *(M)*

To dream of fish indicates success; to catch them means your friends are
false; dead fish signify quarrels and disappointments. *(OM)*

FISHING

Should you dream of catching fish it is a sign of bad luck. Every fish you
hook indicates the death of one of your acquaintances. To dream of eating
fish foretells better fortune, signifying that you will be successful in the
studies which you are currently following, and that you will get a good

reputation for the soundness of your knowledge and the brightness of
your intellect.   *(O)*

To dream that you are fishing signifies that someone will try to draw you
into a plot against a friend. To see other people fishing means a discovery
that will cause you pain.   *(M)*

To dream you are fishing is a sign of sorrow and trouble. If you catch any
fish, you will be successful in love and business. If you catch none, you will
never marry your present sweetheart, nor succeed in your undertakings.
                                                                             (OM)

See also ANGLING.

FISHING NETS

To dream you see fishing nets signifies rain or change of weather.   *(T)*

FISH PONDS

Fish ponds denote that you will do well.   *(OM)*

FITS

To dream of having fits is good or bad, according to the kind of fits they
are. To dream of having a stroke means your physical strength will be
increased. To dream of having fainting fits is bad for a young woman; she
must guard against the consequences of being disappointed in her
expectations. She should try not to become too anxious or it will affect her
health. To dream of having paralytic fits is a bad dream, and the dreamer
should be careful to follow a balanced and a healthy lifestyle.   *(M)*

FLAG

To dream of a flag is a sure sign that one of your friends is in distress, and
that you will hear from that person only just in time to prevent a
disaster.   *(M)*

FLAGON

To dream that you see a flagon of beer, wine or any other alcoholic drink is
a sign that you will be deceived by some unscrupulous person who will tell
you to take useless medicines. You will try them, but they will not benefit
you in the least. To dream that you drink from a flagon of wine or beer
means that you have recently become careless in your tastes and habits.
Indigestion and liver problems will trouble you from time to time.   *(M)*

FLAMES

If in your dream you see flames ascending into the air you will find that
some of your acquaintances are making light of your character by spreading
slanderous reports. Be careful with any gas fittings in your home.   *(M)*

FLATTERY

To dream of flattery administered to some person you know means that slander will soon be busy with his or her reputation, but that, however plausible, take no notice for it will be groundless. *(O)*

To dream you are being flattered denotes that before long you will argue with your sweetheart or spouse for paying too much attention to other people. *(M)*

————— ◆ —————

FLEAS

To dream you eat fleas signifies problems. *(T)*

To dream of fleas indicates weariness of life; to kill one means success over your enemies. *(OM)*

————— ◆ —————

FLEET

To dream you see the naval fleet is a sign that some of your relatives or acquaintances in that branch of the service are about to be promoted. If you dream of seeing a fleet of fishing boats it is a sign of great advancement; you will save money if you are in trade; if you are not in trade, and are married, you will have many healthy children. You will also have great comfort at home, and you will put some schemes into practice which will be financially rewarding in the future. *(M)*

————— ◆ —————

FLESH

If anyone dreams he has grown fat he will gain wealth, according to the quantity of his flesh. On the contrary, if anyone dreams he has grown thin, he will lose whatever money he has. If anyone dreams his flesh has become spotted or black, he will deceive his business colleagues; if a woman dreams this, she will be caught committing adultery, and will split up with her husband. If anyone dreams that his flesh has grown yellow or pale, he will be in danger of falling seriously ill. If anyone dreams his flesh is covered in scabs or corns, he will grow rich proportionately to the number of scabs. If anyone dreams he has eaten the flesh of a man or woman he will enrich himself by injuries and reproach. If anyone dreams his flesh is swollen by an ulcer, that indicates wealth. *(T)*

————— ◆ —————

FLIES

To dream that a swarm of flies are pestering you is a sign that you will experience a loss through someone whom you have trusted. If the insects are merely flying around you, however, without landing, the loss will not be so serious, for you will have your suspicions aroused. To dream of killing flies denotes sickness. *(M)*

To dream of a swarm of flies denotes that you have many enemies; it also denotes that your sweetheart is not sincere. *(OM)*

From such insects or vermin no good we suppose;
For they designate mostly some troublesome woes.   *(MS)*

———————— ◆ ————————

FLIGHT

For a business man to dream that some of his creditors have run away without paying their debts is a sign that he need have no cause to doubt the honesty of his trading partners over the last few months.   *(M)*

———————— ◆ ————————

FLIRTING

For either a young woman or a young man to dream of flirting signifies that their present partner is not a stable person and common sense suggests looking elsewhere.   *(O)*

A flirtation in a dream is a forerunner of two proposals of marriage at, or about, the same time.   *(M)*

———————— ◆ ————————

FLOATING

To see anything floating on water is a warning that you are taking things too easily and missing opportunities of improving your position.   *(M)*

To dream you are floating on water indicates good fortune and speedy success; if you are sinking, look out for reverses of fortune.   *(OM)*

———————— ◆ ————————

FLOOD

This is a bad dream denoting trouble to come.   *(M)*

To dream of a flood shows that you will meet with great opposition from rich neighbours, and that a rich rival will attempt to alienate the affections of your lover.   *(OM)*

———————— ◆ ————————

FLOOR

To dream that you are lying or sitting on the floor is a good omen of success in most of your undertakings. But you must be careful not to get a swollen head; otherwise you will certainly fail. To dream that you are scrubbing or sweeping a floor which refuses to come clean is indicative of petty worries.   *(M)*

———————— ◆ ————————

FLOUR

To dream that you buy flour is a bad omen and indicates the sickness or death of a close friend.   *(M)*

If you are cooking with flour, you will have unexpected happiness.   *(OM)*

———————— ◆ ————————

FLOWERS

To dream of holding or smelling scented flowers in season signifies joy, pleasure and consolation. To dream of seeing and smelling flowers out of season, if they are white, signifies obstruction and failure in business; if yellow, the impediment will not be so considerable; and if they are red, the difficulty and nuisance will be extreme. It usually also signifies death. To dream you are adorned with flowers and posies signifies a short-lived joy and content. To gather flowers signifies happiness and jollity.   *(T)*

To dream that you are gathering sweet-scented flowers is a sign that the person you love best of all truly returns your affection. But should the flowers wither in your hand the other's love will wane before many years have passed. To see flowers growing in profusion is a prediction of a happy future and a well-cared-for life.   *(M)*

To dream you are gathering flowers is a very favourable omen. To see beautiful flowers indicates that you will have much joy and happiness in life. To plant flowers means you will accomplish good work.   *(OM)*

To dream of gathering flowers is a sign of rejoicing, though sometimes it signifies death.   *(D&M2))*

To dream of seeing and smelling red flowers signifies extreme difficulty and nuisance, or even death.   *(A)*

───────── ♦ ─────────

FLUTES

To play or hear someone playing on wind instruments such as flutes signifies trouble and arguments.   *(T)*

Troubles, quarrels and loss.   *(OM)*

───────── ♦ ─────────

FLYING

To dream you fly in the air signifies a speedy journey.   *(P&F)*

To dream you are flying and are afraid denotes you are not as well trusted as you had thought.   *(GFT)*

To dream of flying means that you are destined to succeed in high things, and that every obstacle before you will give way before courage and perseverance.   *(O)*

To dream that you are flying often means that you are conceited, and that this failure will stand in your way of happiness. If you can overcome this, however, and persevere, you will have no cause to complain of the result.   *(M)*

To fly high or a distance means there is much happiness in store for you, as well as success in your undertakings. If while you are flying you suddenly fall, expect disappointments.   *(OM)*

To dream you can fly is a good sign. To fly with wings is generally good, but to fly very high and without wings signifies fear and danger as does to fly over houses and through streets. To dream that you fly with the birds is a sign that you will keep company with strangers; it also signifies pain and punishment to criminals. It is always good after having flown high to descend low and then to wake up, but it is best of all to fly when you want to and come down when you want to for it is a sign that your home and job are well run. To fly backwards is not bad for sailors, but to anyone else it signifies a lack of work and business. To the sick it foretells death. It is very bad to want to fly and yet be unable to do so or to dream that you fly with your head down. To dream that you fly in a bed or chair or are supported in any way signifies great sickness, except to those who want to travel. *(A)*

FOG

To dream of being in a thick fog or mist means that you are destined to develop a taste for metaphysical studies, and that your energies are likely to be spent in speculation and not in practical work in the future. *(O)*

To dream of wandering in a fog predicts a lingering illness, from which, however, you will recover. To a business man or woman it is sometimes indicative of unsuccessful efforts to improve trade. If you are lost in a fog, you will be tempted to stray from the path of virtue, and will need all your courage to keep clear of trouble. *(O)*

This dream warns you to be careful in all your dealings, for it indicates that you will be tempted to questionable undertakings. *(OM)*

FOLIAGE

If green, a great deal of pleasure is in store for you. If it is dead, your undertakings will not succeed. *(OM)*

FOLLY

If you are worried by the thought that you have committed a stupid act, you will be troubled by petty debts contracted through extravagance either on your own part or on that of someone closely connected with you. *(M)*

For a woman to dream she has become foolish and has made a fool of herself in public is a sign that she will have a boy, who in time will grow powerful. *(OM)*

FONT

To dream that you are beside the font when the ceremony of baptism is performed on a child means that you will soon see your child, if you have one, very ill, and you will be compelled to send for the minister to perform the ceremony at your own house before the child dies. *(M)*

FOOL

To see a fool means someone will deceive you. *(OM)*

To dream that you are made a fool is good to anyone who undertakes any business deals in the day following the dream. *(A)*

FOOTBALL
To dream that you are watching a game of football may be taken as a sign that you will be forced to stand by and hear a friend slandered without being able to defend them. *(M)*

———— ♦ ————

FOOTMAN
For a woman of ordinary means to dream that she rides in a wonderful carriage with a footman to attend to her, is a sign that she will never become rich and she and her husband will spend everything they earn. She will need to save and try to avoid running into debt. *(M)*

To dream of a footman means unexpected enemies. *(OM)*

———— ♦ ————

FOP
For a young woman to dream that a gaily dressed young man seeks her company is a sign that she will meet with a very ordinary and unprepossessing young man who has nothing to recommend him to her notice but his honesty and hard-working nature. He is careful and thoughtful, however, and would make her a good husband if she accepts him. *(M)*

———— ♦ ————

FOREHEAD
If anyone dreams they have a large forehead it signifies an ingenious spirit; and if it is very high, it is a sign of solid judgement; it also denotes power and wealth. To dream that your forehead is brass, copper, marble or iron signifies irreconcilable hate against your enemies. If anyone dreams their forehead is injured, they are in danger of losing money. If someone dreams they have a large and fleshy forehead, that signifies freedom of speech, strength and constancy. *(T)*

To dream you have a forehead of brass is good for vintners or bakers but bad to anyone else since it indicates hate. To dream that your brow is hairy is very lucky to everyone, especially to women; but if the brows have no hair, it denotes failure and difficulties. *(D&M)*

If anyone dreams they have a bronze forehead, it denotes hatred. *(D&M2)*

To dream that you have the forehead of a lion is good for anyone, especially someone who wants a son. *(A)*

———— ♦ ————

FOREST
To dream of wandering in a forest predicts a happy married life to a single person, with several children. To a married person it is an omen of a wealthy inheritance. To be lost in a forest indicates uncertainty in love. *(M)*

To dream you are walking in a forest signifies trouble. *(OM)*

FORGE

When a blacksmith's forge figures in a dream beware of dispute and dissension. *(M)*

Denotes a brain full of projects. *(OM)*

————— ♦ —————

FORGERY

To dream you are guilty of this crime denotes that you will never have a very substantial bank account. If you dream that someone else has forged your signature, however, you may look for the reverse. *(M)*

————— ♦ —————

FORGET-ME-NOT

You are loved and remembered by many. *(OM)*

————— ♦ —————

FORK

To dream of a fork indicates that a false friend will attempt your ruin by flattery. *(M)*

Someone will deceive you. *(OM)*

————— ♦ —————

FORTRESS

To see a fortress or castle means hate and sickness. *(OM)*

————— ♦ —————

FORTUNE

To dream you make a sudden fortune is a very bad omen; to the tradesman, it forebodes losses in trade, quarrelling with his creditors, and the loss of liberty; to the lover it denotes that your sweetheart does not return your love; to the sailor it indicates storms and shipwrecks; if you are applying for a job you will not be successful. To dream you are adopting the means of acquiring a fortune is favourable, it indicates a good legacy and success in love. *(GD)*

To dream that you have come into a fortune, or that you have amassed one by your own efforts, is an omen of a period of distress to follow, in which you will contract serious debts. *(M)*

If anyone who has lost a lot of money dreams he has regained it, it signifies that his good fortune will return. *(OM)*

To dream that you make a sudden fortune is a very bad omen; to the tradesman it denotes losses in trade, quarrelling with his creditors and the loss of freedom. *(GD2)*

————— ♦ —————

FORTUNE TELLING

If you are having your fortune told, your favourite ambition will be blighted. To dream of telling a friend's fortune indicates that you will have a serious quarrel with a stranger. *(M)*

————— 148 —————

FOUNTAIN
If a sick person dreams they see a river or fountain of clear running water, that means they will recover, but if the water is muddy, it signifies the opposite. If anyone thinks that a fountain has dried up, that signifies poverty or death. To fall into a clear fountain signifies honour and gain. To fall into a muddy fountain signifies accusation. To see a fountain spring up in your house signifies honour and profit. To see fountains or believe that you are enchanted, signifies sadness. *(T)*

To dream of a fountain is a bad omen. It signifies that you will soon enter a very sad and depressing period of your life. *(O)*

To see a fountain means that you will have your eyes opened in a very unpleasant manner to an intrigue between certain of your friends who have taken a dislike to you. *(M)*

To dream you are at a fountain is a very favourable omen. If the waters are clear, it denotes riches and honours; but if the waters appear dark, muddy or unpleasant then it denotes anxiety and trouble. *(OM)*

FOX
To fight with a fox indicates a disagreement with a wary adversary. If you dream you have a tame fox, the interpretation is the same. If you dream that you have a tame fox at home, you will fall in love with an ill-natured woman. *(T)*

To dream of a fox is a dream of warning for a young woman, intimating that she must not trust the many promises that are now being made to her, because they are insincere. *(O)*

To dream that you see a fox indicates that your confidence will be betrayed, and that this will bring you into trouble with someone in authority. *(M)*

A dead fox is good; a pet fox means danger; to see a fox signifies secret enemies. *(OM)*

Foxes are the heralds of treason. *(MS)*

FOXGLOVES
These flowers are an omen of true friendship. *(M)*

FRAUD
To dream that you commit a fraud is a sure sign that you will have occasion to do a good turn to a stranger who will handsomely reward you. To dream that you have been defrauded is a sign that you will soon be looking for someone to help you out of your problems. *(M)*

To charge someone with fraud signifies that you will be robbed. To commit a fraud indicates you will rise to an honourable position. *(OM)*

FREEMASON

To dream you are a Freemason denotes that you will soon make a number of new friends, who will prove staunch and true. It also foretells you will take a journey to the East. If you are already a member of the Masons and dream you attend a meeting of the lodge it portends sickness and heavy loss of property. To dream that you are expelled from the Order shows you will be promoted. *(M)*

────────── ◆ ──────────

FRIENDS

To see your friends or relations dead signifies joy. *(T)*

To see a friend dead indicates unexpected good news; if you are in love, it indicates a speedy marriage with your lover. *(GD)*

If you dream of a friend, your fortune will improve. *(M)*

To see a friend who is dead, if you are engaged, means there will be a delay to your marriage. *(OM)*

────────── ◆ ──────────

FRIGHTENED and FRIGHT

To dream that you are frightened and yet do not know the cause predicts to a girl that she will receive a proposal of marriage from a very plain-looking man, who will, nevertheless, make a good husband. To a married person such a dream gives warning of slanderous neighbours. *(M)*

Means that you will have no reason to be afraid. *(OM)*

────────── ◆ ──────────

FROGS

Frogs signify flatterers and indiscreet gossips. *(T)*

To the unmarried, the sight of these creatures in a dream foretells a happy married life after a rather trying courtship. To the married, the dream is indicative of happiness in old age. *(M)*

To catch or kill frogs signifies trouble or sudden death. Otherwise this is a good dream, indicating success in business and love, good friends and happiness. *(OM)*

────────── ◆ ──────────

FROST

If you dream of frost, be on your guard against committing a foolish blunder which will lead to a bad accident. *(M)*

Difficulties, troubles and sorrow. *(OM)*

────────── ◆ ──────────

FROWN

To dream that you see a frown on the face of your father, mother or any of your relatives is a sign that you will have greater pleasure in the society of your family and family connections than ever you have had before. Joy, peace and happiness will be enjoyed by you at all times. *(M)*

FRUIT

If anyone dreams that the fruit they have gathered is rotten, that signifies adversity or loss of children. *(T)*

To dream you see fruits in season is good, if they are beautiful; but if rotten and out of season it is bad, especially to a pregnant woman. *(D&M)*

To dream of fruit has a different interpretation according to which fruit it is that you dream of. (See various kinds of fruits.) *(GD)*

If you should be ill when you dream of a collection of fruit, you will quickly recover. If you are already in good health, you will be happy. *(M)*

If you dream of fruits out of season, it denotes sickness. If you dream they are rotten, it foretells poverty. To dream of gathering ripe fruit indicates happiness and wealth. *(OM)*

See also DESSERT.

———— ♦ ————

FRYING PAN

To dream that you see a frying pan full of meat is a sign of a quarrel with your cook, if you have one. You will be strong, intelligent and active. *(M)*

To dream of a frying pan signifies injury and a wife who gossips too much. *(A)*

———— ♦ ————

FUN

To dream that you are having a good time is a sign that you will soon experience problems such as debt or sickness. *(M)*

———— ♦ ————

FUNERAL

To go to the funeral of a relation or friend is a good sign to the dreamer, who will either inherit property or marry into money. *(T)*

To dream of burying denotes a speedy marriage, and you will hear of the death or imprisonment of some close relation or friend. *(GD)*

To dream of being present at a funeral foretells that the unhappiness which you are at present suffering will soon come to an end, and that you will then enter on the happiest period of your life. *(O)*

To dream of a funeral is an omen of success and happiness. If you have children they will be a comfort to you; if you are in love, your affairs will prosper. *(M)*

If you see any particular person attending the funeral either that person or some friend of his will die and leave you something. To dream of a funeral service denotes an inheritance. *(OM)*

———— ♦ ————

FUR

After dreaming of fur in any shape or form be careful not to enter into a serious argument for some time to come. If you disregard this, the argument will lead to a quarrel, and many of your relatives will be involved. *(M)*

———— ♦ ————

FURNITURE
Happiness always follows a dream of furniture. The person in love will soon marry, and the person in business will make money easily. To dream of buying furniture for a home is also a good omen. *(M)*

To dream of getting new furniture that you like, is good. If you do not like it, the dream is a bad one. *(OM)*

GAG

If you dream that your mouth is stopped by a gag it denotes that you will soon after be kissed by a pretty girl. To a young girl such a dream predicts that she will meet and perhaps will fall in love with someone.　*(M)*

———————— ♦ ————————

GAIETY

To dream that you are indulging in riotous gaiety is a sign that you will soon be wearing mourning.　*(M)*

———————— ♦ ————————

GAIN

To dream of gain, if acquired honestly, you may hope for wealth; if by injustice, you will lose your money.　*(M)*

———————— ♦ ————————

GAITERS

For a young woman to see a man wearing gaiters is a sign that she will have an offer of marriage from a labourer. If she dreams of gaiters a second time within a week she will marry soon. The man who wants to marry her is so keen that he will propose to her within six months from the time of the dream.　*(M)*

———————— ♦ ————————

GALL

To dream that you have problems with your gall bladder signifies that you will argue, perhaps violently, with an employee. If you are married, you will have an argument with your wife; and will also be in danger of losing your money by gambling or robbery.　*(T)*

———————— ♦ ————————

GALLOWS

To dream of the gallows is fortunate; it shows that the dreamer will become rich, and be well respected. To the lover it shows the consummation of his deepest wishes; for a pregnant woman to dream of the gallows signifies that she is carrying a son, the birth will be straightforward and the child will become rich.　*(GD)*

To see a gallows in a dream is a clear sign of long life to the dreamer.　*(M)*

GAMES

To play at any party games signifies prosperity, joy, pleasure, and health and concord among friends and relations. *(T)*

To dream you play ball or spinning top signifies hard work and pain. To leap, run or dance signifies prosperity in affairs, but to dance without music foretells a shortage of money. *(OM)*

To dream you play at dice or at cards signifies noise and debate for money. However, it is always good to dream you win, no matter what the game. To see a child so play is good. To a perfectly healthy man, it is bad to dream he plays at dice, except if he hopes for some succession by the death of another; for the dice are made of the bones of the dead. *(A)*

---------- ♦ ----------

GAOL

To dream you are locked in a gaol is a sign that in a short time you will be offered a job as a commercial traveller, and you will have offers of promotion if you go to another part of the country to work. You will do well by the move. *(M)*

---------- ♦ ----------

GARDEN

To dream that you are walking in a garden of flowers and amongst trees shows much pleasure and delight to come from conversation. *(P&F)*

To dream of a curious garden, enclosing delightful fountains, pleasant groves and fruitful orchards is a sign you will marry a woman who is chaste, discrete and beautiful and with whom you will have many lovely children. *(D&M2)*

To dream of a fine garden signifies that you will gain a great deal of pleasure from simple and healthy pursuits and by carefully making sure you spend only what you earn. *(O)*

To dream that you are walking or sitting in a beautiful garden is a proof that your sweetheart or husband is true to you, and will keep his marriage vows. *(M)*

To dream of walking in a garden is a very favourable dream. It indicates increased wealth and position. *(OM)*

> To walk in denotes elevation in life.
> In trade much success and wealth with a wife. *(MS)*

---------- ♦ ----------

GARDENING

To dream you are working in a garden signifies melancholy to those who are normally cheerful; and to labourers it signifies gain and a plentiful crop. *(T)*

---------- ♦ ----------

GARLAND

The young lady who dreams that she is wearing a garland of flowers should be extra careful how she conducts herself for some time to come. Some evil people are watching and waiting for an opportunity to take away her good character. *(M)*

To dream of a garland signifies anticipated pleasures will be realized. *(OM)*

———— ♦ ————

GARLIC
To eat or smell garlic signifies a discovery of hidden secrets and domestic quarrels. *(T)*

To dream you have garlic in the house is good. *(M)*

———— ♦ ————

GARMENTS
If anyone dreams he is wearing a new suit which he likes that signifies joy, profit and success in business. If a woman dreams she is dressed in a hood that indicates damage and dishonour. If someone dreams they are expensively dressed, that signifies honour to the dreamer and his or her partner. If a man or woman dreams they are dressed in rags, it signifies trouble and sadness. To dream you have a red garment on signifies blood or bleeding. *(T)*

See also **APPAREL, CLOTHES, DRESS.**

———— ♦ ————

GARROTER
To dream that you meet a person who tries to rob you by the brutal practice of garroting you is a sign that you will be overcome in your judgement by a person you know well; you will lose money by buying inferior goods; or will be induced to lend money to a friend which you will never be able to recover. *(M)*

———— ♦ ————

GARTER
If a man ties on a girl's garter, it denotes a speedy marriage. *(D&M)*

———— ♦ ————

GAS
To dream of an escape of gas means for a young man that he is about to tell a girl that he will protect her forever, but that he will have quarrelled with her within a week. For a girl to dream of an escape of gas signifies that her too light-hearted behaviour will in the end so excite the fears of her present sensible lover that he will leave her for ever. *(O)*

If you dream of bright and pleasant gas lights it shows success in love. If the gas is dim and looks unnatural your sweetheart will either leave you or die. *(M)*

———— ♦ ————

GATES
To see gates consumed by fire signifies death to the mistress of the house, and sometimes to the dreamer. *(T)*

GAUZE
To dream of gauze signifies concealed feelings.   *(OM)*

———————— ◆ ————————

GEMS
To dream of handling gems of a great brilliance is a sign that you will be blinded by flattery to the evil designs of a person of the opposite sex. To dream that you wear a costly gem in the shape of some precious stone or jewel of some kind is a sign of a falling off of your resources financially; your prosperity in business will not be so good in the future as it has been in the past. It will be better for you to husband your resources and prepare for problems ahead.   *(M)*

———————— ◆ ————————

GERANIUMS
For a young woman to dream she sees a large quantity of geraniums in flower is a sign that she will become more beautiful in personal appearance in the future. Very many eligible offers will be made to her by men of different positions in life. Her perplexity will be increased by the host of admirers who vow their attachment to her. She must guard against those who admire her for her beauty alone, and only listen to those who do not flatter above her merit.   *(M)*

———————— ◆ ————————

GEOGRAPHY
For a young man to dream of his geography lesson is a sign that he will become a better scholar in grammar or arithmetic that he will in geography.   *(M)*

———————— ◆ ————————

GHOSTS
To dream of ghosts and spectres of people you have known shows good news from abroad.   *(D&M)*
If you dream that you are frightened by a ghost it signifies that you will encounter great difficulties; if you are unafraid it signifies good fortune.   *(OM)*

See also **APPARITIONS.**

———————— ◆ ————————

GIANT
To dream you see a giant or a very tall person is a very good sign. *(T)*
If you are in trade you will have a great increase of business from abroad.   *(GD)*

———————— ◆ ————————

GIBBET
To dream you see someone hanging on the gibbet signifies damage and great distress.   *(T)*

GIDDY

To dream that you grow giddy in a dance is a sign that you will lose your present good health. Illness from exposure to cold will shortly overtake you. *(M)*

———— ♦ ————

GIFTS

To dream that you have something given to you is a sign that some good is about to happen to you; it also denotes that a speedy marriage will take place between you and your sweetheart. To dream you have given anything away is the forerunner of adversity; and in love denotes sickness and inconstancy in your partner. *(GD)*

To dream about either receiving or giving a gift means that you will shortly lend a sum of money and will have great difficulty in getting it back; indeed it will only be returned under pressure of legal proceedings. *(O)*

Such things are deceptive as a portrait or locket,
For all is not saved that is put in the pocket. *(MS)*

———— ♦ ————

GIN

To dream of drinking gin indicates a short life and many changes. *(OM)*

———— ♦ ————

GIPSY

To dream that you are talking to a gipsy denotes a wandering nature. You will probably live abroad for some time, but will return to your home when you are approaching old age. *(M)*

Be careful in all your actions for it looks as if some carelessness of yours will bring you trouble. *(OM)*

———— ♦ ————

GIRDLE

To dream you are wearing an old girdle signifies labour and pain. To have a new girdle signifies honour. *(T)*

———— ♦ ————

GIRL

To dream you see a handsome girl in bed is a sign of good fortune. *(D&M2)*

For a man to dream of a girl means that he is engaged, or shortly to be engaged, in paying attentions which may or may not lead to matrimony. It is important to notice whether the girl seen in the dream holds anything in her hand. If she has a bag, which looks like a money bag, it signifies that you are to marry someone who always argues over money. Should the girl hold a notebook in her hand it means that you will end in separating from your lover, but you will easily console yourself. *(O)*

———— ♦ ————

GLADIATOR

Something will happen which will cause you sorrow and anguish. *(OM)*

———— 157 ————

GLASS

If anyone dreams he is given a glass full of water, it signifies his speedy marriage and that he will have children; for anything glass in a dream is applicable to the wife; and water signifies abundance and fruitfulness. if the glass seems to be broken, and the water unspilt, that signifies the death of the wife, but the life of the child, or vice versa.   *(T)*

To dream of a glass being broken shows shipwreck to mariners, and bad luck to anyone in business.   *(D&M)*

For a man to dream that he is presented with a full glass of water shows he will marry suddenly, and have children.   *(D&M2)*

To dream of a glass is a warning sign that you are inclined to be too trusting, and you are not doing yourself any good by talking about your private affairs to everyone you meet. To dream of a broken glass foretells a sudden end of something you have been in the habit of doing for a long time.   *(M)*

To dream of glass marks inconstancy in your sweetheart, and lack of success in business. To dream that you break glass shows that you will unexpectedly meet with misfortunes and troubles. To dream you receive a glassful of water is indicative of a speedy marriage.   *(OM)*

To dream of a drinking glass is bad, for your secrets will be revealed because of your transparency. If the glass is broken, it may also signify the death of a friend.   *(A)*

———— ◆ ————

GLASSES

Good news and an improvement in your position.

———— ◆ ————

GLEAN

To dream that you are gleaning, or that you see gleaners at work, foretells good luck to you and your family.   *(M)*

———— ◆ ————

GLOBE

To see a globe indicates that you will have friends in several different foreign countries.   *(M)*

———— ◆ ————

GLOOM

To dream that you see the sky cloudy and gloomy should give you courage, for by great perseverance you will make a success of your life.   *(M)*

———— ◆ ————

GLOVES

To dream you are wearing gloves signifies honour.   *(T)*

To put on a glove and keep it on indicates marriage.   *(P&F)*

If you dream you have trouble in getting a pair of gloves to fit, you may expect a proposal of marriage at an early date. To dream that you receive a present of a pair of gloves indicates that you will have rival lovers, and have some difficulty in making your choice between them. *(M)*

To dream of gloves signifies transient happiness. *(OM)*

------------- ♦ -------------

GNATS

Back-biters will cause you loss and trouble. *(OM)*

------------- ♦ -------------

GOATS

To see several nanny goats signifies wealth and plenty. To see billy goats signifies that you will be robbed. *(T)*

To dream of goats is both a good and bad omen. You will have petty enemies to worry you, but in spite of their actions, you will become rich and the mainstay of your family. *(M)*

White goats are fortunate; black goats indicate illness; goats on high places mean riches; badly kept animals signify misfortune. *(OM)*

To dream of goats is bad luck, especially to navigators. *(A)*

------------- ♦ -------------

GOBLET

To drink out of one indicates that good times are coming, and you will be happy. *(OM)*

------------- ♦ -------------

GOD

To dream you see God's face, and that He seems to stretch out His arms while you pray signifies joy, comfort, grace, the blessing of God and success in business. To dream you see the body of our Lord signifies respect. *(T)*

To hear His voice, or to dream that He speaks to you means happiness and joy. To see Him or speak to Him indicates anxiety and trouble. *(OM)*

------------- ♦ -------------

GOLD

If anyone dreams he gathers up gold, that signifies deceit and loss. To dream you handle or chew gold signifies anger. *(T)*

To dream of gold signifies that you will be surrounded by great wealth which you will be unable to enjoy because of disappointment and unhappiness. *(O)*

A dream of gold is an indication of prosperity in some cases, but more often it means disappointment and loss. To imagine yourself working in, or exploring a gold mine indicates a spendthrift nature, which will prevent you from accumulating wealth, although a good deal may come your way. *(M)*

To dream of gold is a very good omen. It denotes success in your present undertakings, after experiencing some little difficulties. If you receive sovereigns or any other gold coin, your affairs will prosper, and your sweetheart will be true and marry you. *(OM)*

GOLDFISH
Trouble in business. *(OM)*

------- ♦ -------

GOLD MINE
To dream of a gold mine foretells that an attempt will soon be made to get you to lend money to advance a hazardous speculation, and that if you yield there is small chance of your ever seeing it again. *(O)*

To discover one, great and certain gain. *(OM)*

------- ♦ -------

GOLF
To dream of watching a game of golf, or of taking part in one, means that your health is likely to suffer from too close attention to business; that it is unwise to neglect the enjoyment of the present; and that to a certain extent the future may be left to take care of itself. *(O)*

To dream that you are on the golf links is a sign that you will have little time for recreation in your life. You will be always busy. *(M)*

------- ♦ -------

GONDOLA
To dream that you are travelling in a gondola signifies an easy existence and independence through another's exertions. To the young girl it also foreshadows an early engagement. *(M)*

------- ♦ -------

GOOSE
To dream you cut off the head of a green goose signifies joy and recreation. To hear geese cry signifies profit, and assurance of the completion of business. *(T)*

A young man dreaming that he listens to a goose cackling is informed that he is about to write a letter to a young lady, which he will think the cleverest letter he has ever written, and that the result will fully justify his good opinion of it. A young woman dreaming of a goose may expect to make a fortunate, thought not a brilliant marriage. *(O)*

The goose may be taken as an emblem of sincerity when seen alive. To dream that you are eating geese predicts a wish granted. *(M)*

To dream of geese is a forerunner of good; expect soon to see a long-absent friend. *(OM)*

Of these cacklers to dream is a negative gain.
For tho' your wife's good, oft her tongue gives you pain. *(MS)*

------- ♦ -------

GOOSEBERRIES
To dream of gooseberries indicates many children, chiefly sons, and an accomplishment of your present activities; to the sailor they declare dangers in his next voyage; to the girl, a roving husband; and to the man, a fun-loving wife. *(GD)*

To dream of a gooseberry is bad for the lover. It means that a friend whom he has introduced to his lover will not only endeavour to supplant him in her affection, but will succeed. *(O)*

To see the fruit growing is an omen first of lack of work, and afterwards more work than you can do. The dream that you are eating gooseberries predicts trouble, but it will not be of a very serious nature. *(M)*

------- ◆ -------

GOUT

To dream you have gout signifies fear to the young, and potential physical injury; and to the old, it denotes poverty and lack of energy. *(T)*

------- ◆ -------

GOVERNMENT

To dream that you are employed by the government means that you will have to work hard all your life, and that you will probably have someone else depending upon your exertions. *(M)*

------- ◆ -------

GOWN

For a woman to dream she sees a new gown brought home for her is a sign that some retrenchment will be needed in the expenses of her family; the prevailing fashions are expensive and very much above the income of the family, of which she is constantly reminded by her husband, who will often get cross and bad-tempered about the large amount he will have to pay for her clothes. If a woman has this dream more than once it proves her to be vain and extravagant. For a woman to dream that her gown is torn and mended in several places is a good sign; her husband will make progress in business. *(M)*

------- ◆ -------

GRAIN

To dream you see any kind of grain and gather it, signifies profit and gain. *(OM)*

------- ◆ -------

GRANDCHILD

For a person to dream that he or she sees their grandchildren is a sign that they will remember some of the old pleasures of youth, and they will recount stories about the past to their children. *(M)*

------- ◆ -------

GRAPES

To dream of eating ripe grapes signifies cheerfulness and profit. To dream you gather black grapes signifies damage. To gather white grapes signifies gain. To dream you tread grapes signifies the overthrow of your enemies. *(T)*

To dream of grapes foretells to a girl that her husband will be a cheerful companion and a great singer. *(OM)*

GRASS
You have to fear deceit. *(OM)*

━━━━━━ ◆ ━━━━━━

GRASSHOPPERS
All sorts of grasshoppers signify impertinent gossips and bad musicians. If a sick person dreams of grasshoppers, it means bad luck. *(T)*

To dream of grasshoppers signifies a poor harvest. *(M)*

━━━━━━ ◆ ━━━━━━

GRATER
To dream that you see a nutmeg grater is a sign that you will form a friendship with someone who will prepare many delicious meals for you. *(M)*

━━━━━━ ◆ ━━━━━━

GRAVE
If it seems that you are put in a grave and buried, that indicates that you will die poor. Some believe that to dream you are dead and buried means that you will inherit money or property, according to the amount of earth that is laid on you. *(T)*

To see a grave foretells sickness and disappointment; if you are in love, you will never marry your present sweetheart. *(GD)*

To dream you go into a grave shows you will lose property. If you come out of the grave, it denotes success in your undertakings, and that you will rise in the world. *(OM)*

To dream of taking another out of the grave signifies that you will be the means of saving the life of a person who will be a very great friend to you and you will receive some unexpected legacy. *(GD2)*

See also **BURY.**

━━━━━━ ◆ ━━━━━━

GRAVEL WALK
To dream that you see a smooth gravel walk is a sign that your path of life will be made somewhat rugged by difficulties. You will have to fight with obstacles of a new kind; some of your intimate friends whom you thought would assist you will be shy and reserved towards you, and will refuse you that financial help which would tide you over your present commercial difficulties. *(M)*

━━━━━━ ◆ ━━━━━━

GREENFINCH
Warns you to stick to your work and undertakings if you want to avoid making a loss. *(OM)*

━━━━━━ ◆ ━━━━━━

GRENADIER
For a young woman to dream that she meets with a Grenadier guardsman is a sign that a member of one of the horse regiments will soon want to take her out. *(M)*

GREY HAIRS

To dream that your hair is sprinkled with grey at an early age is a sign that you will carry age very well; you will look younger than you really are.

(M)

GREYHOUNDS

To dream of these dogs racing is good, signifying action and jobs. *(A)*

GRINDING

Grinding corn indicates good fortune; grinding coffee means trouble at home; grinding pepper signifies sickness and sorrow. *(OM)*

GRINDSTONE

To dream of seeing a grindstone is a sign that you will always be in a comfortable position in life; but it will be by your own hard work as you will never receive money from a friend or relation. To dream that you are working at a grindstone means that you will have many debts to pay; but you will meet all your liabilities, and come off with a small income from your work in your old age. *(M)*

GROPING

To dream that you are groping your way in the dark means that you and your partner are not made for each other, and that after marriage you are certain to have continual friction. *(O)*

GROTTO

Your business will improve. To be transported into one indicates a perilous journey. *(OM)*

GROVES

If anyone dreams he owns good lands with pleasant groves and orchards adjoining them, it signifies he will marry a discreet, chaste and beautiful wife, and that they will have very handsome children. *(T)*

GUESTS

To dream that you are embarrassed by receiving a great number of guests predicts that you will be parted from your friends for some time and be forgotten by many. *(M)*

GUITAR

To play the guitar, or hear it played, is for a young man a sign that his thoughts will constantly be occupied by his lover and their marriage will be happy and successful. A woman dreaming of guitar playing may also infer from it a successful marriage. *(O)*

A young man who dreams of playing the guitar should look to it that he is not a flirt, for if he trifles with the affections of the opposite sex he will suffer for it. For a young lady the dream predicts a long engagement with a happy ending. *(M)*

To play a guitar indicates scandal or bad news. *(OM)*

───────── ◆ ─────────

GUN

To dream you see people firing guns or cannons denotes that the dreamer will experience many problems. *(GD)*

To hear the unexpected report of a gun is for a woman a sign that she is likely to be in a position of great danger. For a man it portends the receipt of surprising news. *(O)*

To hear the report of a gun is a sign that you will be the cause of a serious quarrel, and will lose the regard of someone you love. To dream that you are handling a gun is a bad sign. You will do something which you will regret for the rest of your life. *(M)*

If you dream you are firing a gun, it foretells that you will be involved in a law-suit. *(OM)*

───────── ◆ ─────────

GUNPOWDER

If a woman smells gunpowder she will have an offer of marriage from an old, retired half-pay officer. If she sees a great quantity of gunpowder, some dashing young sergeant, either in a horse or foot regiment, will propose to her, and if she accepts him she will find he will make her an excellent husband. If a young soldier sees a quantity of gunpowder it means a removal from his present quarters to do garrison duty. *(M)*

───────── ◆ ─────────

GYMNASTICS

To dream that you take part in some gymnastic exercises is a sign that you will shortly have to give up work through illness. To dream that you see some other people taking this exercise is indicative of some fatal accident to either a friend or an acquaintance. *(M)*

HADDOCK
To dream of this fish indicates that you have a contented mind which will prevent you from stirring yourself to achieve great things. You will always be in flourishing circumstances. *(M)*

———————— ♦ ————————

HAIL
Dreams of hailstorms signifies rest, repose. *(T)*

To dream that you are caught in a hailstorm foretells that you will form a subject for envious remarks on the part of many who have not been so successful in the world as yourself, and whether these remarks are to prove injurious or not may be judged by the severity of the storm. *(O)*

To dream of hail is a good omen, although it may not appear to be so at the time. But persevere with whatever you have in hand, no matter how many obstacles may stand in the way of success, and you will be rewarded sooner or later. *(M)*

To dream that you are in a hailstorm indicates great sorrow in life. *(OM)*

———————— ♦ ————————

HAIR
If you imagine you see a strange woman with long and beautiful hair, it is a very good sign as it denotes friendship, joy and prosperity. If a man dreams his hair is long, like a woman's, that signifies cowardice and effeminacy, and that he will be deceived by a woman. To see a woman without hair signifies famine, poverty and sickness. To see a bald man signifies the opposite. To see plaited hair signifies annoyance and grief, and sometimes injuries and quarrels. To see black hair, short and curled, signifies sadness and loss. To see well-combed hair signifies friendship. To lose your hair signifies annoyance and loss of money. If your hair seems to be longer and blacker than usual, your wealth and reputation will increase. If anyone dreams that their hair has grown thinner than it was before, it is a sign of affliction and poverty. If you dream you perfume your hair, that signifies vanity and conceit. If a woman dreams this, she will deceive her husband, and 'wear the trousers' at home. If you dream your hair is permed, it signifies that you are in some danger either from sickness or injury. *(T)*

To dream you have long tidy hair is good for a woman, but if the hair is untidy, it indicates anger and sullenness. To have a head of beautiful hair is good; and to be bald is bad. To dream you have a thick beard and some boys pull it off shows you must take care against danger.   *(D&M)*

To dream that your hair is long is good; if it is untidy, long and brittle, it shows disturbance and trouble. To dream a man has no hair on his face denotes shamefacedness. If a seaman dreams his head is shaven, he is in danger of being shipwrecked.   *(D&M2)*

Dreaming of losing hair means you will lose something; either friends, property, a law-suit, or perhaps even your reputation.   *(O)*

To dream that your hair is falling out is an indication that something is wrong with your love affairs or domestic arrangements. Try to find out what it is, and put it right before it is too late. A girl who dreams of combing her hair may expect a proposal of marriage; a married woman a present from her husband. To dream that your hair is growing rapidly is a sign of fickleness.   *(M)*

To dream you plait or curl your hair is only good for a woman; to others it signifies debt and impeachment for money and sometimes imprisonment. If you dream you have fair long hair and you seem to take a pride in it, it is a good sign especially to a woman or a man who normally wears his hair long. To dream you have wool instead of hair foretells a long sickness.   *(A)*

> To comb is to profit in every pursuit;
> But should it fall off, friends are hollow at root,
> If ever grown long and pendant o'er shoulders,
> You'll please all friends and astonish beholders.   *(MS)*

---◆---

HAM

To dream of ham implies cruel enemies. Be on your guard against them. To dream of eating ham is a sign of discontent in later life.   *(M)*

To dream of a ham signifies joy and pleasure.   *(OM)*

---◆---

HAMMER

To dream that you are using a hammer denotes that one of your wishes will be realized. To hear the clang of a hammer foretells unpleasantness.   *(M)*

---◆---

HANDCUFFS

To dream that you are handcuffed is a sign to a girl that she will marry a man connected with the law; to a married woman that her husband will have need of a lawyer's advice. To see another person handcuffed is an indication that one of your friends will shortly find themselves in serious trouble, in which you will be involved.   *(M)*

---◆---

HANDS

If anyone dreams his hands are more attractive and stronger than usual, he will be employed in some important affair, which he will bring to a happy conclusion, and gain reputation and advantage from it; and his employees will work for him cheerfully and loyally. If anyone dreams that his hand is cut off, that it has become thin and dry or that it has been burned, he will lose his most faithful employee. If he has none, he will not be able to work, but will become poor. If a woman dreams this, she will lose her husband, her eldest son, or fall ill. If anyone dreams he works with his right hand, that is a sign of good fortune to him and his family; if with the left that denotes bad luck. Some also attribute the arm and the right hand to the father, son, brother and friend, and the success that may happen to them; and the left arm or hand signifies the mother, daughter, wife or employees. To dream your hand is hairy signifies trouble and imprisonment. To dream that you have clear and white hands signifies friendship if you are rich or idleness and necessity if you are poor. To dream you have many hands signifies good luck, strength and wealth. To dream you look at your hands signifies sickness. To dream you wash your hands signifies anxiety and vexation. *(T)*

To dream of your hands being fine and strong shows prosperity to tradesmen; but is bad for criminals. To dream of the right hand means you will gain something; the left, that you have already received it. *(D&M)*

> To dream a cold hand is put to you in bed,
> And your next news, a relation will be dead.
> And yet to dream, your hands you wash, 'tis clear
> Your troubles now, soon will all disappear. *(N)*

To dream that you have hurt your hand signifies that you will soon be receiving a present of money as a reward for some good action. *(M)*

To dream your hands are strong and attractive shows prosperity to tradesmen. To dream you have hair on the backs of your hands signifies captivity, but if it comes on the palm it denotes idleness. *(A)*

HANDWRITING

To see the handwriting of a dead friend is a warning to stop indulging in your accustomed bad habits or there will be dreadful consequences. For a young woman to dream that she sees the handwriting of her lover is a sign that he will soon experience some accident or injury. He may fall out of a boat, be accidentally shot with a firearm, or fall from a rock or a tree and be seriously injured. For a young man to dream that he sees the handwriting of his sweetheart is a sign that she is secretly going out with someone else in his absence.

HANGING

If anyone dreams they condemned someone to be hanged, it signifies they will be angry with that person for a short time, but will be reconciled with them. If anyone dreams that they were taken to the bottom of the gibbet to be hanged, they will lose their property and dignity. *(T)*

To dream of seeing people hanged, or that you are going to be hanged yourself, is a sign you will rise above your present condition by marriage; or you will be asked a favour by someone in need. *(GD)*

> To see people hanged, or to feel hung yourself,
> Is the manifest proof of the increase of wealth
> And however awkward we own the sensation
> You scarcely dare doubt of a just elevation. *(MS)*

———— ♦ ————

HAPPINESS

To dream of being extremely happy signifies that in your waking hours you are, perhaps quite unconsciously, walking the brink of a precipice, and that you should therefore exercise the greatest caution in all you do. *(O)*

If during a period of distress, you dream that you are very happy, your problems will increase for a short time, but then everything will come right. But you must meet your troubles head on and sort them out. *(M)*

———— ♦ ————

HARBOUR

To see a harbour signifies that you will have joy, profit and good news.
(T)

———— ♦ ————

HARES

To dream you see a hare running signifies great wealth gained by application and intelligence. *(T)*

To dream of hunting a hare which escapes shows losses. *(P&F)*

> A dream that you pursue a hare,
> Of cruel sports, bids you beware;
> Some accident perchance you'll meet,
> Great or small in lane or street. *(N)*

To dream of seeing a hare is a bad omen, and indicates that a death will shortly occur of one near and dear to you. Should you, however, see two or more hares in company, the dream is of no such melancholy significance, but merely indicates that you will shortly make a pleasant excursion to a popular rural haunt. *(O)*

To dream you see a hare running signifies loss of money. *(OM)*

———— ♦ ————

HARP

To dream you play or see another play a harp signifies the death of relations.
(T)

To dream of playing the harp denotes that through envy you will make an enemy. To hear the music of the harp is significant of a nervous breakdown. *(M)*

To dream you play on a harp is good for weddings or those contracting engagements; but it is bad for other affairs since to many it signifies the gout. *(A)*

HARPIES
To dream you see harpies, those legendary half-woman and half-serpents, signifies troubles and pain caused by envious and treacherous people. *(T)*

———— ♦ ————

HAT
If anyone dreams he has a hat on which he likes that signifies joy, profit and success in business. To dream your hat is torn or dirty signifies damage and dishonour.   *(T)*

———— ♦ ————

HATE
It is a good dream that someone hates you, for it is a sure sign of success. On the contrary, to dream of someone you hate is unlucky, and brings sorrow.   *(M)*
To dream of hatred, whether of friends or enemies, is bad.   *(OM)*

———— ♦ ————

HAWKS
To dream you see birds of prey or falconry signifies increase of wealth to the rich, but the opposite to the poor.   *(T)*
After dreaming of a hawk beware of a dark man, who will endeavour to harm you. Keep a tight hold on your money.   *(M)*
Someone will be jealous of you.   *(OM)*

———— ♦ ————

HAWTHORN
For a young woman to dream that a young man presents her with a piece of hawthorn blossom is a sign that she is highly respected by a young man living nearby who is too shy to speak to her.   *(M)*

———— ♦ ————

HAY
The man who dreams of working in the hay will become famous throughout the country. For a woman, the dream gives promise of comfort and an exalted station in life.   *(M)*
To dream of hay signifies happiness and success; to mow it denotes sorrow.   *(OM)*

———— ♦ ————

HAY-MAKING
No inference important can be hereby impart,
As it emanates merely from pureness of heart.   *(MS)*

———— ♦ ————

HAZEL NUTS
To see and eat hazel nuts signifies difficulties and trouble.   *(T)*
See also NUTS.

———— 169 ————

HEAD

If anyone dreams their head is bigger than usual, that signifies that they will be promoted to a powerful job. It sometimes also indicates victory over enemies and overthrowing adversaries at law; and to merchants and bankers, collecting money or recovering treasure. If a sick person dreams this, it indicates a serious and violent fever. To dream you have a small, light or sharp head signifies lack of spirit and disgrace. To dream you have three heads on one neck signifies authority, power and reputation. To dream that you have the head of a lion, wolf or some other wild animal, is a good sign; the dreamer will accomplish his intentions, will overcome problems and be respected by friends and colleagues. To dream you are holding your head in your hands signifies the loss of your wife and children. If the dreamer is not married, it means good luck; and if he does his hair and puts on a hat, his business will succeed. To dream you have two heads signifies company. To dream you wash your head signifies escape from danger. *(T)*

To dream your head is turned back to front is a warning to leave the country, otherwise there will be dire consequences. *(D&M)*

For a man to dream that his head is very large signifies good fortune. *(D&M2)*

HEADACHE

To dream of having a headache foretells that you are about to be tempted to do wrong, but the temptation must be resisted at any cost, for if you yield, your conscience will trouble you continually. *(O)*

To dream of a headache signifies loss of memory. *(OM)*

HEARSE

To dream of a hearse ornamented with feathers signifies that you will marry a rich person, or help at a relation's wedding, who will marry well and be a friend to you. *(DSG)*

HEART

If anyone dreams they have a pain in the heart, it is a sign of dangerous illness approaching, according to the level of pain. If anyone dreams they have lost their heart, it is a sign of sudden death, or that they will fall completely under the power of their most bitter enemies. To dream your heart is more lively, large and vigorous than usual is a sign of long life, that you will overcome your enemies and be prosperous in your enterprises. In the opinion of some, the heart in dreams signifies man, and chiefly the husband, so that if a woman dreams she has pains in her heart, the evil indicated will happen to her husband; if it is a girl the evil will happen to her father. *(T)*

HEARTH
To be cooking over a fire means you will successfully carve out your own fortunes.   *(OM)*

———— ♦ ————

HEAT
To dream you feel very hot signifies grief.   *(T)*

———— ♦ ————

HEATHENS
To have any dealings with heathens, or to dream of them in any way, is a warning of treachery in a person you would suspect least of anyone you know. Be careful whom you trust until you have found the guilty party. *(M)*

———— ♦ ————

HEATHER
Good fortune and a pleasant journey follow a dream of heather.   *(M)*
    Indicates hope; although if it is withered, your hopes are vain.   *(OM)*

———— ♦ ————

HEAVEN
To dream you ascend up to heaven, signifies authority and power. *(T)*
    To dream of heaven is an assurance that you will have no cause to complain of lack of comfort in your married life.   *(M)*

———— ♦ ————

HEDGE
To dream of a high hedge indicates that you will have to fight hard to gain success in something you have undertaken, and unless you put your best efforts into it you will be overwhelmed by the opposition you will encounter.   *(M)*
    If the hedge is green, it indicates prosperity and success.   *(OM)*

———— ♦ ————

HEDGEHOG
To dream of a hedgehog signifies that your kindness will be taken advantage of.   *(OM)*

———— ♦ ————

HELL
To dream you see hell as it is described and hear the damned souls groan, and complain of the extremity of their torments is an indication from God that you must improve your morals and way of life. To dream you see the damned plunged in the fire and flames, and suffer great torture signifies sadness, repentance, grief and a melancholy. To dream you have descended into hell and returned signifies misfortunes to the rich and powerful, but is a good sign to the poor or weak.   *(T)*

———— ♦ ————

HENS
To dream of a hen and her chickens signifies loss and damage. To dream

that a capon or hen crows signifies sadness and trouble. To dream you hear hens cackle, or geese honk signifies profit and assurance of the completion of a business project. To dream you catch hens signifies joy. *(T)*

To dream of hens is very unfavourable; it indicates loss of property, friends and reputation; in love it denotes misery and disappointment. After such a dream I would advise the dreamer to change his residence. To dream you hear hens cackling foretells success in love, and an accumulation of riches from female relations. *(GD)*

A dream in which a hen forms a prominent figure means that throughout life you are likely to be protected from all trouble and to have your bread buttered on both sides. *(O)*

To hear the cackling of hens means that a secret which you have confided in a friend has been passed on further. To see a number of hens foreshadows a visit to the country. *(M)*

———— ◆ ————

HERBS

To dream you eat any herb indicates good health and long life. To be hunting for herbs means gain in business or your profession. *(OM)*

To dream of smelling herbs such as marjoram, hyssop, rosemary, sage, etc. signifies hard work, trouble, sadness and weakness to anyone but a doctor to whom such dreams are propitious. *(A)*

———— ◆ ————

HERMIT

To have dealings with a hermit is a sign of a loveless marriage. *(M)*

To dream of a hermit signifies sorrow. *(OM)*

———— ◆ ————

HERRING

To dream of herrings, whether of catching them or eating them, is a dream for the economical and signifies that by frugal living they will soon become the owners of a vast amount of property. *(O)*

To dream of eating this fish is an indication that, unless you are more frugal and save money now, you will suffer a fall in your standard of living later in life. *(M)*

———— ◆ ————

HIDING

To dream you are hiding denotes obscurity and blighted hopes. *(D&M)*

To dream you are hiding denotes that bad news will soon reach you. *(OM)*

———— ◆ ————

HIGHLANDER

To dream that you see a Highlander in full Scottish costume is a sign that you will be a cool and calculating trader and a careful and plodding contriver in all your business transactions. *(M)*

HILLS

To dream of travelling over steep hills shows that you will encounter many difficulties, and enter upon some arduous undertaking. If you descend the hill easily, you will get the better of all your problems and become rich.
(GD)

To dream you climb a steep hill and never get to the top signifies your life will be one of difficulties and troubles. *(OM)*

———— ♦ ————

HIPS

If anyone dreams his hips have grown larger and stronger than usual, he will be very happy and healthy; and if he marries, will have lovely children. To dream your hips are broken, and that you cannot walk, denotes affliction, sickness and loss of children. If anyone dreams that his hips are black and blue with whipping, or blows with a stick or sword, that means his death in a short time, or at least that he will hate his wife and have several grievances. If he dreams his hips are cut half through, his hopes in his wife and relations will be utterly lost. *(T)*

———— ♦ ————

HIPS and HAWS

This indicates poverty or loss of money; especially if you are eating them in your dream. *(OM)*

———— ♦ ————

HOE

To dream that you see this agricultural implement is a sign that you will have good health and spirits for a long time. If a young woman has this dream she will have a lover who is engaged in agriculture. *(M)*

———— ♦ ————

HOG'S BRISTLES

To dream of these signifies great and violent dangers. *(A)*

———— ♦ ————

HOLE

To dream you creep into or fall into a hole means you will come in contact with undesirable people. *(OM)*

———— ♦ ————

HOLLY

To dream of holly signifies vexations and disagreements. *(OM)*

———— ♦ ————

HOMESICK

If you are away from home and dream of those you love and have left there, and have intense feelings of homesickness, it is a sign of great wealth coming to you from an unexpected source. Someone who has no family has taken a fancy to you and will leave you the largest portion of his fortune. *(M)*

HONEY

Signifies prosperity, honour and renown. But be careful to be honest in all your dealings. If, however, the honey is surrounded by bees, beware of jealous people who will attempt to snatch away your success.   *(M)*

    To dream of honey signifies profitable enterprises.   *(OM)*

———————— ◆ ————————

HONOUR

To dream that you have been the recipient of some special honour is a sign that you will be humiliated in the presence of someone who will be pleased to see you embarrassed.   *(M)*

———————— ◆ ————————

HOOP

To dream of a hoop foretells a pleasant surprise or a visit from two friends whom you have almost forgotten.   *(M)*

———————— ◆ ————————

HORNETS

To dream of hornets attacking you is an omen that you will shortly meet a person of the opposite sex who will fascinate you.   *(M)*

    To dream of hornets signifies assault and discredit to the dreamer.   *(A)*

———————— ◆ ————————

HORNS

If anyone dreams he has horns on his head, it signifies dominion, grandeur and royalty; nevertheless some authors say that to dream you have the horns of an ox, or any other potentially dangerous creature, denotes anger, pride and violent death by the hand of justice. To dream you see a man with horns on his head signifies he is in danger both of the loss of his life and property.   *(T)*

    To hear a horn blowing is a sign that your help is wanted by someone living a long distance away. To see the horns of a bull or any other animal indicates that you have vicious enemies.   *(M)*

———————— ◆ ————————

HORSE

To dream you see many horses signifies wealth and plenty. The horse is a good sign, for if anyone dreams they see, take or mount a horse, that is a happy omen to the dreamer. If anyone dreams that he is mounted on a stately horse, nimble, full of metal and well harnessed, he will have a handsome, noble and rich wife, provided the horse is his own; if it belongs to someone else, he will receive comfort, property and honour through a woman who is a stranger. If anyone dreams that he is riding and he passes a place without making his horse rest by dismounting, he will gain honour, dignity and fame. If anyone dreams he rides a horse with a long tail, it is a sign he will find many friends to assist him in his undertakings. Some say that it promises him a noble woman, by whose means he will be successful in his affairs proportionately to the greatness of the tail; quite the opposite, if he thinks his horse's tail is cut off—then his friends or colleagues will fail him when he stands in most need of them. If his horse stops, he will meet with obstruction in his designs. If anyone dreams that another rides his horse without his consent, it signifies that some person will commit adultery with his wife. Some authors are of the opinion that if anyone dreams he is mounted on a nimble, sprightly, active and well-managed horse, he will be honoured by everyone. If he dreams he spurred the horse too violently and forced him to what he did, he shall be advanced to a position of authority. If anyone dreams he has a young, well-harnessed mare, it is a sign he will soon be married to a beautiful, young and rich woman, and they will be very happy. If it is a poorly-formed mare without a saddle, that denotes his wife will have no money of her own. To dream that you ride on a white, grey or dappled horse signifies prosperity. To dream you see white horses signifies joy; black horses signify sadness. To see horses pace signifies mirth. To see horses of several colours signifies success in business. To see red or roan-coloured horses signifies prosperity. To see a gelding signifies accusation. To see a horse mount signifies prosperity.   *(T)*

To dream you are on horseback, and the horse runs away with you shows you will be called away on something contrary to your liking. *(P&F)*

To dream of riding a horse indicates a change of scene, change of friends, new lovers, new rivals, in fact, quite a sensational upsetting of everything in your life.   *(O)*

To dream that you are dealing in horses denotes that good luck awaits you in connection with a favourite project. If you dream you are riding on a black horse, you will rise to a position of trust in your neighbourhood. If the horse is white, you will not be so successful, but you will be happy. To dream of a horse kicking is an indication that someone you love will be taken with a sudden illness. A horseshoe means good news.   *(M)*

To dream you see a horse running signifies prosperity. To dream of riding on a tired horse shows that you will fall desperately in love. To dream you see a horse dead is a sign that stagnation will take place on your business with some losses.   *(OM)*

HORSE HAIR
To dream of horsehair is a sign of servitude and misery.   *(A)*

HORSEMAN
To dream of a horseman signifies a dangerous journey.   *(OM)*

HOSPITAL
To be in a hospital indicates you will suffer a long illness.   *(OM)*

HOTEL

To dream of living in an hotel signifies to a man that he will shortly be compelled by an accident to reside for a time in an hotel in a strange town, and that he will end by marrying the best girl in the neighbourhood. A girl dreaming of hotel life may conclude that she will marry a husband who will be of a roving disposition. *(O)*

━━━━━ ♦ ━━━━━

HOTHOUSE

Anyone who dreams of a hothouse may look for a rapid improvement in financial affairs. *(M)*

━━━━━ ♦ ━━━━━

HOUR GLASS

Forewarns that whate'er be your health or your state,
You've arrived at an epoch—the crisis of fate;
Reflect then, be wise—yet act with decision
Or impudence may plunge you 'ere long into prison. *(MS)*

━━━━━ ♦ ━━━━━

HOUSE

To dream you build a house signifies comfort. To dream you burn a house and see it burning signifies scandals that will occur around you, and loss of property. *(T)*

To dream of building a house means that single people will marry, but those who are already married will encounter trouble and anxiety. A dream of a house falling down denotes to the businessman that he ought to look into his affairs, the balancing of his books has been too long neglected. *(O)*

If you dream of your own house, domestic happiness will be yours; but should the house be in a dilapidated state, illness will occur in the family. To dream that you are building or buying a house generally means that you will have to cut down expenses by moving to a cheaper residence. *(M)*

To dream you see a home on fire foretells hasty news. *(OM)*

━━━━━ ♦ ━━━━━

HUNGER

If anyone dreams he is extraordinarily hungry he will be ingenious, hard-working and eager to advance in his job in proportion to the greatness of his hunger. *(T)*

To dream you are very hungry is a very favourite omen. To the lover it denotes that your sweetheart will undertake a journey before you marry. *(DSG)*

For a woman to dream that she is hungry is a good sign. She will have a good husband and good children, and command the respect of all her friends. To a man, the dream gives warning that he is aspiring to perform an impossible task. He will do well to be less ambitious. *(M)*

HUNTING

To dream you go hunting signifies an accusation. *(Y)*

To dream you are hunting and that the game is killed shows much trouble. *(OM)*

To dream you are hunting a fox and that he is killed shows much trouble through the pretentions of false friends, but that nevertheless you will discover them and overcome all their deceits. To dream that you are hunting a hare is indicative of failure and that you will be disappointed in your favourite object, whatever it may be. To dream, however, that you are hunting a stag is good if he is caught alive; you will be successful in all your present undertakings. *(GD2)*

———————— ♦ ————————

HURRICANE

Be on your guard, otherwise you will be led into a serious quarrel, ending in the law courts. The quarrel will not concern you personally, but the contending parties will do their best to include you in the mutual recriminations, and you will have to take a firm stand. *(M)*

———————— ♦ ————————

HUSBAND

For a wife to dream of her husband is a sign of growing affection. A widow dreaming of her deceased husband may safely anticipate receiving a proposal. *(O)*

For a wife to dream of an absent husband is a sign that he is well and will soon return to her. The girl who dreams she sees the man she is destined to marry will not find a partner until late in life. *(M)*

———————— ♦ ————————

HUSSAR

For a young unmarried woman to dream that she meets a hussar is a sign that she will fall desperately in love with a soldier, who has never shown any attachment towards her, but who has known her for a long time. She will do her best to gain his attention, for in her case 'love is blind', but she will not be able to win his love, and the consequence will be that she will spend many days in a gloomy love-sick state of mind. *(M)*

———————— ♦ ————————

HYPNOTISM

To dream that you have been hypnotised indicates that you will reveal some secrets which will cause unpleasantness to some of your friends. *(M)*

———————— ♦ ————————

HYSSOP

To dream that you smell of hyssop signifies hard work, trouble, sadness and weakness; unless you are a doctor in which case the dream is propitious. *(T)*

ICE

When you dream of ice and snow in winter, that has no particular meaning for you are thinking about the cold of the preceding day. But if it is in another season, that denotes a good harvest to farmers; to merchants and other businessmen, it signifies hindrance in their negotiations and voyages; and to soldiers, that their designs will be frustrated. *(T)*

To dream you are sliding or skating on ice denotes that you will pursue some unprofitable concern, and lose out; in love, it shows that your sweetheart is fickle and deceiving, and that you will never marry your present one. *(GD)*

To dream of being on the ice signifies losses of various kinds, especially of money. For a man to dream of ice melting signifies that he will fall madly in love with a young woman, and that his passion will last no longer than fourteen days. *(O)*

To see a sheet of thin ice is a sign that you will make and break a promise on the same day, which will lead to a coolness between yourself and your sweetheart. Should the ice be thick, however, and you see people skating on it, you will have a desire to travel, but will not be able to gratify it. *(M)*

> This dream like a parable ought to remind,
> In youth of the friendship and guile of mankind
> When sliding so gaily and thoughtless along,
> In whistling a tune, or in chanting a song;
> Your hopes all expectant may meet a frustration,
> For all those who slide must hazard prostration. *(MS)*

———— ◆ ————

ICEBERG

Denotes an enemy who will take advantage of his superior position to do you harm. *(M)*

———— ◆ ————

ICICLES

To dream of icicles denotes good luck, happiness and success in love. *(OM)*

———— ◆ ————

IDIOT

If anyone dreams he has become an idiot, or mad, and is guilty of stupid behaviour in public, he will live long and be popular. *(OM)*

IDLE

To dream that you are idle in your character and habits is a sign of having great profits, both in money and intelligence, from your industry. You will only need to persevere in your daily hard work at your job to gain a position of influence. *(M)*

————— ♦ —————

ILLNESS

To dream you see yourself sick signifies sadness and imprisonment. *(T)*

To dream you are ill and in pain indicates misery and unhappiness. To tend or visit the sick means joy and happiness. To dream you have a lingering illness signifies that you will become rich. *(OM)*

————— ♦ —————

ILLUMINATION

It is a certain sign of war when a person dreams of seeing a city illuminated. To dream your own house is illuminated means much quarrelling among relatives. *(OM)*

————— ♦ —————

IMPALE

To dream one of your relatives or friends falls from a window or the top of the house and is impaled upon the rails beneath is a sign that something will fall from a housetop and injure your head. *(M)*

————— ♦ —————

IMPRISONMENT

To dream you are imprisoned signifies enjoyment and happiness. *(OM)*

————— ♦ —————

IMPS

To dream of imps signifies grief and disappointment. *(OM)*

————— ♦ —————

INCEST

For a man to dream he is in bed with his mother means he should make haste to complete his business arrangements. *(D&M2)*

————— ♦ —————

INFANT

If an unmarried woman dreams of an infant, it means that she will go through some trouble. *(OM)*

————— ♦ —————

INJURY

To dream you receive an injury warns you to beware of enemies. If in business, you will meet with overwhelming competition. *(OM)*

————— ♦ —————

INK

To dream of ink being spilt, or of your being soiled with ink, means that someone is harbouring evil against you, and that you will shortly receive an anonymous letter of which it would be unwise to take any notice.   *(O)*

To a girl spilt ink gives a warning that she will receive a confession of love, and possibly a proposal by post. To a married person the dream predicts libel and slander.   *(M)*

To dream of spilled ink signifies separation and losses.   *(OM)*

———————— ◆ ————————

INN

To dream that one is in an inn or pub and eating with your companions signifies joy and comfort.   *(T)*

To dream of being in an inn is a very unfavourable sign; it denotes poverty and failure. Expect yourself or one of your family to be committed to prison. If you are sick, you will never recover. To the tradesman, loss of credit and bad employees.   *(DSG)*

To dream of an inn signifies loss of money. If you are in love you will be disappointed.   *(OM)*

———————— ◆ ————————

INN KEEPER

To dream of an inn keeper signifies death to the sick. To those who are seriously ill it foretells the approach of their death.   *(A)*

———————— ◆ ————————

INQUEST

To dream of being at an inquest denotes prosperity.   *(OM)*

———————— ◆ ————————

INSANITY

To dream that you are insane is an omen of good fortune. To dream that you are watching another person who has lost his or her senses indicates coming mild sickness in your family.   *(M)*

———————— ◆ ————————

INSECTS

To dream of insects crawling over you is a good omen of prosperity. To see them running away from you predicts disappointment.   *(M)*

To dream of insects signifies illness and loss.   *(OM)*

———————— ◆ ————————

INSTRUMENTS

To dream of musical instruments or to see one instrument alone being played or to play one yourself, indicates mourning and sorrow.   *(OM)*

———————— ◆ ————————

INSULT

To dream that you have been insulted is a sure sign that someone will be flattering you before long, and by that means trying to make you commit a foolish indiscretion. be careful of the person, and have as little as possible to do with them. *(M)*

To dream you are insulted signifies quarrels, loss of a lover and opposition. *(OM)*

———— ♦ ————

INTESTINES

To dream of intestines signifies sickness and anxiety. *(OM)*

———— ♦ ————

INVALIDS

To dream you comfort invalids and prescribe remedies and medicines for them signifies profit and good luck. *(T)*

To dream you are an invalid and unable to leave your bed is a really good omen, for although you may expect a bad illness soon, it will pass quickly, and you will afterwards enjoy a long spell of good health. To dream that someone you know is an invalid foretells bad news concerning a brother or sister. *(M)*

To dream of invalids signifies that you will fall ill. *(OM)*

———— ♦ ————

INVITATION

The person who dreams of receiving an invitation to a party or social function may expect to lose someone close to them. *(M)*

———— ♦ ————

IRON

To dream you buy and sell iron goods with a stranger signifies loss and misfortune. To dream you see yourself hurt with iron signifies damage. *(T)*

To dream of iron signifies quarrels and disputes. *(OM)*

———— ♦ ————

ISLAND

To dream you are on an island signifies that you will lose the friendship of someone. *(OM)*

———— ♦ ————

ITCH

To dream you itch signifies that your fears and anxieties are groundless. *(OM)*

———— ♦ ————

IVORY

To dream of ivory signifies riches, success, abundance, prosperity; this is a very good dream. *(OM)*

———— ♦ ————

IVY

Dreaming of ivy means that your present lover will soon have to take a back seat, and that your next partner will be the one with whom you will

———— 181 ————

form a lasting and serious relationship. *(O)*

An especially good omen for sweethearts. Should you dream that your lover is picking ivy for you, you will marry a faithful husband. *(M)*

Your friends and everyone you love will cling to you. It also signifies good health and happiness. *(OM)*

JACKAL
To dream of this bird signifies that some enemy will talk about you behind your back and cause you trouble. *(OM)*

————— ♦ —————

JACKASS
For a young woman to dream that she sees a jackass is indicative of her meeting with a young man who is patient in character and dull in intelligence, but who will be true to his vows of attachment. He will prefer meeting her in private, for he will be of a reserved and shy temperament. It is possible for her to meet with a worse match than a marriage with him would prove. *(M)*

————— ♦ —————

JACKDAW
The person who dreams of a jackdaw must be wary of a jealous enemy who will not rest until he has done that person an injury. *(M)*

To dream you catch one signifies you have enemies, but you will overcome them. *(OM)*

————— ♦ —————

JAM
To dream of eating jam foretells a short illness. To dream that you are making jam is an omen of prosperity. *(M)*

————— ♦ —————

JAR
To dream of receiving the present of an ornamental jar means that you are in danger of a close relative causing arguments in your family. *(O)*

To dream that a house is jarred or shaken by an earthquake, an explosion, or anything that may occur outside is a sign that the head of the family in that house will be ill. Jars of preserved fruit or jellies are good omens; if you dream you are presented with one or more of them it denotes you will be long-lived and thrifty. *(M)*

————— ♦ —————

JASMINE
This foretells good luck. Lovers will soon marry. *(OM)*

————— ♦ —————

JAUNDICE
To dream of this complaint signifies sickness and poverty. *(OM)*

JAWS
The jaws represent cellars, shops and places used to store goods.   *(A)*

———— ◆ ————

JEALOUSY
Signifies trouble and anxiety.   *(OM)*

———— ◆ ————

JELLY
To dream that you are eating jelly is a sign of approaching physical weakness, but not severe illness. Give careful attention to your children, as one of them will have weak ankles. For a young man to have this dream is a sign that his special object will not be so easily attained. Difficulties will be presented which will require great patience and perseverance to be exercised by him.   *(M)*

———— ◆ ————

JEOPARDY
If you dream you are in jeopardy, it will be fortunate for you.   *(OM)*

———— ◆ ————

JEWEL and JEWELLERY
To dream of chains, pearls or precious stones and jewellery for the heads and necks of women, are good dreams for women. To widows and girls they signify marriage; to those without children, that they will have a child; to those who are married with children, purchases and riches.   *(D&M2)*

To dream of looking at but not possessing, a rare jewel means that you will shortly meet someone whose worth you will at first fail to recognize, and whose friendship you will reject, and that the rejected friendship can never afterwards be yours.   *(O)*

To dream that you are the owner of many valuable jewels is a sign of joy to come. Should there be many emeralds, however, your jubilation will be tempered with bad news which will bring many tears.   *(M)*

To dream of jewellery signifies that you may expect a handsome present.   *(OM)*

———— ◆ ————

JILTED
The girl who dreams she has been jilted may rest assured that her lover is very faithful to her, but she must not trifle with his affections, otherwise his love will turn to hatred.   *(M)*

———— ◆ ————

JOCKEY
For a girl to dream that she is in love with a jockey is an omen of a gay life for some time, then poverty.   *(M)*

If a woman dreams she sees a jockey riding at full speed, she will have an offer of marriage made to her very unexpectedly.   *(OM)*

JOLLITY
To dream of jollity, feasts and celebrations is a good sign and a prosperous
dream. *(OM)*

───────── ♦ ─────────

JOURNEY
To dream of going on a journey, by whatever form of transport, means that
you are about to have a change in your circumstances. To ascertain
whether it will be for the better or for the worse, recall the style in which
you were travelling. *(OM)*

To dream that you are forced to undertake a journey gives promise of an
invitation to a social function where the dreamer will meet someone who
will be very useful later in life. *(M)*

───────── ♦ ─────────

JOY
To dream of sudden joy shows the arrival of a friend. *(P&F)*

A dream of being overjoyed about anything is in many instances, but
not always, a bad omen, denoting the approach of grief. *(O)*

To dream you are taking part in some joyous festivity, or that you have
cause for feeling particularly happy, is a bad omen; minor troubles are
sure to arise. *(M)*

To dream of joy and festivity is a token of good for anyone about to
marry, or it indicates enjoyment for those fond of society. *(OM)*

───────── ♦ ─────────

JUBILEE
To dream you are at a jubilee is a sure sign that you will have a fortune left
you by some rich relatives. *(OM)*

───────── ♦ ─────────

JUDGE
To dream of seeing a judge on the bench means that you will shortly find
yourself engaged in a law-suit, in which if the judge sits with the window of
the court to the right, you will be successful, if to the left you will come off
second best. Should the court be lighted from the roof the jury in your case
will be unable to agree. *(O)*

To dream of a judge is a sign that you will be likely to grow discontented
with your lot, and in trying to improve matters you will go from bad to
worse. *(M)*

To dream of a judge signifies malice and cruelty. To dream you are
judge signifies annoyance. *(OM)*

───────── ♦ ─────────

JUG
The person who breaks a jug will receive a great surprise. *(M)*

To dream of drinking out of a jug is a sign of going on a journey. If the
jug is large, the journey will be long; if small, the journey will be short. *(OM)*

JUMPER
This dream signifies that someone will speak evil of you, and warns you to be circumspect in all your dealings. *(OM)*

———— ♦ ————

JUMPING
To dream that you are jumping from a high position or over obstacles is a sign that you will meet with lasting success if only you will put your heart and soul into your work. *(M)*

   To dream of jumping signifies that you will overcome all obstacles. *(OM)*

———— ♦ ————

JUNGLE
If you dream of being lost in a jungle, be careful to whom you speak, for someone will be trying to lead you astray. Should you meet a wild animal when you are lost you will be pestered by this person for some time. *(M)*

———— ♦ ————

JURY
In the preceding dream the judge will be the most prominent figure, but in a dream in which your attention is mostly given to the jury you are about to suffer a good deal of annoyance from the unreasonable conduct of one of your neighbours, and that it will only come to an end by your instituting legal proceedings. *(O)*

   For a man to dream that he has been summoned to serve on a jury is a sign that he will have trouble with his fellow workmen, which will lead to grave charges being levelled against him. *(M)*

———— ♦ ————

JUSTICE
To be brought to justice signifies happiness. To be condemned by a judge signifies a love affair. *(OM0*

KEG

To dream you see a keg of whisky is a sign of your children being placed in danger in the streets; some kind friend will rescue them from being run over by a lorry. To see a keg of gunpowder is a sign of your having false friends. Your conduct will be the subject of ridicule in the company of your friends. *(M)*

———— ♦ ————

KETTLE

To dream that you see a bright copper kettle is a sign of great domestic comfort. You will have much peace and joy in everyday life. Your wife will strive to make your home attractive by her winning ways and cheerful smiles. Your children will welcome you home with shouts of joy and happiness and they will chatter about what they have been doing all day. At home you will be exceptionally happy. If a young man has this dream it means that his intended will be neat, tidy and a good housekeeper. *(M)*

———— ♦ ————

KEY

To dream you lose your keys signifies anger. *(T)*

To dream you find a key denotes admission to a position of trust. *(GFT)*

To dream your keys are gone or lost
Shows that you'll soon be vexed or crossed. *(N)*

To dream of carrying about a bunch of keys means for a man that he is shortly to be placed in a situation of great responsibility, leading to proposals which will greatly influence his future fortunes. For a young woman, a similar dream signifies that she is about to enter a life-long situation as the wife of an industrious and devoted lover. *(O)*

To dream of keys is favourable to a person in trade and to a sailor, as they denote a gift and that the dreamer will become rich. *(OM)*

To dream of seeing a key signifies a good and handsome wife to someone wanting to marry. It is also good for those who arrange other men's business, but is bad for travellers because it signifies that they will be delayed. *(A)*

———— ♦ ————

KEYHOLE

To dream that you see a person looking through the keyhole of your door is a sign that your house will be burgled, but the thieves will be frightened away before they can force an entrance. *(M)*

◆

KHAKI

If you see a khaki uniform or imagine you are ordering a suit of that material or colour, be sure that you will shortly be mixed up in a serious quarrel which will make you very unhappy. Should you already be dressed in khaki, however, expect good news; possibly of an improvement in your affairs. *(M)*

◆

KILL

To dream you kill a man signifies success in business. To dream you kill your father is a very bad sign. To kill a stranger signifies loss. To dream you are killed denotes loss to the person who has killed you. *(OM)*

◆

KING

To dream you are talking with a king signifies good reputation. To dream that you receive an audience of a king signifies gain. To receive a gift from a king signifies great joy. To see a king signifies honour and joy. *(T)*

To dream you see or speak to a king signifies that you will rise to honour and will acquire riches. Your business will improve. *(OM)*

◆

KISS

To dream you are kissed by men of great quality signifies consolation. To dream you kiss a deceased person signifies long life. *(T)*

To dream of kissing a father or mother denotes a good friend. To dream of one woman kissing another denotes disappointments in love; if she has a crying child in her arms it shows affection through loss of her parents. To kiss without power of speech signifies the dreamer shall fall in love, but not possess his lover. *(D&M)*

For a woman to dream of kissing another woman denotes infertility. *(P&F)*

To dream you are kissing a pretty girl is good as it denotes that a friend will do you an unexpected favour. To dream of kissing a married woman is a sign of poverty, and that you will fail in your present undertakings, but it usually means deceit; and the day will not pass without quarrels. *(GD)*

To dream of kissing may be pleasant enough while is lasts, but it indicates that in waking hours there will be arguments, and that words will run more or less high in proportion to the warmth and enthusiasm recognized in the dream. *(O)*

For a man to dream of kissing a girl denotes that the next day he will have a particularly happy day. *(OM)*

To dream that you kiss the dead signifies death to anyone who is ill. To anyone who is healthy, it means he should not tell anyone about his business dealings, unless the dead person was a particular friend.   *(A)*

> Though pleasing sensations from kissing must spring,
> In spite of its honey it carries a sting,
> Indeed with all craft intimately replete
> It embraces hypocrisy, fraud and deceit
> And taken in all views to all sexes and ages,
> This dream disappointment and crosses presages.   *(MS)*

————— ♦ —————

KITCHEN
If one dreams that the kitchen is on fire, that denotes death to whoever does the cooking.   *(T)*

To dream of a kitchen signifies that you will receive a visit from relatives.   *(OM)*

————— ♦ —————

KITE
Dreaming of flying a kite indicates advancement in business and ultimate prosperity. To watch kites flying is a sign that you will meet with many bad debts, and experience all the bad fortune that results from trusting customers without making proper inquiries.   *(O)*

> If flying on high it will plainly appear,
> Your fond wishes soar much beyond your own sphere
> But if it should pitch and most rapid descend,
> Your chastity, lassie, may prudence defend,
> For should you once lose it—I solve but the dream,
> More disasters thro' life will surround you I deem.   *(MS)*

————— ♦ —————

KNAVE
To dream of the knave of hearts indicates a lover. The knave of spades, widowhood. The knave of clubs, business.   *(OM)*

————— ♦ —————

KNEE
The knee denotes hard work, therefore if anyone dreams that they themselves, or any other person has hurt their knee, they will be prevented from working efficiently by malicious and envious people. If anyone dreams that their knees are cut and they cannot walk, they will be reduced to poverty and be unable to work. If their knees heal and they recover their strength, the bad luck will alter, and they will grow rich and live happily. If anyone dreams they can run swiftly, they will be happy in all their undertakings. If a man dreams his knees are weary, that signifies sickness. If anyone dreams that they are kneeling, that denotes devotion and humility, and sometimes vexation and trouble in business. To dream the knee is swollen and painful signifies sickness, pain, loss and bad business, or problems in business.   *(T)*

To dream of strong, sturdy knees signifies journeys and healthy activity. To dream that a tree or branch grows out of your knees signifies slowness and hindrance, to a sick man, sometimes death. *(A)*

To dream you are wounded in the knee denotes anxiety or business problems caused by envy. A knee swollen or painful indicates grief, sickness, trouble and sometimes a delay in business affairs. To feel your knees tired or sore indicates sickness. To dream of walking on your knees because you have no feet signifies distress for yourself or a near and dear friend. *(M)*

───────── ♦ ─────────

KNEEL

To dream you kneel signifies anxiety in your affairs. *(OM)*

───────── ♦ ─────────

KNICK-KNACKS

To a woman a dream of knick-knacks portends domestic worries; but should she be arranging them in a room and have trouble over the task, the worries will be slight. To a man the dream foretells bickering and arguments. *(M)*

───────── ♦ ─────────

KNIFE

To dream you give someone a knife signifies injustice and contention. *(T)*

To dream of knives and forks denotes great contention. *(D&M)*

To dream of receiving a present of a knife is a bad omen, for it signifies that many ties in which you take pleasure are about to be cut, and that death and indifference and misunderstandings will cause havoc in the circle of your friends. *(O)*

It is a bad omen to dream of giving a knife as a present. To dream that you are using a knife for any purpose denotes deceit and tears. If you cut yourself, be prepared for sickness. *(M)*

To dream of knives is a very unpropitious omen. It signifies law-suits, poverty, disgrace, strife and failure. *(OM)*

Generally to dream of knives is very unpropitious; it indicates law-suits, poverty, disgrace and strife. Should you, however, be in love, it denotes a happy marriage with your lover and that you will be comfortably off through hard work. *(GD2)*

───────── ♦ ─────────

KNIGHT

To dream of a knight is an omen of success in love and domestic affairs. *(M)*

───────── ♦ ─────────

KNIT

To dream you are knitting signifies that your undertaking will be successful. To see someone knitting signifies that you will be deceived. *(OM)*

───────── ♦ ─────────

KNOTS

To dream of knots signifies that you will meet with much to cause you anxiety. *(OM)*

LABORATORY
To dream of a laboratory signifies danger and sickness. *(OM)*

◆

LABOURER
To dream of a labourer signifies that you will have increased wealth. *(OM)*

◆

LABYRINTH
To dream you are in a labyrinth signifies that you will unravel a mystery.
(OM)

◆

LACE
The woman who dreams she is buying lace will need in future to be more careful with her money. She is probably a spendthrift and will live to regret it. To dream of bootlaces is a sign that you will rise much higher than your present position, though the change will not come until you are older. *(M)*

To dream of lace signifies extravagance. *(OM)*

◆

LADDER
To dream you climb a ladder signifies honour. To descend one signifies damage. *(T)*

To dream of a ladder signifies a journey. *(A)*

To dream you climb a ladder is a very good omen. It denotes that you will better your position in life and gain a good reputation; in love, it denotes a happy marriage. *(GD)*

To ascend a ladder in a dream indicates your success in the world, but shows that it will not be rapid, for you will go up the ladder of fortune only step by step. *(O)*

A ladder is a sign of good luck, and to dream that you are climbing one predicts that if you keep plodding along you will reach your goal. Should you dream of descending a ladder, however, you will have several ups and downs before success ultimately comes to you. *(M)*

◆

LAKE
To dream of a lake of clear water is an omen that life will hold more joys than sorrows for you; and should you be in a boat on the lake, your lover will be successful. If the water is rough, you will have a serious illness, but it will not permanently affect your good fortune. *(M)*

To sail on a smooth lake signifies comfort, happiness and success in business. If the water is dirty, muddy or rough it foretells trouble and loss.

(OM)

LAMB
To feed or bring a lamb to the slaughter signifies that you will suffer problems. To dream you see a lamb or young kid signifies extraordinary comfort. *(T)*

To dream of watching lambs feeding or playing about means approaching grief and pain from a quite unexpected quarter. *(O)*

To dream of a lamb is a sign that your worst enemy is a person whom you trust more than any of your friends, chiefly because that person is for ever boasting of their faithfulness. If you can discover the false one, obtain good proof of the deceit, and then have nothing more to do with them. *(M)*

LAME
To dream of a lame man means you will have business problems. *(OM)*

If anyone dreams that he has become lame that denotes disgrace; or if he is a prisoner, it foretells the punishment of his faults, or if rich, loss of goods by fire. *(T)*

LAMP
To dream of a brass lamp signifies either great goods, or great evils, according to the disposition of the light. *(A)*

LANCE
To dream of a lance signifies hatred. *(OM)*

LAND
If a man dreams he owns considerable lands, enclosed with pastures, it signifies that he will have a handsome wife. *(OM)*

LANDLADY
If a man dreams of the landlady of a public house it is a sign that he will not care for his wife. He will give his attention to anything but his home, and will carry misery with him wherever he goes. *(M)*

LANDSCAPE
To dream of a landscape signifies great good fortune. *(OM)*

LANTERN
To see a clear, shining lantern on a table or cabinet is a good sign to the sick since it denotes recovery and health. A single person who dreams of a lamp will soon marry, will be successful and prosper in his undertakings. *(T)*

If anyone dreams that he sees a lantern with a light in it extinguished, that signifies sadness, sickness and poverty. *(OM)*

------ ♦ ------

LAP DOGS
To dream of little dogs signifies delight and enjoyable pastimes. *(A)*

------ ♦ ------

LARD
To dream of lard signifies that you will triumph over your enemies. *(OM)*

------ ♦ ------

LARDER
To dream of a larder foretells that you may expect happiness and a joyful time. *(OM)*

------ ♦ ------

LARKS
To dream of larks signifies that you will soon be richer than you are. *(OM)*

------ ♦ ------

LASH
To dream that you see a criminal being flogged is a sign that someone you love will be punished because he has fallen into bad company, and been present when his companions have broken the law by committing a felony or an assault. *(M)*

------ ♦ ------

LAUGHTER
To dream of laughter brings tears. *(M)*
   To dream of laughter signifies grief and pain. *(OM)*

------ ♦ ------

LAUREL
If a woman sees or smells laurels, it means she will have children; she will be married suddenly or will be happy, successful and prosperous. To dream you see a laurel tree is a token of victory and pleasure; and if you are married, it denotes the inheritance of possessions by your wife. *(T)*

------ ♦ ------

LAW
To dream you have a law-suit signifies that you will have occasion to fight for your rights, but there will be joy, consolation and good news. *(OM)*

------ ♦ ------

LAWYER
To dream of meeting a lawyer brings bad news; if you speak to him you will lose some property; if you hear someone speaking in his favour you will meet with misfortunes. *(M)*
   To dream of a lawyer foretells the marriage of a friend. *(OM)*

LEAD

To dream you trade in lead signifies sickness. *(T)*

To dream of handling lead is a bad dream, and signifies death. In all probability a succeeding dream will indicate whether the death will occur within your own family, or of a friend or acquaintance. *(O)*

The person who dreams of lead in any shape or form will hear of someone afflicted with mental illness. To a girl engaged to be married such a dream foretells broken promises and deceit. To a business man it indicates a down-turn in his affairs. *(M)*

───────◆───────

LEANNESS

If anyone dreams he has grown very thin he will either become ill or lose money or property. *(T)*

───────◆───────

LEAPING

To dream you are leaping over walls, bars or gates is a sign that you will encounter many difficulties in your present occupation, and that your lover will not marry you. *(GD)*

───────◆───────

LEARNING

To learn a lesson of any kind denotes that you will not make a great success of your life. You should better yourself and try to get out of the rut into which you have fallen. *(M)*

───────◆───────

LEASE

The person who dreams that he or she has taken over the lease of some premises will shortly have occasion to move into another area. *(M)*

───────◆───────

LEATHER

To see a quantity of leather or any article made of leather is a sign that you will have to suffer many insults without being able to avenge them. *(M)*

───────◆───────

LEAVES

To dream that the ground is covered with green leaves is a sign of wealth and a large family. If the leaves are withered, however, the dream indicates loss and unrequited love. *(M)*

───────◆───────

LEECH

To dream of a leech signifies fortunate friends and happiness awaits you. *(OM)*

───────◆───────

LEEKS

If anyone dreams that he eats or smells roots which have a strong smell like

───────────────194───────────────

leeks, it signifies a discovery of hidden secrets and domestic arguments at home. *(T)*

To dream of leeks signifies that perseverance in your project will bring its reward in due course. *(OM)*

———— ♦ ————

LEGS

To dream your legs are scabby or itchy signifies pointless worry and care. To dream that your legs are perfectly well signifies joy and good fortune, that you will be prosperous in your business. To dream that your legs are swollen or cut off signifies the loss or damage of employees and of best friends, who will either fall sick or die. If anyone dreams that his leg is dislocated or broken, it signifies that an employee will be injured or die. *(T)*

To dream you have a wooden leg signifies the alteration of your condition; from good to bad, and from bad to worse. *(OM)*

———— ♦ ————

LEMONS

To dream of lemons denotes arguments in your family. *(OM)*

———— ♦ ————

LENTILS

Lentils signify corruption. *(T)*

———— ♦ ————

LEOPARDS

Dreams of leopards have the same interpretation as those of lions, only they are more subtle and malicious than the lion, who is always generous. *(T)*

Dreaming of leopards foretells honour. *(OM)*

———— ♦ ————

LEPROSY

If anyone dreams he is a leper, that denotes profit and wealth with notoriety. If a woman has this dream, she will be acquainted with a rich and powerful man who will be very generous to her. *(T)*

———— ♦ ————

LETTERS

To dream you write letters to your friends, or receive letters from them, signifies good news. *(T)*

To dream of receiving letters is demonstrative of your being loved by a person of the opposite sex, who is very much your friend, and will do all in their power to make you happy. To dream of writing letters shows success in enterprises, and that you will receive some very pleasant news. *(GD)*

To dream of receiving and reading a letter means that you are at present in doubt as to what course of action to follow, and that the first words spoken by the first person you meet on the following morning will indicate what you should do. *(O)*

LETTUCE
To dream you eat raw salad, such as lettuce, signifies trouble and difficulty in the management of affairs. *(T)*

———— ♦ ————

LIBEL
To dream that a person has libelled you means that your character is above suspicion, but you will be single minded in political controversy, rash in your expressions when in debate, and full of eccentricities. The religious sect which you will join will be small in number, but very dogmatic in their teachings. To dream that you have libelled a person is a sign that you will express your opinion quietly on any subject. You will be mild, gentle and peaceful in your behaviour. *(M)*

———— ♦ ————

LIBRARY
To dream of sitting in the library means that you have abilities which, rightly cultivated, would enable you to attain literary distinction. *(O)*

———— ♦ ————

LICE
To dream of killing a few lice shows you will have no worries; but to have a large number foretells long sickness. *(D&M)*

To dream that you are lousy and killing a large number of them, is a very good omen. *(OM)*

———— ♦ ————

LICENCE
To dream that you take out a licence to sell any article is a sign that you will be very desirous of getting a livelihood by some other occupation than your present one. *(M)*

———— ♦ ————

LIFEBOAT
If a young woman dreams that she sees a lifeboat at anchor it is a sign that a sailor will fall in love with her, but will be prevented from seeing her more than once, because he will be under orders to return to his ship, which is about to sail to a distant country, where he will be absent for a great number of years. If she dreams that she sees a lifeboat at sea it is a sign that she will become a sailor's bride before many months are over. If a young man has this dream it means that one of his brothers or cousins who has emigrated will be shipwrecked on returning but will be saved by a passing vessel, and will arrive safely in England a few months later than he was first expected.

———— ♦ ————

(M)

LIGHT
To dream you see a great light is a happy omen which denotes that you will become powerful and rich; in love, it shows a sweetheart of an amiable disposition; and that you will marry well, have children, and be very happy.

If the light disappears all of a sudden, it means a great change in your present situation, much for the worse; it portends imprisonment and loss of goods, with unexpected misfortunes. *(GD)*

To dream of a light being suddenly extinguished means that you are about to lose sight of a friend, who will disappear as effectually as if the ground had opened and swallowed them up. To dream of a light gradually increasing means for a man that he will marry a woman of limited education, but that by self-teaching she will become as valuable as she has always been a sympathetic partner. The same dream occurring to a woman signifies growing affection both on her own part and on that of her husband. *(O)*

━━━━━ ♦ ━━━━━

LIGHTHOUSE

To dream of a lighthouse is an indication that you will be forced, much against your will, to take a journey by water. *(M)*

━━━━━ ♦ ━━━━━

LIGHTNING

To see lightning in a dream means much the same as hearing thunder, except that what is to happen will come sooner, light travelling much faster than sound. *(O)*

To dream of lightning signifies change of place. *(OM)*

━━━━━ ♦ ━━━━━

LILIES

To see, hold or smell lilies out of season signifies your hopes of obtaining something will be frustrated. *(T)*

━━━━━ ♦ ━━━━━

LILY of the VALLEY

A young man dreaming of the lily of the valley may safely conclude that his matrimonial choice is a wise one, and he will be happily married. To dream of the lily of the valley means for a young woman that her fiancé will never distinguish himself in anything, but may be trusted to go through the world quietly and respectably. *(O)*

━━━━━ ♦ ━━━━━

LIME

To dream that you see a quantity of lime is a sign that you will have some property left you; a few old houses in a dilapidated condition will be your inheritance in the will of a wealthy relative. *(M)*

━━━━━ ♦ ━━━━━

LIMP

To dream that you limp is a sign that you will have to take a long journey on foot. *(M)*

━━━━━ ♦ ━━━━━

LINEN

To dream of linen signifies loss and misfortune. *(T)*

To dream you are dressed in clean linen denotes that you will shortly receive some good news; that your lover is faithful, and will marry you; that you will be successful in all your present undertakings; and that you will receive a handsome present from an agreeable young man. If your linen is checkered, you will get a legacy from a friend, and marry a very industrious person; if it is dirty, then it denotes poverty, a prison and disappointment in love, with the loss of something valuable.   *(GD)*

------------ ♦ ------------

LINSEED

If you dream that you have a poultice of linseed put on any part of your body it is a sign that you will have an attack of inflammation of the lungs or chest.   *(M)*

------------ ♦ ------------

LION

If you dream you see a lion, that signifies a meeting with someone in authority. If anyone dreams they fight with a lion, that signifies a quarrel with a strong opponent; if they won in the dream, they will win the argument. To ride on the back of a lion signifies protection from someone in authority. To be afraid of a lion signifies you will feel the anger of someone in authority. If anyone dreams that they have eaten lion's flesh, they will grow rich through the king's or someone powerful's means. If anyone dreams that they have found the skin, liver or marrow of a lion, they will suddenly grow rich. To dream you have the ears of a lion signifies treachery or deceit from your enemies and those that envy you. To dream you have the head of a lion is a good sign as the dreamer will accomplish his ambitions.   *(T)*

To dream of a lion fawning on you denotes the favour of a noble person.   *(D&M)*

To dream of seing a lion denotes that you will appear before someone powerful and be promoted to a lucrative office, accumulate riches, and marry a woman of great spirit.   *(GD)*

To dream of meeting a lion indicates that you are about to have strange adventures, the recounting of which, in later life, will give great amusement both to yourself and your friends.   *(O)*

------------ ♦ ------------

LION CUB

To dream of a lion cub foretells protection and friendship.   *(OM)*

------------ ♦ ------------

LIONESS

Dreaming of seeing a lioness is good.   *(OM)*

------------ ♦ ------------

LIPS

To dream that you have beautiful lips is a sign that your friends are healthy; and to have them dry and chapped, the opposite.   *(T)*

The lips represent those people who kiss and embrace us and are often near us, such as wife, children, parents, friends. *(A)*

For a man to dream that his lips have grown larger signifies that he will have fine children. *(D&M2)*

———— ♦ ————

LIQUEUR

To dream of liqueur warns you to beware of flattery. *(OM)*

———— ♦ ————

LITTER

For a newly-married woman to dream that she sees a litter of pigs is a sign that she will have a large good-looking family. She will have twins once or twice and her children will grow up to be attractive and respected. *(M)*

———— ♦ ————

LIVER

If anyone dreams that he has a liver complaint his money will be wasted and he will die suddenly. If anyone dreams he has seen or found the liver of any of his enemies, and carried it away, he will defeat those who wish him ill. *(T)*

To dream you eat liver signifies good health. *(OM)*

———— ♦ ————

LIVERY

This foretells annoyance. *(OM)*

———— ♦ ————

LIZARDS

To dream of lizards signifies bad luck and misfortune caused by unknown enemies. *(T)*

To dream of a lizard indicates great change in your business and affairs. *(OM)*

———— ♦ ————

LOAD

To dream you are loaded down signifies that your business will soon come to an end. *(OM)*

———— ♦ ————

LOCK

To dream of a lock foretells difficulties. If you can open the lock, you will succeed in life. *(OM)*

———— ♦ ————

LOCKJAW

For a married man to dream that his wife is suffering from lockjaw is a sign that she will be one of the greatest gossips in the neighbourhood. For a woman to dream that her husband has lockjaw means that she will drive him from his home to seek pleasures elsewhere, because of her bad management and untidy habits. *(M)*

LOCUST
A locust signifies that you will be short-lived. *(OM)*

———————— ♦ ————————

LODGINGS
To dream of looking for lodgings means that your present ideas on the choice of an occupation for life are wrong. If the lodgings you are inspecting are on the ground floor, it may be taken as a sign that you would succeed in one of the professions. The floor above that indicates a prosperous career in mercantile life. The top floor points to distinction as an author, artist or musician. *(O)*

———————— ♦ ————————

LOGS
To dream that you are chopping logs is a sign that strangers will come to your house. *(OM)*

———————— ♦ ————————

LONELY
To dream that you are meditating in a lonely place is a sign that you will become a proficient scholar in languages and theology; you will be fond of solitude, and study much by moonlight. *(M)*

———————— ♦ ————————

LORD
To talk to a lord or that you go anywhere with him signifies honour.
(OM)

———————— ♦ ————————

LOSS
To dream that you have lost something of value predicts a find. *(M)*

———————— ♦ ————————

LOTTERY
To dream of a lottery signifies a heavy loss. *(OM)*

———————— ♦ ————————

LOVE
It is a bad omen for a girl to dream that she is in love before she is in love actually. She will in all probability die unmarried. To dream that you are loved by someone whom you dislike is a warning that you will one day need a friend and will not know where to turn for one. *(M)*

To dream of love signifies prosperity and happiness and success in love. *(OM)*

———————— ♦ ————————

LUCK
To dream that you have experienced a stroke of good luck is a sign that you are inclined to leave too much to chance. You should rely more upon your own judgement.

To dream you are lucky signifies that you will be disappointed.   *(OM)*

———————— ♦ ————————

LUGGAGE
To dream of luggage signifies trials, difficulties and danger.   *(OM)*

———————— ♦ ————————

LUNGS
If anyone dreams they have the lungs of a bull, goat, ram or any other horned animal, they will become the heir of a wealthy and distinguished person. If anyone dreams that somebody has taken out their lungs, or that they are injured or ill, their designs will be frustrated, and they will run the risk of a great danger.   *(T)*

———————— ♦ ————————

LUTE
To play or see someone else play a lute signifies good news, harmony, and a good relationship between man and wife, master and servants, prince and subjects or among friends.   *(T)*

To dream of a lute indicates that you will go into delightful company and that you will have success and happiness.   *(OM)*

———————— ♦ ————————

LUXURY
To dream of luxury denotes a late wealthy marriage after many hardships. To the person who is already married it is significant of approaching troubles connected with the home.   *(M)*

To dream of luxury signifies poverty, sickness and disappointment. *(OM)*

———————— ♦ ————————

LYING
To tell a lie is a bad omen.   *(OM)*

———————— ♦ ————————

LYNX
Several of these animals denote vicious enemies, who will one day do you harm. If only one appears in your dream, you will hear of something which will cause you pain.   *(M)*

To dream of a lynx foretells you that you will discover the secret hatred of someone.   *(OM)*

MACHINERY

To dream that you are working machinery is a sign that you will not always need to earn your living. For a girl to dream that she is working a sewing-machine is a sign of happiness in love and an early marriage. *(T)*

To dream of machinery signifies prosperity. To inspect it signifies wealth. *(OM)*

———— ♦ ————

MACKEREL

To dream of eating this fish is a sign that you will be disappointed in long-held expectations. *(M)*

To dream of seeing mackerel in clear water signifies success and prosperity; if not fresh, it signifies disappointment in love. *(OM)*

———— ♦ ————

MADNESS

If anyone dreams that he is mad and commits ludicrous behaviour in public, he will live to an old age, and will be well-liked and powerful. If a woman dreams this it is a sign she will have a boy, who in time will grow powerful; if she is a girl, she will soon marry an honest man. *(T)*

To dream of madness in any form is extremely fortunate, indicating that all your undertakings, however unpromising or foolish they may at times appear, will in the end bring you success and command admiration from your friends. *(O)*

If you dream you meet with, or are in danger of being waylaid and injured by, a madman it is a sign that you will have a friend calling upon you whom you have not seen for years because he has been travelling abroad. He will offer you help and advice, and behave very kindly to you. If you dream that you see a madman it is a sign that you will become more reconciled to the disappointments in life; they will not have as bad an effect upon you as they had before, but you will have learned how to bear the difficulties of life without undue sorrow. *(M)*

To dream you are mad, and that you are with other mad people, is very good. It promises long life, riches, happy marriage, success in trade and good children. *(OM)*

———— ♦ ————

MAGAZINE

Dreaming of reading a magazine is a luckier dream than that of writing one. The former means that you will shortly have the opportunity of

———————————— ————————————

greatly extending your education, and sphere of influence; the latter indicates that you will experience a run of bad luck.   *(O)*

──────── ◆ ────────

MAGGOT
To dream of a maggot signifies that there will be a dispute in your home. *(OM)*

──────── ◆ ────────

MAGIC
To dream that you are under a magic spell is a sure sign that you are making a great mistake in thinking that a certain person is worthy of your regard. *(M)*
   This dream warns you to beware of rogues, for you should fear loss. *(OM)*

──────── ◆ ────────

MAGISTRATE
A magistrate is a warning that, unless you are more careful in the way in which you conduct yourself, people will begin to suspect you of a vice of which you are quite innocent.   *(M)*

──────── ◆ ────────

MAGPIE
If you see several of these birds congregated together, beware of foolish gossip, otherwise it will lead you into trouble. If only one bird appears in your dream, it is a good omen, foretelling celebration.   *(M)*

──────── ◆ ────────

MALICE
It is good to dream of anyone bearing malice towards you because it is a sign that a particular person likes you and would do you a good turn if ever it lay in his or her power.   *(O)*

──────── ◆ ────────

MALLOWS
To dream of eating mallows signifies freedom from trouble and expedition of business.   *(T)*

──────── ◆ ────────

MAN
To see a man publicly burned signifies loss of merchandise or sickness. To dream you see a dead man signifies that you will be subject to the same passions and fortune as the dead man. To dream a man who is alive is dead signifies troubles to come. To dream you see armed men is a good sign. To dream you ruin a man signifies sadness.   *(T)*
   If an unmarried woman dreams of being a man, she will have a husband, or if without children, have a son; but to a girl it indicates difficulties. *(D&M)*
   For a young woman to dream of talking confidently to a young man is a happy sign in love affairs. It is all the more promising if he is handsome with soft eyes and a serious expression. For a man to dream of talking to a man foreshadows rivalry in business or in love, perhaps in both. An old man means that you will shortly receive a legacy, the amount of which may

be guessed by noticing whether the old man has long or short hair.   *(O)*

For a young woman to dream of receiving the attentions of a man she does not know is a good omen for her future happiness. If the man is very old, she will not marry until after experiencing a disappointment in love. *(M)*

MANACLES
To dream that you are held helpless by heavy manacles is a sign that someone will help you to a good position in life.   *(M)*

MANURE
To dream you manure and cultivate the earth signifies melancholy to those who are usually happy, and to labourers it signifies gain and a plentiful crop.
   (T)

MAP
To dream that you are studying a map of a foreign country foretells a short journey to meet a stranger. If the map is of your own country, you will meet an old acquaintance whom you have not seen for some time.   *(M)*

MARBLE
To dream of marble in any shape or form denotes that you will triumph over your enemies, also that at some time you will live beyond your income and come very near to financial ruin.   *(M)*

MARE
If anyone dreams they are mounted on a mare that signifies they will gain reputation, dignity and fame.   *(T)*
See also **HORSE.**

MARKET
To dream of being at a market denotes that you will shortly have difficulty in disposing of something you want to sell, but if in your dream you are with other people you will succeed in your attempt after a while.   *(O)*

To dream that you are in a market place is a sign of plenty. You will never want for the necessities of life.   *(M)*

MARRIAGE
To dream you are married signifies sickness or melancholy. If a man dreams he is married to an ugly woman, that signifies death or some unhappiness; if to an attractive woman, that denotes joy and profit. To dream you marry your sister signifies danger. To dream you marry a wife signifies loss and sometimes death.   *(T)*

For a sick person to dream of marriage is a sign of death.   *(D&M)*

To dream you are married is ominous of death, and very unfavourable; it denotes poverty, a prison and misfortunes. To dream you help at a wedding is the forerunner of good news and great success. To dream of lying with your newly-married husband or wife threatens danger or sudden misfortunes, and also that you will lose a part of your property; to the sailor it indicates storms and shipwrecks, with a narrow escape from death. *(GD)*

> This dream is too often the presage if death,
> 'Id est,' that a cord would soon strangle your breath;
> Tho' at times it denotes great misfortune and care,
> Yet attending at weddings will change the affair;
> And to lie with your husband or wife the first night
> Implies some disaster, nay, some sudden fright. *(MS)*

If you dream of being present as a bride or groom at a marriage it is a bad dream, and warns of death or long sickness to a member of your family. But a dream of being either a bridesmaid, best man or guest is encouraging, for it announces that you will shortly enter into an advantageous and agreeable friendship. *(O)*

It is extremely unlucky for a young woman to dream that she is married when she is not. She will be crossed in love, and lose all faith in the opposite sex. *(M)*

MASK

To dream of a man in a mask indicates that the word of one of your friends in whom you place implicit confidence is not quite to be relied on. *(O)*

MASS

To dream you go to mass signifies honour and joy to the dreamer. *(T)*

MEADOW

To dream of being in a meadow is a good sign to farmers and shepherds, but to others it denotes business problems. *(T)*

To walk through a meadow, especially in the evening, is a good omen. It announces the approach of a happy interview which may make a favourable change in your fortunes. *(O)*

To dream of meadows signifies a pleasant journey and happiness, especially if you are walking through them. *(OM)*

MEAL

To dream you are eating a good meal signifies meanness and poverty. Judge the opposite if there is nothing for you to eat. *(OM)*

MEASLES

If anyone dreams he has the measles, it denotes he will gain profit and wealth. *(OM)*

MEAT

To eat roast meat signifies falling into sin. To see the meat you have eaten signifies loss. *(T)*

———————— ◆ ————————

MEDICINE

To dream you prescribe medicines signifies profit and happiness. To dream you give or take medicine signifies living in poverty. *(T)*

To dream of taking medicine denotes that unless you make a change in your present situation you will have to swallow a great deal that is disagreeable, and put up with a great deal that might be resented, if you are to become a success in life. *(O)*

To dream you take medicine signifies loss of money. If it is bitter you will overcome your enemies. *(OM)*

———————— ◆ ————————

MELONS

For a sick person to dream of melons is considered by some to be an indication of recovery. *(A)*

———————— ◆ ————————

MENAGERIE

To dream that you visit an exhibition of wild animals means peace at home and greater friendship with your acquaintances. Someone you love will want to emigrate and nothing that you say to dissuade them will have any effect. *(M)*

———————— ◆ ————————

MERMAID

For a married woman to dream that she sees a mermaid is a sign that either she or some of her neighbours will have a child that will be quite different from the usual run of children, either for better or for worse. *(M)*

———————— ◆ ————————

METEORS

After dreaming of meteors you may expect all sorts of trouble and loss. *(OM)*

———————— ◆ ————————

MICE

The woman who dreams of mice may look forward to hearing good news, and taking part in some happy celebration. To a man the dream is indicative of prosperity. *(M)*

———————— ◆ ————————

MIDWIFE

A midwife means secrets and problems will be revealed. It means death to the sick. *(A)*

———————— ◆ ————————

MIGNONETTE

To see and smell this fragrant little plant is a good sign. Your life for the future will be full of gladness, you will have many good friends; your health will be sound, and you will have plenty of good food; you will also have plenty of holidays. *(M)*

MILESTONE
To dream of a milestone signifies the end of considerable problems. *(A)*

MILK
To dream you drink milk is an extraordinarily good sign. *(T)*

To dream you are selling milk denotes that you will be crossed in love, and that you will be unsuccessful in business. To dream you are drinking milk is the forerunner of good news and great success; if you are giving milk away, it shows you will be successful in love, marry happily, have children and do very well; to see milk flowing from the breasts of a woman denotes success in trade, that you will have many children, and that they will become rich by the hard work of their parents. *(GD)*

To the married, seduction, from Hymen announces,
And a bad course of life to most females pronounces. *(MS)*

To dream of milk in any form, even adulterated, is very fortunate and indicates increase both in money and goods. Bit it is bad luck to dream of spilling milk, for that indicates scattered fortunes, bankruptcy and on the whole a melancholy and dismal future. *(O)*

To dream you are carrying milk is a good sign; but if you fall and spill it, you will suffer problems. *(OM)*

MILLET
To see the land sown with millet signifies vast riches to be easily gained. *(T)*

MILLIONAIRE
For a young woman to dream that she marries a millionaire is a sign that when the wedding does come off it will be a union with a man who has been wealthy, but who has lost his money. He will be intelligent, however, and do well in business. *(M)*

MILLS
To dream of mills signifies that you will inherit a fortune. *(OM)*

MILLSTONE
To dream of a millstone signifies an increase of family. *(OM)*

MINCE PIES
To dream you eat or make them indicates your wedding or that you will go to one. *(OM)*

MINISTER

It is not a good sign to see a minister in your dream. Expect a serious disappointment. *(M)*

────── ♦ ──────

MIRE

> To dream you wade in mire and muddle,
> Ever predicts you toil and trouble,
> Yet perseverance will avail,
> And against this spell prevail. *(N)*

────── ♦ ──────

MIRROR

For a girl to dream of a mirror is a sign that she is in danger of being too vain and neglecting her intellect. It is ominous of future unhappiness, especially if dreamed on a Sunday. For a young man, dreaming of a mirror means personal appearance will be important to his job. *(O)*

If you are in good health when you dream of a mirror it indicates joy and honours, lovers and children. If you are ill, expect a relapse. *(OM)*

To see yourself in a mirror means you will have many children. *(D&M)*

To see a mirror indicates sickness and even death. If you are admiring yourself in the mirror, be careful that your vanity does not lead you into problems. *(M)*

────── ♦ ──────

MISER

To dream of being a miser indicates, for a man, that he will grow rich if he only confines himself to one enterprise, and exercises a proper economy and control over that. When a woman dreams of being miserly it foreshadows an account in a healthy state at the bank. *(O)*

────── ♦ ──────

MISFORTUNE

This dream indicates prosperity.

> Content and happy may they be
> Who dream of cold adversity,
> To married man and married wife,
> It promises a happy life. *(O)*

────── ♦ ──────

MOLE

To dream of a mole signifies that your work will be in vain. *(A)*

To dream of moles indicates deceit. Be careful to whom you tell your secrets, otherwise you will find them broadcast. *(M)*

To dream of a mole signifies that you will come to grief. *(OM)*

────── ♦ ──────

MONEY

If a man dreams that he has found gold and does not know where to hide it, or that he has found a purse of money and is afraid of being arrested with it, it means that a woman will cause him to lose money. *(A)*

To dream that you are paying money foretells the birth of a son, destined to cut a great figure in life. *(DSG)*

To dream of gathering small bits of money shows great losses; but receiving money, great advantage. *(P&F)*

To dream you pick up loose change from the ground denotes want and hard work; but if a large sum is put into your hands it shows that you will receive some money unexpectedly or will be relieved by a friend. To dream of money in your hand and not know how you came by it denotes finding a precious thing. *(D&M)*

To dream of receiving money denotes success. *(GD)*

If gold, it is lucky; but should it be copper,

It claps on your fortune a sad weighty stopper. *(MS)*

A person who dreams of making a present of a sum of money to a stranger will soon have a valuable find. To receive money denotes illness. To see a lot of money and not touch it foretells quarrelling and deceit. *(M)*

If you dream you lose money, it is a proof you will be deceived in love and be unsuccessful in some favourite pursuit. *(OM)*

———— ♦ ————

MONEY LENDER

A dream of a money lender is significant of bad luck. *(OM)*

———— ♦ ————

MONKEY

To an engaged person this animal denotes a speedy marriage. A married person who dreams of seeing a monkey will soon be rejoicing over some domestic event. *(M)*

To dream of monkeys is ominous of evil. *(OM)*

See also **APE**.

———— ♦ ————

MONSTER

To dream of monsters signifies the vain hopes of things which will never happen. *(A)*

To dream you see a monster in the sea is not good; but every fish and a great monster seen out of the sea is good. *(OM)*

———— ♦ ————

MOON

If anyone dreams he sees the moon shine, it signifies his wife loves him and that she is healthy; it also denotes that he will come into silver. To dream you see the moon darkened signifies the death or sickness of your wife, mother, sister or daughter; it can also mean loss of money, or danger on a journey, especially by water; or an illness in the brain or eyes. To dream you see the moon darkened then grow clear and bright again signifies profit to the woman who dreams and to the man joy and prosperity; the moon first clear and afterwards clouded, indicates the opposite. To dream you see the moon in the form of a full white face signifies speedy marriage to a girl; to a married woman, that she will have a handsome daughter. If a husband dreams it, it signifies that his wife will have a son. Such a dream is prosperous to goldsmiths, merchants, jewellers and bankers. To dream you see the full moon is a good sign to handsome women, but it is bad for people who conceal themselves, such as criminals, for they will be discovered. It also signifies death to the sick or to sailors. To dream the moon shines on your bed signifies grace, pardon and deliverance by means of a woman. To dream you see the moon pale is joyfulness. To see the moon fall from the sky signifies sickness. To see the moon decrease signifies the death of a powerful man. To see the moon dyed with blood signifies travel or a pilgrimage. To see the moon darkened signifies sadness. To see the new moon signifies expedition of business. To see two moons appear is increase of reputation. To see the sun and the moon fall together is a bad sign.   *(T)*

To dream of moons battling in the sky signifies divisions among near friends and relatives.   *(P&F)*

To dream of the moon denotes general good luck. If it sets it indicates a tranquil, happy existence; if it rises you may expect to meet someone at a friend's house who will have a great influence over your future.   *(O)*

MOTHER

To dream you lie with your mother signifies completion of business. To dream you see your mother living signifies joy. To see her dead signifies misfortune.   *(T)*

To dream you see your mother, is a sign of some agreeable adventure about to happen to you, and that you will hear from a friend abroad. *(GD)*

MOTHER'S MILK

For a young woman to see in a dream that she has milk in her breasts signifies that she will conceive and give birth to a child. To an old woman it signifies riches. To a girl, that her marriage is near, but if she is a pretty girl and has been unmarried for a long time, it signifies her death. To a poor man it means plenty of money and possessions by which he will help others, but to travellers it signifies sickness.   *(A)*

MOTHS

To see a number of moths flying around the flame of a candle, then flying into the flame and falling, is a sign that you had better be on your guard, as a deception is about to be practised upon you. A grand scheme for making money will be presented to you, which will be described in glowing terms, but if you look into it, you will see that those who float the new company or scheme have an eye to filling their pockets at the expense of dupes. Do not enter into any scheme without careful consideration, or you may buy your own experience at a very high price, and become both a wiser and a poorer man. *(M)*

————————— ◆ —————————

MOUNTAINS

To dream you ascend a very high mountain signifies honour. *(T)*

To dream you travel over high hills and rocky mountains signifies advancement, obtained with much difficulty. If you meet anyone who directs you the right way, a friend will help you. *(A)*

Dreaming of climbing a mountain denotes that you are either having, or are going to have, a great struggle, but that you will get the better of all your troubles, and your life will become as happy as before it was desolate. *(O)*

To dream that you are climbing a mountain is a sign that you will have every opportunity of becoming powerful. To dream of descending a mountain, however, denotes a change in your affairs for the worse. *(M)*

To dream you see steep and craggy mountains indicates difficulties in accomplishing your ambitions. If you ascend them and gain the top, you will be successful in whatever you undertake and become rich. *(OM)*

————————— ◆ —————————

MOURNERS

To dream of mourners denotes the death of a friend. *(D&M)*

————————— ◆ —————————

MOURNING

To dream of being dressed in mourning is a lucky omen, as it foreshadows joy and prosperity. To the young it indicates that they will shortly be happily married. *(O)*

The married person who dreams that she is dressed in mourning will lead a joyful and prosperous life for some time to come. *(M)*

————————— ◆ —————————

MOUSE

To dream of a mouse or mice means that someone will try to interfere with your business affairs, and will not be shaken off except by the most vigorous measures. *(O)*

————————— ◆ —————————

MOUTH

If anyone dreams their mouth is wider than usual, their family will become rich. If anyone dreams that their mouth has closed up, in such a way that they cannot open it, they are in danger of a sudden death. *(T)*

————————— ◆ —————————

MOVING

Be careful after dreaming that you are moving from one house to another. It is indicative of enemies who will do their best to cause you some serious loss. *(M)*

MOWING
To dream that you are mowing grass foretells a gain of money, and conveys a warning that someone will try to cheat and rob you of it.   *(M)*

———————— ♦ ————————

MUD
To dream of mud foretells that you will soon be hearing good news which will make a big change in your life.   *(M)*
    To dream of mud is an omen of good fortune.   *(OM)*

———————— ♦ ————————

MUFF
To dream of a muff warns you to beware of inconstancy.   *(OM)*

———————— ♦ ————————

MULBERRIES
The person who dreams of eating this fruit will soon have to undertake a journey which will prove most advantageous to his or her position. *(M)*

———————— ♦ ————————

MULES
To dream of mules signifies good for farmers and labourers.   *(A)*
    The mule signifies malice and foolish imagination.   *(T)*
    To dream of a mule signifies bad news of a law-suit; if you are riding on one it either signifies that you will never be married or that you will be childless.   *(OM)*

———————— ♦ ————————

MURDER
To dream you murder a man signifies success in business. To dream you kill your father is a bad sign.   *(T)*
    To dream you see a murder shows poverty and sadness.   *(D&M)*
    To dream of this crime denotes that you will live a long life in spite of many trials and difficulties.   *(M)*

———————— ♦ ————————

MUSHROOMS
To dream of gathering mushrooms foretells that several little surprises await you.   *(M)*

———————— ♦ ————————

MUSIC
To dream you hear music played signifies consolation in adversity and recovery of health to those who are sick.   *(T)*
    To dream you hear beautiful music is a very favourable omen as it indicates happy news from a long-absent friend; to married people it denotes good-tempered children; in love, it shows that your sweetheart is very fond of you, is good-tempered, sincere and faithful. Rough and discordant music foretells trouble, vexation and disappointment.   *(GD)*
    To dream of music is lucky or unlucky according to the kind of music.

Dance music and all light and frivolous music indicates bad luck; but slow music means coming joy. *(O)*

To dream that you hear sweet music indicates that good news is already on the way to you. *(M)*

———— ♦ ————

MUSTARD

To dream you see or eat mustard seed is a bad sign, unless you are a doctor. *(T)*

———— ♦ ————

MYRTLE

To dream of myrtle indicates a love vow. *(OM)*

NAILS

To dream of knocking nails into a wall or some article you are making is a sign that all your life you will have to rely on your own endeavours, and it will be as well if you work hard while you are young so that you have something to fall back on later in life. The woman who dreams that she is trimming her nails must be wary of a hidden enemy.   *(M)*

If anyone dreams that his nails are longer than usual, that signifies profit; and the contrary, loss and discontent. If anyone dreams that his finger tips or nails have been cut off, that signifies loss, disgrace and arguments with his relations and friends. If anyone dreams that his nails have been pulled off he is threatened by all sorts of misery and affliction and is also in danger of death. To dream you bite your nails signifies arguments and annoyance.   *(T)*

To dream your nails have grown long is very good, and denotes riches, prosperity, success in love, a good industrious husband or wife, with dutiful children; it also foretells that you will suddenly receive a sum of money that will be very useful.   *(GD)*

———————— ♦ ————————

NAKEDNESS

To dream you see a naked man signifies fear and terror. To dream you see a naked woman signifies honour and joy, provided she is fair, clear skinned and beautiful. But if on the contrary you dream you see a naked woman who is old, wrinkled or ugly that signifies shame, repentance and bad luck. But if a man dreams he sees a woman painted, the luck will not be as bad. If you see a naked woman painted or in a beautiful statue of marble, gold, silver or brass, that signifies good luck and success in business. If a husband dreams he sees his wife naked, it signifies deceit. If a wife dreams she sees her husband naked, it signifies assurance and success in her enterprises. To dream you see a whore naked signifies peril and danger by the craft and deceit of that woman. To dream you see a friend naked signifies arguments. To dream that a man sees himself naked signifies sickness or poverty, and most commonly shame by means of some other person. If anyone dreams he is naked in a bath with a person he fancies, it signifies joy, pleasure and health. If a woman dreams that she is stark naked in her husband's arms, that indicates sadness to her by bad news; but when the husband has the same dream, it signifies happiness and profit. If a woman dreams she is in bed with someone she does not like, it predicts sickness or discontent; if the husband dreams the same thing, that signifies sickness or death to his wife or mother. To dream that a man is naked in bed with a beautiful woman signifies deceit; and with a handsome man, pain, trouble, loss, damage and deceit. To dream you are stark naked signifies loss and damage to your property. *(T)*

To dream of nakedness denotes scandal; to dream you see a naked woman is lucky; it foretells that some unexpected honours await you. *(GD)*

To dream that you are naked in church is bad. For a girl to dream she sees a naked man shows that she will quickly fall in love and be married, have many male children, who will be great cowards. *(DSG)*

> This omen's no good, 'tis with scandal propense,
> And argues a habit to envy intense;
> To see women naked sad whimsies obtrudes,
> Which clothes not your back or affords you some food;
> Tho' still some old women obstinaciously prate you,
> That some expected high honours await you. *(MS)*

To dream that you are naked is a sign of poverty. You should be more thrifty and spend less on your appearance. *(M)*

———— ◆ ————

NAVAL BATTLE
To dream that you witness a naval battle is a sign that you will have more than one relative on board a naval vessel. They will prosper in their situations, be promoted and distinguished in the service. If a young woman dreams that she meets an officer who has won distinction in a naval engagement, who proposes marriage to her, it is a sign that she will have her own lover who will be an officer in the Marines. *(M)*

———— ◆ ————

NAVEL
If anyone dreams he has severe pain in his navel he will receive bad news of his father and mother, who will be in danger of death; if he has neither father or mother, he will lose any money he inherited from them or be forced to leave his native country. *(T)*

To dream of the navel signifies loss of father and mother, or being forced to leave the country. *(A)*

———— ◆ ————

NAVIGATION
If anyone dreams that he is sailing in a boat, he will have comfort and success in his affairs; but if the water is rough it means the opposite. To dream of being in danger of overturning or shipwreck is a sign of danger. *(OM)*

———— ◆ ————

NECK
The neck signifies power, honour, wealth and inheritances. To dream that

the neck has become larger than usual but not deformed, it means you will be well known for good deeds, and grow richer. The slender neck signifies the opposite. If anyone dreams that someone is trying to strangle him, it is a bad sign and the dreamer will be injured in some way by that person. To dream that you have a crick in your neck so that you hold your neck on one side is a sign of misfortune, shame and loss. To dream the neck is swollen signifies sickness. To dream you have three heads on one neck signifies domination, power and reputation. *(T)*

If a woman or girl dreams that her neck is large and thick it is a sure sign she will have many children; if it seems smaller than usual it denotes health trouble to a married woman, and loss of her sweetheart to a girl. If a woman dreams that her neck is beautiful it foretells that some gentleman will make love to her. *(M)*

NECKLACE
To dream of wearing an expensive necklace is an unfortunate sign for a woman, denoting that she will probably have more money than happiness in her marriage. To dream of breaking a necklace is still worse, since it signifies that she may in the end experience poverty and neglect. *(O)*

To dream that you have received a necklace as a present foretells that you will not always be content with your lot; you will aspire to higher things. If you are wearing a necklace and it is particularly gorgeous, be careful you are not led astray by someone who, while protesting great friendship, is really jealous of you. *(OM)*

To dream of a necklace signifies jealousy and quarrels. *(OM)*

NEEDLE
For a girl to dream of using a needle denotes that she is of an industrious nature, and will reap the rewards of her hard work. Her husband and children will praise her as she will ensure their comfort and success. *(O)*

The woman who dreams that she is using a needle will be happy in the possession of good and trusted friends. Should she prick herself with the needle, however, it foretells trivial annoyances which will cause her some anxiety in the future. *(M)*

To dream of needles signifies misfortune in love. *(OM)*

NEIGH
The neighing of a horse foretells serious illness for someone dear to you. To a business man it denotes a falling off of business. *(M)*

To dream you hear horses neigh augurs that you will have new and powerful friends. *(OM)*

NEIGHBOURS
To dream you see your neighbours at the street corner gossiping is a sign

that you will be the subject of a practical joke, in which you will lose your temper, and make yourself more ridiculous than if you took the matter calmly. *(M)*

This dream warns you of danger of some kind, therefore be cautious in all your actions. *(OM)*

————— ♦ —————

NEST
To dream of seeing a nest with neither eggs nor young birds in it means for a young man that when he has nothing he will marry a girl with nothing. The same dream for a young woman is of a more cheering character; it denotes she will shortly go to brighten up the life of one she dearly loves. *(O)*

A nest full of eggs foretells gain and profit. If empty, your business will soon run into difficulties. *(OM)*

————— ♦ —————

NETS
To dream you see fishing nets signifies rain and change of weather. *(T)*

————— ♦ —————

NETTLES
To dream of stinging yourself on nettles shows that you will work hard to achieve your ambitions. *(OM)*

————— ♦ —————

NEWSPAPER
> May prove by hypothesis of some amount,
> If insurance in lottery you'd turn to account;
> For the date of its year, if your memory supplies,
> Insure, and that number will claim a great prize. *(MS)*

To dream of reading a newspaper indicates than an expected letter is sure to arrive, though its content will not be to your liking. *(O)*

When a newspaper figures in your dream you may expect someone to deceive you. According to some writers this dream indicates that you will have good news from an absent friend. *(OM)*

————— ♦ —————

NICKNAME
To dream either that you are being called by a nickname, or that you yourself are calling someone by theirs, is an educational dream, since it is a lesson that if you are too straightforward you will upset other people. Exercise a little tact. *(O)*

To dream that you hear yourself called by a nickname is a sign that you will be liked by nearly all your friends and neighbours because of your abilities as a workman or tradesman and your generous character; you will always be ready to help anyone in distress. *(M)*

NIGHT

Dreaming of the approach of night means that you are about to lose something of great value, and not to recover it again for a long time, if ever.

(O)

To dream of night signifies anxiety and sadness. If you are walking on a dark night it indicates grief and disappointment as well as financial loss.

(OM)

———— ♦ ————

NIGHT BIRDS

To dream of any kind of night birds, such as the owl, is ominous.   *(OM)*

———— ♦ ————

NIGHTCAP

For a girl to dream that she is wearing a nightcap in company is a sign that she will be kissed by a strange gentleman, or that a stranger will fall in love with her. If a married woman dreams this it foretells that her husband will be jealous of her, and perhaps not without cause.   *(M)*

———— ♦ ————

NIGHTINGALE

To dream of a nightingale indicates weddings and music.   *(A)*

To dream of this pretty warbler is the forerunner of good news, a success in business, plentiful crops and of a sweet-tempered lover. For a married woman to dream of a nightingale shows that she will have children who will be great singers.   *(GD)*

This is a bird of good fortune, and to dream of it is a good omen sometimes meaning a successful marriage, at other times a contented home and great prosperity in business.   *(O)*

———— ♦ ————

NIGHTMARE

To dream of having a nightmare is a sign that a woman will be domineered over by a fool.   *(OM)*

———— ♦ ————

NOBLES

To dream you talk with great lords and nobles, or go anywhere with them, signifies honour.   *(T)*

———— ♦ ————

NOISES

To dream you hear strange noises signifies that your position will be influenced by someone who is dying.   *(OM)*

———— ♦ ————

NOSE

If anyone dreams their nose is larger than usual, they will become rich and powerful, and will be provident and subtle; but to dream losing their nose signifies the contrary. To dream you have two noses signifies quarrels. If anyone dreams that their nose has grown large and deformed, they will live in prosperity, but never gain the love of people. If anyone dreams his nose is blocked so that he cannot smell, he is in danger of being deceived by his wife, who will commit adultery with one of his friends. If it is a woman, her husband will deceive her. To dream you take hold of your nose signifies fornication. *(T)*

To dream you have a large, attractive nose is good to anyone except a sick person, for then it is a sign of death. *(D&M)*

For a man to dream that he has a long nose means mirth. To dream you have a large nose is unfortunate. To dream you have no nose is lucky, and if you are sick it means you will escape death. *(D&M2)*

To dream of anyone having a long nose means the coming of death, and the longer the nose the more speedy the end. *(O)*

NOSEGAYS
Gathering a nosegay, giving or receiving one, are all three favourable dreams, and should put the dreamers on good terms with themselves and with the rest of the world. They all point to long-continued happiness and prosperity unless some of the flowers are withered in which case occasional troubles may be expected. *(O)*

NOVEL
For a young woman to dream that she is reading a light novel is a sign that she will become a favourite in the company of many of the young men in the neighbourhood where she lives. If the novel is a very serious one she will be of a very retiring and sullen character and will not gain many admirers. *(M)*

NURSE
To dream that you are a nurse is a sign that you will end your days in peace and happiness at a ripe old age. The girl who dreams she has become a Red Cross nurse and is tending wounded soldiers in the battle line will become famous by some deed of heroism performed in her everyday life. *(M)*

NURSERY
To dream that you spend some time in a nursery means that you will not be fond of children, but will avoid them and only be fit for the company of old people. You will be rather short-tempered and fidgety when the least thing goes wrong with you; you will magnify any problems and a molehill of trouble will be made to look like a mountain. *(M)*

NURSING

To dream you are nursing a sick friend is a sign that you will meet that friend strong and well when you least expect to do so. Should your patient be a stranger, you will experience a great deal of trouble by offending a person of the opposite sex. To dream that your soldier lover has been wounded in battle and that you are nursing him back to health and strength to fight again is a sign that he will be promoted on the field for some deed of bravery, probably for rescuing a comrade or an officer under fire. *(M)*

———— ◆ ————

NUTS

If you see clusters of nuts, it denotes riches and happiness; to the lover, success, and a good-tempered sweetheart. If you are gathering them, it is not a good omen, for you will pursue an action that will not turn out to your advantage. If you crack them, your lover will treat you with indifference, and be very unfaithful. *(GD)*

To dream of eating nuts is a sign that you will succeed in solving many difficult problems, and become distinguished for wisdom and common sense. Dreams of gathering nuts, however, are not favourable: they indicate that your present efforts in courtship will not turn out as successfully as you sometimes hope. *(O)*

To dream of eating nuts denotes that you will enjoy both wealth and good health. To a young girl the latter dream foretells a love match in a much higher sphere than her present one. *(M)*
See also **FILBERTS, HAZELNUTS.**

———— ◆ ————

NUT TREE

To dream you see nut trees and that you eat their fruit signifies riches and content, gained through hard work. To find nuts that have been hidden signifies you will find some treasure. *(T)*

OAKS

To see a stately oak signifies riches, profit and a long life.   *(T)*
   If in your dream you see an oak felled to the ground it signifies losses.
(OM)
   To dream of an oak tree is a sign that you will shortly be entertaining a number of people in your house. To dream that you see an oak withered and dead denotes that you will receive a sum of money through the death of a distant relative.   *(M)*
   Should the oak be in leaf it signifies losses of various kinds, but should the tree be bare then you may expect many gains in money, pleasure and friendship.   *(O)*

———————— ◆ ————————

OAR

If you dream of being in a boat and losing one or more of the oars it is a sign of the death of your father, mother or of someone to whom you look for protection; if an engaged young girl or a married woman dreams this it foretells of the death of a lover or husband.   *(M)*

———————— ◆ ————————

OATMEAL

To dream of either seeing, handling or eating oatmeal means that you will all through life discover that 'economy is the best revenue', and that by the exercise of judicious thrift you will attain to a position of honour.   *(O)*

———————— ◆ ————————

OBITUARY

To dream that you read in the columns of a newspaper an account of the death of a friend is a sign that you will soon read of the wedding of a friend who said he would never marry. If an unmarried woman has this dream it is a sign that she will be deeply wounded by reading of the marriage of an old sweetheart who some time ago jilted her, or left her for another young woman.   *(M)*

———————— ◆ ————————

OBSERVATORY

To dream that you visit an observatory to view the stars or for astronomical study is a sign that you will be fond of solitude and retirement, and be devoted to a study such as geometry, which will require close application.
(M)

OCEAN
Should you see a calm ocean in a dream you may infer that your circumstances for the present will continue without change or disturbance, but should the sea be stormy you can expect that your life will shortly become unsettled. *(O)*

It is unlucky to dream you swim, walk on or catch fish in the ocean. But it is nevertheless lucky to dream of the ocean to any one about to go on a journey. *(OM)*

———— ♦ ————

OFFENCE
To dream you have given offence, or that you have had cause for taking offence, indicates that a friendship will probably grow before long into a warmer attachment. *(O)*

———— ♦ ————

OFFICE
To dream you are turned out of your office foretells death and loss of property. *(OM)*

———— ♦ ————

OFFICERS
To dream of officers signifies anger and authority. *(T)*

———— ♦ ————

OIL
If someone dreams he perfumes his head with oils, it signifies he is vain and conceited. If it is a woman, she will deceive her husband, and wear the trousers. *(T)*

After dreaming of oil look after your money. If you have any investments take steps to see that they are safe and, above all, be careful not to lend any money for some time to come. Whoever borrows from you will have no intention of paying you back. *(M)*

To dream of oil or its use means that you will shortly be in danger of getting into trouble through a too free use of your tongue. *(O)*

———— ♦ ————

OINTMENT
To dream you make an ointment signifies anxiety and trouble. *(T)*

A forewarning of coming trivial illnesses, but nothing serious. *(M)*

———— ♦ ————

OLD
Honour awaits the person who dreams he or she has grown very old. A dream of old buildings is a forewarning of danger, and a dream of old clothes denotes that someone holds you in contempt because you are too shy. *(M)*

For a woman to dream she is courted by an old man is a sure sign that she will receive a sum of money. *(OM)*
See also **AGE.**

OLIVE and OLIVE TREES

If anyone dreams they see or smell an olive, if she is a woman she will have children; if a girl, she will soon marry; if a man, it signifies happiness, prosperity, abundance and success in business. To dream you see an olive tree with olives denotes peace, delight, harmony, freedom, dignity and fulfilment of your desires. To dream of gathering olives off the ground signifies hard work. *(T)*

To dream of eating olives indicates that you will be called upon to undertake a morally distasteful duty. *(M)*

――――――― ♦ ―――――――

ONIONS

To dream of this vegetable denotes a mixture of good and bad luck; if you are eating them, you will receive some money, recover something lost or stolen, or discover a hidden treasure; your lover will be faithful, but of a cross temper. It also denotes attacks of thieves and a failure of crops; it shows that you will be engaged in some disagreeable quarrels, perhaps with your own family. If you are throwing onions away it is the forerunner of quarrels; if you are in love, you will fall out with your sweetheart; if you are in trade, you will quarrel with your customers and employees. If you are gathering onions, it indicates the recovery of a sick person in your family; the receipt of some unexpected good news and a quick removal from your present situation. *(GD)*

If anyone dreams he eats or smells onions, it signifies a discovery of hidden secrets and domestic quarrels. *(T)*

If you dream of eating onions it foretells that you are about to have a quarrel with someone whose influence you need, and that it will all begin about nothing. *(O)*

The sight of onions in a dream should be taken as a warning against wasting your money. Should you be a spendthrift, you will live to want what you are now throwing away. To an unmarried woman a dream of onions denotes a poor marriage and a large family. *(M)*

> Any root or strong herb by experience foretells
> The discovery of secrets and 'en famille' quarrels. *(MS)*

――――――― ♦ ―――――――

OPAL

Good luck should follow a dream in which an opal figures. To a person engaged to be married it promises a happy life. *(M)*

――――――― ♦ ―――――――

OPERA

For an unmarried woman to dream that she is at the opera with her lover is a sign that he will try to blind her to his faults by flattery and boasting. To a married woman the dream is a sign that she will have cause for serious complaint regarding her husband's attentions to other ladies unless she does more to retain his love. *(M)*

ORANGE

To dream that you see or eat oranges signifies wounds, grief and anxiety. *(T)*

Oranges are very bad omens; they indicate loss of goods and reputation, burglaries, wounds and unfaithful lovers. *(GD)*

To dream of eating a sour orange is a sign of happiness. A sweet one denotes discontent with your lot and an early attempt to change it. *(M)*

To dream about oranges is especially unfortunate to lovers. It indicates jealousy and bad temper. For people in business it is also a bad dream, meaning losses of various kinds and a serious diminution of profits for the current year. *(O)*

------ ♦ ------

ORANGE BLOSSOM

Nothing could be more unlucky than for a single woman to dream of this bridal decoration. It denotes disappointment in love and marriage. To a married person the dream comes as a sign that trouble and sickness will enter the house. *(M)*

This is not a good subject to dream about. It foretells the death of someone of your family. *(O)*

------ ♦ ------

ORCHARD

This signifies that you will marry a discreet and beautiful wife and that you will have very attractive children. *(T)*

To dream that you are in an orchard denotes that although you will have many small cares, no serious trouble will spoil your happiness. If the trees are unusually well-laden with fruit, you will have either a small family or no family at all. *(M)*

It is lucky to dream of being in an orchard because it means prosperity in all your affairs. To a young woman it tells that she will soon be married to the man of her choice, and that almost all her future life will be happy. *(O)*

------ ♦ ------

ORCHESTRA

To dream that you hear or see an orchestra playing is an omen of bad news already on its way to you. *(M)*

------ ♦ ------

ORGAN

To dream you play or see someone else play an organ signifies the death of relations. To dream you hear the sound of organs signifies joy. *(T)*

To hear the music of a church organ is a forewarning that you will have a serious illness, which will make you alter your life considerably. To dream that you are playing a church organ, however, is indicative of fair dealing and honesty. Should you see a church organ without hearing any music, you will hear bad news from a friend whom you have recently visited. *(M)*

ORNAMENTS

To dream that you see a great number of ornaments is a sign that in spite of all your thrift you will only be able just to keep your head above water financially. You will have many debts and financial problems. To dream that you buy a number of ornaments is a sign that you will suffer financial hardship because of your extravagance. *(M)*

◆

ORPHANS

Whoever dreams of orphans will receive profits and riches from a stranger.
(OM)

OSTRICH

To see this bird in your dreams is a sign that you are inclined to be conceited. Unless you think less of yourself and more of others you will have a serious fall socially. *(M)*

◆

OTTER

To dream that you see an otter is a sign that you will be the subject of intense spite of people you have long thought to be your best friends. You will experience not only slighting remarks, but expressions of positive hatred from some of your relatives or those you thought had some affection for you. Your feelings will be hurt, as you never had a bad thought of those friends before. *(M)*

◆

OVEN

To dream you see an oven foretells that you are about to be separated from your family by changing your present home; it also shows you an attack by thieves and that your sweetheart is flighty and unlikely to make you happy. *(GD)*

To dream of kindling a fire easily in an oven or hearth is a sign of generation, but for it to go out straight after lighting it signifies injury. *(A)*

To dream of an oven denotes to a single woman that she will never have much luxury in life. She will always have to do all her own work. To a married person the dream comes as a forewarning of arguments with neighbours. *(M)*

To dream of an oven and cooking in an oven is meant to convey the fact that nothing can be done well without preparation, and to indicate that your affairs will prosper as long as you continue to exercise hard work and intelligence. *(O)*

◆

OVERCOAT

To dream of an overcoat is a sign that the time will come when you will suffer great shame and remorse and will try to hide from your friends and relatives. *(M)*

To dream of an overcoat, either putting it on or taking it off, means that you are about to undergo a change of circumstances which may or may not end well for you. Be prepared for considerable change in your life. *(O)*

———— ♦ ————

OVERTURNED

If a woman dreams she is overturned while riding it is a sign that she will be greatly distressed for a short time. For a man to have this dream denotes that an animal to which he is attached will sicken and perhaps die.   *(OM)*

———— ♦ ————

OWL

To dream of night birds such as the owl is a bad omen, and those who dream of such birds must undertake no business on that day.   *(T)*

This bird denotes poverty and misfortune, although to an unmarried woman it also indicates that she will one day marry a clever man who will possibly give her an easy life.   *(M)*

For the young it predicts that they are in danger of marrying someone stupid. For the middle-aged and the old it denotes the approach of poverty.   *(O)*

———— ♦ ————

OXEN

To dream you have the horns of an ox denotes anger, pride, violent death by the hand of justice. To dream you feed oxen is a good sign. To see fat oxen signifies a fruitful year. Lean oxen signify scarcity of provisions and famine. To see oxen ploughing in the field signifies gain. To see black oxen signifies danger. To see oxen drinking is a bad sign.   *(T)*

To dream of seeing strong white cattle shows virtuous inclinations; to see fat and thin oxen signifies gain or misfortune.   *(GD)*

To those who dream of cattle should notice whether they are thin or fat. Thin cattle indicate poverty, famine and the loss of comfort and happiness. Fat oxen, on the contrary, indicate plenty of everything, enough and more.   *(O)*

See also **CATTLE.**

———— ♦ ————

OYSTERS

To dream that you are eating oysters is a very favourable omen; if you are married, your wife or husband will be very fond of you, and you will have many children. To an unmarried man it denotes that his future wife will be very fond of him, and they will have many children.   *(DSG)*

If you are in trade your business will increase very fast, and you will become rich; if you are a farmer, you will have plentiful crops. For a girl to dream of eating oysters shows that she will soon be married to a young man who will do well by hard work, and they will have many children. To dream that you have difficulty opening oysters is a sign that by your own endeavours alone you will obtain much enjoyment late in life. To dream that you are eating oysters is an omen of good health. *(M)*

To dream of oysters is an indication that your expenses will shortly, from an unforeseen cause, be greatly increased. *(O)*

PACKING

To dream that you are packing luggage for a journey indicates that you will never see much of the world. You will be a home bird rather than a traveller. To dream that you are packing a present to send to a friend is a sign that you will shortly receive a communication from a person you have not seen for some years. *(M)*

———— ◆ ————

PADLOCK

The person who dreams of a padlock will never have much valuable property to guard, although he will probably never be in real financial trouble. *(M)*

———— ◆ ————

PAIN

To dream that your shoulders are painful or swollen signifies trouble and displeasure from relations. If anyone dreams his stomach aches, he will have family problems. If anyone dreams he has a severe pain at his navel he will receive bad news of his father and mother, who will be in danger of death. If he has neither father nor mother, he will lose the money or property they left to him or will be forced to leave his native country. If anyone dreams he has a pain in his heart, it is a sign of some dangerous illness approaching, according to the proportion of the imagined pain. *(T)*

To dream that you are suffering pain is a warning of trouble in your domestic affairs. To a person in love this dream is an especially bad omen. *(M)*

———— ◆ ————

PAINTING

To dream you see your picture painted signifies long life. To see tapestry or pictures signifies treachery and deceit. *(T)*

To dream of painting your house is a sign of sickness in the family, but at the same time thrift and good luck in business. If you see a white house newly painted outside, you will probably have to attend a funeral; to see any other coloured house newly painted indicates that you will hear of the sickness of a friend or relative. Dreaming of beautiful paintings of landscapes, portraits etc. is an omen of bad luck and poverty. *(M)*

To dream of painting, whether it is the walls of your house or anything else, is a good sign, meaning that what mistakes you have committed in the

earlier part of your life will all be forgotten and that you will come to
occupy an honourable position in the world. *(O)*

———— ♦ ————

PALACE
The woman who dreams she is in a palace or sees one from outside will
experience a shock which will temporarily injure her health. To a man the
dream is an omen of bad business and losing customers. *(M)*

To dream of living in a palace signifies that you are about to experience a
change of circumstances for the better. *(O)*

———— ♦ ————

PALM
To dream you hold or smell a palm means that a woman will have children,
a girl will soon be married, or a man will find happiness, prosperity,
abundance and success in his business. *(T)*

To dream you are gathering palms denotes plenty, money and success
in undertakings, and is a very good omen indeed. *(GD)*

A dream of a palm is indicative of success and triumph over enemies. *(M)*

———— ♦ ————

PANCAKES
To dream of eating pancakes is a good omen both for business and love.
The woman who dreams of cooking pancakes will rule her home and have
few troubles to contend with. *(M)*

———— ♦ ————

PANSY
Denotes modesty of spirit. You are too bashful to rise much in life, but you
will be happy and stand high in other persons' esteem. *(M)*

———— ♦ ————

PANTOMIME
Beware of joking with one of your friends who is of a particularly jovial
nature. Something you say will be misconstrued, perhaps purposely, and
you will be caused much pain and annoyance. *(M)*

———— ♦ ————

PANTRY
If a young woman dreams that she is at work in a pantry it means that she
will meet an untidy young man who will want to take her out. He will be
lazy, and make a precarious livelihood by getting a job where he can; he
will try to borrow money from her, and will con her if she gives him
money. She will do well to avoid him, and have nothing to do with him. If a
young man dreams that he is in a pantry it is a sign that he will never
become wealthy, but always remain poor because he does not look ahead.
(M)

———— ♦ ————

PAPER
To dream you blot or tear paper signifies that your business will be well
run. *(T)*

To dream of paper is a good omen; if it is clean you will be successful in your undertakings; marry the person you love; have good children, and be very happy. If it is dirty or scribbled on, then it shows temporary want and an unpleasant argument. If it is plainly written, you will receive good news, make an advantageous bargain, and inherit some money. If it appears crumpled and carelessly folded up, it shows that some difficulties will occur, which will cause pain. If it is neatly folded, you will obtain whatever you most want. *(GD)*

> To dream that you on paper write,
> Denotes accusers, hate and spite. *(N)*

To dream that you see a great deal of paper is a sure sign that you will receive money either in payment of a debt or as a present. Should the paper be dirty, however, you will soon be wishing that the money had never come your way, for it will lead you to commit some foolish indiscretion which you will have cause to remember for the rest of your life. *(M)*

It depends altogether on what sort of paper you dream about. If it is white paper it means that your life for some time will be without incident, colour or importance. To dream, however, of printed paper, especially of seeing countless newspapers, signifies great agitation and uncertainty in all your affairs for some time to come. *(O)*

———— ♦ ————

PARADISE

To dream of being in paradise signifies that by the exercise of good principles, you will experience lasting happiness, make large profits and no, or at least only trifling, bad debts in business. *(O)*

———— ♦ ————

PARASOL

To dream that you are walking with your parasol, or your umbrella, open indicates that although you may shortly fall ill, you will quickly recover your health. *(M)*

———— ♦ ————

PARCEL

The person who dreams of carrying a parcel will shortly be guarding a secret of vital interest to their own and other people's happiness. To dream of receiving a parcel indicates the loss of a valued possession. *(M)*

Dreaming of a parcel signifies that there is something coming to you in the shape of a fortune, but whether good or bad depends on the appearance of the parcel. A neat parcel means prosperity, an untidy one, troubles. Brown paper wrapping signifies that the gift will come from an unexpected source, and white means that the fortune is exactly both what you deserve and what you might naturally expect. *(O)*

PARENTS

For a young person to dream of his parents is a good or bad dream, according to the circumstances. To dream that you see both your parents in comfortable circumstances is a sign that you will live to an old age and never need money. To dream of quarrelling with your parents indicates that you will one day be guilty of a serious crime. If your parents are dead and you dream you receive a visit from them, it means that you are about to undertake a new calling or speculation and that you must be careful or give up your new project. If you have been guilty of any act of indiscretion, and you see your parents in a dream, it is meant as a rebuke, and if your actions have made other people suffer, you must try to make some reparation to them for it. If a young woman is about to be married, and her parents appear to her smiling, she can be sure that her marriage will be a happy one; but if they appear to be frowning it means that it will be best to break off the engagement, for nothing but bad will come of it.   *(M)*

───────── ♦ ─────────

PARROT

To dream of a parrot means that if you are wise you will keep your own secrets, because several you have lately told have been published abroad by those in whose reticence you reposed confidence.   *(O)*

A dream in which parrots appear signifies that you have dangerous neighbours.   *(OM)*

───────── ♦ ─────────

PARTRIDGES

To dream of partridges foretells entanglements with women who are devoid of conscience and are ungrateful and hard.   *(A)*

───────── ♦ ─────────

PARTY

To dream you have received an invitation to a party is a sign that you will soon hear of a wedding. To dream that you are present at an evening party denotes that you will move to a new neighbourhood before very long and have to make new friends. To dream of giving a large and sumptuous party to your friends is a sign of losses and poverty.   *(M)*

───────── ♦ ─────────

PASTRY

To dream of pastry signifies that you are about to fall ill and will endure great pain.   *(OM)*

───────── ♦ ─────────

PATH

To dream you are walking in a good broad path denotes health.   *(GD)*

> To dream a path is straight and fair
> Doth health and happiness declare.
> But crooked ways denote much ill
> To those who have a headstrong will.   *(N)*

PAWNBROKER

To dream that you have been forced to pay a visit to a pawnbroker foretells first success and afterwards reverses—the latter brought about by your own foolishness. Be careful not to waste, and you may possibly steer clear of the unpleasant part of this prediction. *(M)*

———— ♦ ————

PEACHES

To dream of peaches in season denotes content, health and pleasure; but if you seem to eat them out of season, they signify vain hopes and failure in business. *(T)*

———— ♦ ————

PEACOCKS

To dream you see a peacock is a sign you will marry an attractive wife, that you will grow rich and be well respected. *(T)*

To dream of seeing this beautiful bird is a very good omen. It denotes success in trade; to a girl, a good and rich husband; to a widow, that she will be courted by someone who will tell her many fine tales, without being sincere; it also denotes great prosperity by sea. *(GD)*

For an unmarried man to dream of a peacock indicates that he will marry a woman fond of extravagant, loud clothes. To an unmarried woman the dream foretells a grand wedding. To married persons it denotes wealth and good reputation. *(M)*

To dream of seeing a peacock means that your husband or wife will be attractive but not particularly intelligent. *(O)*

———— ♦ ————

PEAR

To see or eat ripe pears signifies joy or pleasure; if they are sour or wild, the opposite. *(T)*

To dream of pears indicates elevation in life, accumulation of riches, success in business and constancy in love. If a pregnant woman dreams of them she will have a girl who will marry someone far above her class before she is seventeen. *(D&M2)*

To dream of pears means that an opportunity for advancement will shortly present itself, of which you should unhesitatingly avail yourself; should you let it slip the rest of your career will be comparatively unimportant. *(O)*

Well-baked pears signify great success. *(OM)*

———— ♦ ————

PEARLS

To dream of pearls is a bad omen. You will hear of the illness and subsequent death of a dear friend; and should you be wearing pearls, the shock of the news will cause a breakdown in your own health unless you remember the warning and steel yourself for the worst. *(M)*

PEAS

To dream of eating peas denotes success in business. *(T)*

To dream of peas is a sign of prosperity; to dream you gather peas shows great happiness and content. Peas dried for seed denote wealth. *(GD)*

To dream of either green peas or sweet peas means that you will have many children, who in their youth will be a cause of care and anxiety, but later on in life will be both a credit and a comfort to you. *(O)*

———— ♦ ————

PEN

For a young woman to dream of a pen means that she will shortly receive a proposal of marriage from someone who lives at a distance, and with whom she cannot meet at present. For a man to dream of a pen signifies that he will experience great difficulty in declaring to the girl he loves how he feels for her. *(O)*

———— ♦ ————

PENSION

To dream that you have a pension from a friend or a company for which you used to work is a sign that you will hear many degrading expressions and much conversation that will be offensive to you, because of your being dependent on other people who will be overbearing towards you. *(M)*

———— ♦ ————

PEOPLE

To dream of seeing a great crowd of people means affliction in connection with your family. From the age of the chief person in the crowd you can conclude which family is going to suffer. *(O)*

———— ♦ ————

PEPPER

To dream you grind pepper signifies melancholy. *(T)*

———— ♦ ————

PERFUMES

If you dream you perfume your head with essences or sweet-scented powders it signifies that you have too great an opinion of yourself. If a woman dreams this, she will deceive her husband and wear the trousers. If anyone dreams they are presented with sweet perfumes, they will receive some welcome news, according to the proportion of the scent in quality and quantity; and will gain profit, advantage and honour among their acquaintances. If a person dreams they make perfumes and give them to their friends, they will be the messenger of good news which will prove advantageous to themselves and their friends. *(T)*

———— ♦ ————

PHEASANTS

To dream of a pheasant signifies that you are about to have some good fortune. If you carry one, you will receive a great honour. *(OM)*

PHILOSOPHERS

To dream you argue with philosophers signifies profit and gain.　　*(T)*

———— ♦ ————

PHOTOGRAPH

To dream of receiving the photograph of anyone is a sign that there is a danger of your friendship with that particular person coming to a speedy end. When anyone dreams of receiving their sweetheart's photograph, let them be on their guard against rivals and quarrels.　　*(O)*

———— ♦ ————

PIANO

A dream of playing a piano or an organ is a favourable omen and means the discovery of something of great value in a surprising place.　　*(O)*

———— ♦ ————

PICNIC

For a young woman to dream that she goes to a picnic and meets with a sweetheart there, who is gaily dressed, full of attention and attractive is a sign that one who is not considered very intelligent will hanker after her, and do his utmost, in his way, to gain her love. She may do worse than allow herself to be courted by him.　　*(M)*

———— ♦ ————

PICTURES

To dream you are looking at beautiful pictures indicates that you will be allured by false appearances into an unprofitable concern, that you will waste your time on an idle project, and that you will always be in pursuit of happiness without attaining it. In love, it denotes great pleasure in the enjoyment of your lover and promises a handsome wife, a good husband and dutiful children.　　*(GD)*

For a man to dream he sees his own picture is a sign of longevity. *(D&M2)*

It is very lucky to dream of pictures, whether they are paintings or engravings. To the young it means a marriage of affection, and that the home after marriage will be loving. The business man dreaming of pictures is assured that his present transactions will result profitably, but at the same time warned that he must not trust too much to appearances. *(O)*

———— ♦ ————

PIES

To dream of watching a woman making pies means that your experience in love is likely to prove disastrous, and that you may come in the end to have as many wounds in your heart as there will be wrinkles on your face. Dreaming of eating pies, whether they are meat pies or fruit, signifies that you will shortly have an opportunity of laughing at something till your head aches.　　*(O)*

PIGEONS

To dream you see pigeons is a good sign that you will have delight and content at home, and success in affairs abroad. To dream you see a white pigeon flying signifies consolation, devotion and success in undertakings; provided they are done for the glory of God, and the good of your neighbour. *(T)*

To dream you see pigeons flying denotes unexpected, pleasant news and success in undertakings. They are very favourable to lovers, as they announce constancy in your partner, but also that the person you love will be absent from you for a long while on a journey; if your lover is at sea, they denote that he has a pleasant voyage, continues faithful and will return rich. *(GD)*

Dreaming of pigeons denotes that a young child of your acquaintance, but not of your family, will suddenly fall ill; he will recover, however, from very serious illness to become a great man. *(O)*

————— ◆ —————

PIGS

Pigs denote idle and lazy people, who live doing nothing, and thinking of nothing, but how to prey upon other people's goods, so they can live at ease. They also signify envious people who are in no way useful to society. To dream you trade in pigs signifies sickness. *(T)*

To dream of a sow with a litter denotes fruitfulness. *(P&F)*

To dream of seeing a pig is not good, no matter whether it is alive or dead. It portends a married life spent without comfort, and trade pursued without any satisfactory result. *(O)*

————— ◆ —————

PILGRIM

To dream you see a pilgrim or talk with one signifies that you will have a successful future. *(OM)*

————— ◆ —————

PILLOW

To dream that your pillow is covered with blood means that the head of someone in the family will be severely injured in an accident. To dream that your pillow is torn means that the reasoning faculties of either yourself or those who are dear to you will become deranged; but to dream that your pillow is clean and white means prosperity, success and happiness. *(M)*

————— ◆ —————

PIN

To dream of anyone taking a pin from you signifies that you will soon receive a present, trifling in value, but indicating a growing affection towards you on the part of the giver. *(O)*

PIN CUSHION

For a housewife to dream that she sees a pin cushion with many pins stuck in it is a sign that her house will not be as orderly as it should be.   *(M)*

———— ◆ ————

PINE TREES

To dream you see a pine tree signifies idleness and forgetfulness.   *(T)*

———— ◆ ————

PISTOL

The report of a pistol heard in a dream foretells the arrival of news of great importance from a distant quarter.   *(O)*

———— ◆ ————

PIT

It is a good sign to dream you see a pit full of clear water in a field where there is none at all, since it indicates that you will thrive, marry suddenly and have good and obedient children. If you see a pit whose water overflows the banks, that predicts loss of property, the death of wife and children; and if the wife has the same dream, that denotes her death or the loss of her property.   *(T)*

To dream of falling into a deep pit shows that some very unhappy misfortune is about to happen to you; that your lover is false and prefers someone else; to a sailor it forbodes a sad disaster at the next port. To dream you are in a pit, and that you climb easily out of it indicates that you will have many enemies and experience much trouble, but that you will overcome them, and surmount your difficulties, marry well and become rich. To a sailor it denotes that he will be hospitably received, fall in love, marry a rich and attractive wife, leave the sea, and live at ease on the shore.   *(GD)*

———— ◆ ————

PLAGUE

If anyone dreams he has the plague, his hidden store will be recovered and he will run the risk of losing it.   *(T)*

———— ◆ ————

PLANTS

To dream of watching plants growing in a garden means that you ought to move from the place you live as you have lived there long enough for any good it is likely to do you.   *(O)*

———— ◆ ————

PLAYS

To dream you see a comedy, farce or some other play signifies success in business. To dream you see a tragedy acted signifies hard work, loss of friends and property, with grief and suffering. To dream you play with animals is a good sign.   *(T)*

To dream that you are at a play is the forerunner of great good luck, it indicates great happiness in marriage and very great success in business.

(GD)

PLOUGH

To dream of a plough signifies success in life and a good marriage.

(DSG)

To dream of a plough indicates that you will have many children, although perhaps later in life. *(GD)*

POETRY

To dream of writing verses and having a young lady criticise them denotes that you are never likely to marry, even though you fall in love countless times and write poetry about all your lovers. *(O)*

POLICEMAN

> To view of the law these dire caitiffs approach
> Proves clearly your conscience's not void of reproach. *(MS)*

To dream of being in the custody of a policeman signifies that you may expect to be unjustly blamed by one who wishes you ill, but that in the end the false accusation will do you more good than it ever did harm. *(M)*

POMEGRANATES

If you have gathered pomegranates you will be made rich by a rich person; but if the pomegranates are not ripe, that denotes sickness or anxiety caused by someone wickedly disposed. If anyone dreams that the fruit he has gathered is rotten, that signifies adversity or loss of children. *(T)*

POND

To dream you see a small pond signifies that you will enjoy the love of a beautiful woman or handsome man, and will see your dreams realised. *(T)*

For a married woman to dream of a pond signifies that she will shortly become pregnant; if there are many fish, she will have twins; if the fish are small her next child will be a girl; if large, a boy. To a widow it denotes that she will re-marry and be very happy. *(DSG)*

PORCUPINE

To dream of a porcupine signifies that you will encounter difficulties in business. *(OM)*

PORK

To dream of pork is a good dream for all engaged in money-making, It denotes quick profit, and that customers will as a rule prefer to pay cash rather than take credit. *(O)*

* * *

POSTMAN
You will receive little correspondence for some time after dreaming that a postman has handed you a letter or letters. If, however, you dream that you see a postman delivering letters at other houses and missing your own, you will hear important news. *(M)*

Dreaming of a postman means that there is a letter already written to you, and perhaps even posted, and informing you of something of considerable importance. *(O)*

* * *

POST OFFICE
To dream of being in a post office on any errand signifies that you are in danger from the gossiping tongues of people you think your friends, and that if you want your secrets preserved you had better keep them to yourself. *(O)*

* * *

POT
To dream of watching a pot boiling is a sign of approaching instability, particularly in your love affairs. You will shortly discover that you will have cause for jealousy, and will make the most of it. *(O)*

* * *

POTATOES
To dream of planting potatoes means that at present you are neglecting your opportunities, and that you have a power and ability which only needs to be cultivated to lead you on to fortune. *(O)*

* * *

POVERTY
To dream of being poor means that you are on the eve of marrying someone fairly well off, or receive a legacy. *(O)*

* * *

PRAISE
Dreaming of praising someone, or of someone praising you, indicates that you are about to be abandoned by someone to whom you have given your affections, although you should remember that there are 'other fish in the sea'. *(O)*

* * *

PRAYER
To dream you pray devoutly to God signifies joy, comfort and happiness. To dream you make promises and offerings to God signifies love. *(T)*

To dream of prayer or requests for alms or of a poor and miserable beggar denotes anxiety and loss. If you receive alms it is a sign of damage and even death to you or to a close friend. If the beggar enters your house and steals anything or is given anything, it shows adversity. *(D&M)*

PRECIPICE
To fall over a precipice signifies that you will suffer an injury, risk your life and your property will be in danger from fire. *(T)*

To dream of climbing precipices denotes problems. *(D&M)*

To be on the brink of a precipice with the danger of falling over is a dream of warning, the meaning of which is that if you are in trade you should look carefully into your accounts, and if in private life, that you should consider the character of your present associates. *(O)*

PREGNANCY
Being pregnant in a dream indicates sorrow and sadness. *(D&M)*

PRESENT
To dream of receiving a present from a friend signifies that the first advice you receive from anyone on getting up that morning should be followed, because it will have an important effect in securing a result you are at present aiming at. *(O)*

PRIEST
To dream of a priest foretells the settlement of quarrels. *(OM)*

PRINTER
For most people, to dream of a printer means that their names will soon appear in the newspapers in connection with an event of great importance. To an author, however, it signifies that a period of general disturbance will soon arrive, resulting mostly from his or her own fault. *(O)*

PRISON
To dream of being confined in prison it means that you will make money and succeed in life, but it will be by pursuing things against your will. *(O)*

PRISONERS
To dream of seeing prisoners executed is a good dream. *(OM)*

PROCESSION
To dream that you are watching a procession foretells steadfast affection from the person you love. *(OM)*

PROSTITUTES
To dream you are in the company of a prostitute signifies completion of business. *(T)*

———— ♦ ————

PUBLIC HOUSE
To dream you are in a pub with friends indicates happiness and comfort. *(T)*

———— ♦ ————

PUDDING
To dream of eating pudding is an unwelcome omen, meaning that you are about to have an illness and that your complete recovery will be only possible by your following a strict diet. *(O)*

———— ♦ ————

PURSE
To dream of finding a purse is a very favourable omen. It denotes great happiness and unlooked-for prosperity; in love, it is a sure token of an early and happy marriage. To dream you lose your purse shows the loss of a friend; in other respects it denotes some unpleasant adventure is about to happen to you by which you will gain; to a sailor it denotes the loss of his sweetheart while at sea. *(GD)*

To dream of losing your purse is unlucky. It foretells that you will be cheated out of a large sum of money, and will not know about it until it is too late to recover it. *(M)*

To dream of taking money out of a purse signifies that you will shortly be tempted to invest in government which does not pay interest or repay capital. *(O)*

QUACK

To dream that you are under the care of quacks is unfortunate and indicates that you should be wary of anyone making false medical claims. *(OM)*

———— ♦ ————

QUAILS

To dream of quails signifies messengers bringing bad news from across the sea. *(A)*

———— ♦ ————

QUARREL

To dream of quarrelling indicates unexpected news. *(GD)*

To dream that you are involved in a serious quarrel foretells that you will never lack for friends and will lead a peaceful life. *(M)*

To dream of taking part in a quarrel signifies bad luck and indicates that you may expect to overhear a conversation in which you will hear no good of yourself. *(O)*

———— ♦ ————

QUARRY

To dream that your fall down a quarry is a sign that some sudden and violent death will take place before many months are over among some of your friends or relatives. *(M)*

———— ♦ ————

QUAY

To dream that you stand on the quay of a seaport town and see the ships load and unload their goods is a sign that you will shortly receive very costly presents from a relative or friend either in America, Canada or Australia. *(M)*

———— ♦ ————

QUEEN

To dream you see a queen signifies honour, joy and prosperity. *(GD)*

If you dream a queen speaks to you, your joy will be short-lived and sorrow will quickly follow. *(M)*

To dream of seeing a queen means for a man that he will shortly marry a woman who will rule his house and his conduct. *(O)*

QUICKSANDS

Be especially careful of your health after dreaming of walking on quicksand. On no account go near a house where a person is ill from an infectious disease. To dream that you are sinking in quicksands indicates that you are too easily led astray by flatterers. Try to ignore them. *(M)*

———— ♦ ————

QUOITS

To dream that you are watching a game of quoits foretells a holiday in the country. To dream that you play a game of quoits is a sign that you will, unless you are careful, become a gambler, at first for small, but then for larger stakes. *(M)*

For a woman to dream of quoits signifies her undertaking a disagreeable and laborious task. For a man it is a sign of quarrelling. *(OM)*

RABBITS

For a girl to dream of a rabbit is a sign that someone has fallen in love with her but is too shy to tell her. *(O)*

To dream that you see many rabbits alive is a warning against unknown enemies who will try, by underhand methods, to disgrace you. To dream that you are eating rabbit is a sign that you will be a hard worker all your life and taste few real joys without working hard to attain them. *(M)*

To dream of a rabbit warren signifies expensive enjoyments. To see rabbits signifies an increase in your family. *(OM)*

———— ♦ ————

RACE HORSE

This denotes that you will lose a sum of money through trying to make money. *(M)*

———— ♦ ————

RACING

To dream you are running a race is a good token, presages success in life, and that you will soon hear some very happy news. In love, it denotes that you will conquer all your rivals, and be very happy with your partner. To dream you are riding in a race shows disappointments, anger and business problems. To a married woman it denotes the loss of her husband's affections, and that her children will be in trouble. *(GD)*

To win a race is indicative of good fortune at the end of a long and hard struggle for success; to lose a race is a warning that you will experience many disappointments and never climb to the top of the tree. The girl in love who dreams that she has won a race may rest assured that her love is returned and is faithful; but to dream of running a race and losing is a bad omen for all love affairs and relationships. *(M)*

———— ♦ ————

RADISHES

To dream of radishes signifies a discovery of hidden secrets and can indicate domestic quarrels. *(T)*

———— ♦ ————

RAGS

Beware of too much frivolity after dreaming of rags. Try to take life a little more seriously, or you will one day have reason for repentance. *(M)*

RAILWAY TICKET

To dream you have taken a railway ticket to any destination signifies that an unwelcome visitor is about to arrive, and that prudence suggests you should be out of the way. A dream of having lost a railway ticket, on the other hand, means that a journey you are about to take will be prosperous, and that everyone you meet will be good to you. *(O)*

———— ◆ ————

RAIN

Dreams of heavy rain and storms signify problems, troubles, danger, losses and peril. To dream you see it rain signifies great riches. *(T)*

To dream of thunder and rain which do no damage denotes that you have some dangerous enemies, but will overcome them. *(D&M)*

To dream of being in a gentle shower of rain denotes great success in your present undertakings; it is particularly favourable to lovers, as it denotes constancy, affection and a sweet temper; to the sailor it promises good fortune at sea. If it is very heavy rain with thunder and lightning, then expect to experience disappointment and misfortunes. *(GD)*

To dream of rain, especially if it is a sudden shower, indicates good luck. It signifies that prosperity is about to smile upon you, but that you must hurry to take advantage of its favours or you will miss your chance. *(O)*

To see rain falling while the sun is shining is a sign that whatever troubles you may have at that time will soon be swept away and brighter days will arrive. *(M)*

———— ◆ ————

RAINBOW

To dream you see a rainbow in the east is a good omen to the poor and sick, for the former will make money and the latter will recover their health. If you see a rainbow in the west it is a good sign to the rich but a bad sign to the poor. To dream you see the rainbow directly over your head or nearly signifies a change of fortune, and most commonly the death of the dreamer, and the ruin of his family. *(T)*

To dream you see a rainbow denotes travelling; it also denotes unexpected good news. It denotes that your lover is good-tempered and constant, and that you will be very happy in marriage, and be successful in business through foreign trading. *(GD)*

To dream of seeing a rainbow means that no reliance can be placed on your present condition continuing, whether that be good or bad, and that you are on the eve of a change. *(O)*

To dream of a rainbow is indicative of good news which you may expect to receive through a stranger. *(M)*

———— ◆ ————

RAKE

It is a fortunate omen to dream that you are going over ground with a rake, signifying that you will be well educated and will use your knowledge for the benefit of others. *(O)*

To dream that you are using a rake in your garden denotes a persevering nature, which should bring you success in some important undertakings. For a young woman to dream that her lover is a rake, or a wild character is a sign that she will have comfort and happiness in her courtship, no one will be able to find fault with her lover, because he will be attentive to business, straightforward and honest. *(M)*

───────── ◆ ─────────

RAMS
To dream of a ram signifies misfortune for the dreamer. *(OM)*

───────── ◆ ─────────

RASPBERRIES
To dream of raspberries signifies a successful marriage and also that you will receive news from overseas. *(OM)*

───────── ◆ ─────────

RAT
To dream of seeing many rats playing is good because rats signify employees. *(A)*

To dream of rats means that you may expect to be injured by the interference of someone who thinks he knows your business much better than you do yourself, but by the exercise of courtesy, good humour and common sense you will in all probability soon get rid of them. *(O)*

To see rats signifies that you will have many enemies. If you are attacked by rats and get the better of them it means that you will overcome your difficulties. If they bite you and make you run away, then you must expect some serious misfortune. *(OM)*

───────── ◆ ─────────

RAVENS
If anyone sees a raven, it indicates mischief, particularly to a husband or wife who will be discontented by his adulterous partner. To hear a raven croak signifies sadness. To see ravens flying signifies complaint and sadness. To see a raven fly over you signifies danger and damage. *(T)*

To dream you see a raven is a very unfavourable token; to the sailor, they indicate shipwreck, and distress on a foreign shore. *(GD)*

───────── ◆ ─────────

RAZOR
Be careful not to interfere in any quarrel among your friends after dreaming of a razor. If you attempt to smooth matters you will find yourself in an awkward predicament, and both parties will be offended by your conduct. *(M)*

───────── ◆ ─────────

READING
To dream you read romances, comedies or other diverting books signifies

joy and comfort. To dream you read serious books signifies wisdom and knowledge. *(T)*

To dream that you read well signifies that you will go into the country and have goods and honours given to you there, but to read badly signifies the opposite. *(A)*

To dream that you are reading is a sign that you have a very determined spirit, and although this will sometimes lead you into trouble, it will bring you success in most things you undertake. *(M)*

To dream you are reading signifies riches to the dreamer, not only in love but also in money. *(OM)*

───── ♦ ─────

REAPING

To dream you are reaping or that you see others engaged in this occupation, cannot be taken as an altogether good omen. Although you will one day know what it is to live in affluence, you will have many trials and experience much sorrow before that time comes. *(M)*

To dream of reaping signifies that you should aim for a simple life in order to be happy. *(OM)*

───── ♦ ─────

REFLECTION

To dream you see yourself mirrored in water signifies death to the dreamer, or some close friend. *(A)*

See also **MIRROR**.

───── ♦ ─────

RELATIONS

To dream you see or talk with your father, mother, wife, brother, sister, or other of your relations and friends, even though they are dead, signifies you should mind your affairs, and behave yourself. *(T)*

───── ♦ ─────

REMOVAL

To dream that you are changing your house is a sign that you will soon receive intelligence of someone in a distant town of whom you have long lost sight. *(O)*

───── ♦ ─────

REPTILE

To dream of any reptile is a sign of a quarrel; if you imagine you are bitten it shows that you will come out second best, or badly injured, either physically or by reputation. *(M)*

To dream of any reptile signifies that you have a subtle enemy of whom you must beware. *(OM)*

───── ♦ ─────

RESURRECTION

To dream of the dead reviving signifies troubles and injury. To dream of the dead dying again signifies the death of anyone whose name is called in the dream. *(A)*

------- ♦ -------

RESOLUTION

All civil commotions anticipate feuds,
And among friends and families discord includes. *(MS)*

------- ♦ -------

RHUBARB

To dream of rhubarb either growing in the garden or cooked on the table, means that your affection for someone from whom you expected some return is hopeless, and that you would be better to finish the relationship. *(O)*

To dream you handle good rhubarb is a portent of firm friendship with a former enemy. *(OM)*

------- ♦ -------

RIB

All the ribs or intestines signify wealth if they are healthy or the opposite if they are diseased. *(A)*

For a man to dream his upper ribs are broken shows disagreement between him and his wife in which he will come off the worst. But if his lower ribs are broken it shows arguments with female relatives. If you dream your ribs have grown larger and stronger it shows you will be happily married. *(D&M2)*

------- ♦ -------

RIBBON

For a young woman to dream of ribbons is a sign that she is about to have a new partner but he will soon leave her for someone with more money. *(O)*

To dream that you are purchasing ribbon of a bright colour is a sign that you will shortly have to wear mourning for a valued friend. A girl engaged to be married who dreams of a yellow ribbon should be careful in her dealings with the opposite sex. Her sweetheart is inclined to be jealous, and he will break the engagement for the least cause. *(M)*

This dream signifies that you are spending your money on foolish expenditure. *(OM)*

------- ♦ -------

RICE

To dream of rice signifies many difficulties which will cost you money. *(A)*

Whoever dreams of rice may rest assured that they will have a large family, but enough money to bring them up comfortably. *(O)*

If you dream you are eating rice you will one day possess great wealth. *(M)*

RICHES

To dream of riches means you may for some time be short of money but that in the end you will be comfortably off. *(O)*

To dream that you have inherited a fortune is a bad omen. You will probably lose all your money through the failure of some concern in which you are interested, and feel the loss all your life. To dream that you save a fortune is almost as bad; but in this instance there is a chance for you to retrieve your loss by hard work and patient effort. *(M)*

---◆---

RIDING

To ride a horse is good because the horse signifies a person even a ship, to guide and govern. If you dream of a horse you will become powerful. To ride a horse through a town is good for anyone who takes a risk or is sick; the first will gain the prize, the other be healed. To ride out of a town is the opposite. To dream you ride a wild horse and can govern it and stay in the saddle signifies rule and dignity, but to fall or be thrown signifies disgrace. *(A)*

To dream you are riding with a woman is very unfortunate: expect to be crossed in love. If you are in trade, your business will fail and you may be brought near to bankruptcy; if you are a sailor, it denotes your lover is unfaithful. *(GD)*

---◆---

RIGGING

To dream you see the rigging of a ship signifies news from debtors. *(T)*

---◆---

RING

To dream a ring falls off your finger indicates evil and a prison, also the death of a close friend or relation. To a pregnant woman it shows that her child will encounter may difficulties, and be far from happy. To a girl, it is a warning to beware of her present lover, who will use her then abandon her. *(DSG)*

To dream of losing a ring or rings signifies the loss of someone in charge of your property, such as a husband or wife, tenant or employee; and also your goods, and possessions. To many this dream has foretold the loss of eyesight, because the eyes have an association with the stones in a ring. *(A)*

To dream of a gold ring dropping from your finger shows the loss of a lover or close relation; to put a ring on anyone's finger denotes an early marriage. *(D&M)*

To dream of having rings on your fingers denotes honour and dignity. *(D&M2)*

For a woman to dream a ring is put on her finger shows success in love; but if taken off, the opposite. *(P&F)*

To dream you give a ring to anyone signifies damage. *(T)*

To dream of an engagement ring is not a favourable omen and means that many quarrels are likely to take place between you and your partner and that in the end one disagreement more serious than the rest will separate you for ever. *(O)*

The married woman who dreams she is wearing a new ring may expect to receive an invitation to a wedding at an early date. It is a bad omen for a young woman who is engaged to be married to dream that she is wearing a wedding ring. She will not have all the success she might wish for in her love affairs, and if she marries early in life the match will not be a good one. To dream that you receive a ring as a present foretells unexpected news, causing you to take a journey to visit a friend in trouble. To dream that you lose a ring indicates that you will have serious troubles, but will be able to surmount them with the help of someone very dear to you. *(M)*

───────── ◆ ─────────

RIVAL

To dream of the discovery of a rival is one of the best omens in love affairs. It means that you will shortly be united with your loved one, and few couples anywhere will be happier than you two. *(O)*

───────── ◆ ─────────

RIVER

To dream you see a flowing river, and that the waters are smooth and clear indicates happiness and success in life. To the lover it shows constancy and affection in your partner and that if you marry, you will be very happy and contented, and have five children, mostly girls, who will be very beautiful; to the tradesman and farmer, it shows prosperity and gain; to the sailor, that his sweetheart will be kind and faithful, and that his next voyage will be lucrative and pleasant. If the water appears disturbed and muddy, or has a yellow tinge, then it denotes that you will acquire considerable riches; if you have a law-suit, such a dream foretells that you will win. *(GD)*

To dream of being in a rough river, and not to escape, signifies danger and sickness. To dream of swimming in a large river signifies future peril and danger. To dream you see a clear river run by your bedroom indicates the arrival of a rich and generous person, who will do something to your advantage; but if the water is rough or dirty and seemed to spoil the furniture in the room, that signifies violence, quarrels and chaos caused by enemies. A rich man who dreams he sees a stream of clear water run by his house will be unexpectedly appointed to a position of responsibility which will be financially advantageous and will offer a refuge and asylum to the oppressed. *(T)*

To dream of a river and find it difficult to cross shows that you will experience many delays in your undertakings. *(D&M)*

A dream by a man of sailing up or down a river denotes that he will shortly be married to someone imperious and bossy. *(O)*

If the river is flowing quietly between its banks, it may be taken as a sign that you will live to a ripe old age and have little to trouble you. If the water is rough, however, you will experience difficulties in life. To dream that you have fallen into a river is a promise of good news. *(M)*

———————— ♦ ————————

ROADS

To dream that you stand at a spot where several roads meet indicates that you will not always go on in the steady way you are doing now. Several changes will come into your life, and you will not live long in one neighbourhood. To dream that you see a broad and even road stretching before you is lucky, but narrow and crooked roads are bad omens. *(M)*

———————— ♦ ————————

ROAST MEAT

To see or eat roast meat signifies that you will be shortly greeted by one you love. *(OM)*

———————— ♦ ————————

ROBBER

To dream that you are attacked by a robber indicates a calamity in which you will lose some valuable property. To a person in love this dream brings a warning that a rival is in the field striving to gain the affections of your lover. *(M)*

———————— ♦ ————————

ROBIN

To see a robin denotes that you will make many friends, but that your character and temper are such that you are not likely to form a lasting union with anyone. *(T)*

———————— ♦ ————————

ROCK

To dream of a rock signifies that you will experience great annoyance. To climb over one signifies that you will overcome the dangers that are before you. *(OM)*

———————— ♦ ————————

RODS

To dream you have rods in your hand signifies jollity. *(T)*

To dream you are whipped with rods denotes that you will meet with a treacherous friend who will almost ruin you. It also indicates your being shortly at a celebration, where you must be careful of quarrelling; if you do it will be to your disadvantage. If you are in love, it denotes your sweetheart will be fickle and hardly likely to make you happy. *(GD)*

———————— ♦ ————————

ROOF

To dream you see the roof of a house destroyed by fire denotes loss of goods, law-suits or friends. *(T)*

ROOKS

To dream you see a rock signifies a successful conclusion of business.

(T)

◆

ROOM

To dream you are in a strange room signifies that you will accomplish your ambitions. *(OM)*

◆

ROOTS

To dream you eat roots signifies arguments. *(T)*

◆

ROPE

It is a bad sign to dream of rope. You may infer from it that you are in danger of being restricted in your actions, willingly no doubt at first, but from which restraints you will soon wish to escape. *(O)*

To dream you are tied with rope denotes happiness, marriage and many children; it also denotes that you will be very angry with someone for a trifling reason. To dream you see many ropes is a very bad sign indeed; it portends some dreadful accident. To the lover it also denotes the loss of the affections of your sweetheart; to the tradesman, poor success in business. *(M)*

◆

ROSE

To dream of roses in season is a token of happiness and success. To dream of these, or any flowers out of season indicates distress, sickness and disappointment. To the tradesman, they forebode bankruptcy and prison; to the married, loss of their spouse and children. *(GD)*

Few dreams are more fortunate than those in which a rose, of any colour, plays a leading part. To dream of a rose indicates to a young woman a loving marriage in which money will not be scarce; and to a young man indicates that he will be particularly lucky in his business speculations. *(O)*

◆

ROSEMARY

To dream you smell rosemary signifies hard work, trouble, sadness and weakness to anyone but a doctor, to whom such dreams are propitious. *(T)*

◆

ROUGE

To dream you are using rouge to make up your face is a very favourable omen, denoting success in life. To the lover it indicates her sweetheart to be faithful, good-tempered and keen to marry. If you are married, it denotes children, who will be very happy, become rich and be a great comfort in your later years. To dream you see another person using rouge shows that pretended friends are endeavouring to do you an injury, and that your children will meet with persecution and problems. In love such a dream shows your sweetheart to be fickle and hardly likely to make you happy. To dream that the rouge comes off your face is indicative of loss of property and the affections of the person you love. *(M)*

---◆---

ROUSE

To dream you rouse a person from sleep is good. *(OM)*

---◆---

ROWING

To dream that you are rowing a boat on a river gives promise that your dearest wish will be fulfilled. To be rowing on the sea denotes a life of trials and misfortunes. *(M)*

---◆---

ROYALTY

To dream you are a king or emperor indicates death to the sick, but that others will do admirable work and gain a good salary as well as a good reputation. *(A)*

To dream of royalty signifies that you will receive a great honour. To receive an audience with a king signifies gain. To receive a gift from a king signifies great joy. *(T)*

---◆---

RUB

To dream that you are rubbing anything signifies success in marriage or business. *(OM)*

---◆---

RUNNING

To dream you want to run but cannot means that your affairs will be difficult and your ambitions hard to accomplish. *(A)*

To dream of running is a good omen; except if you are rich, in which case if you dream of coming to the end of the race, it signifies that the end of your life is near. *(D&M)*

To dream you are running a race is good, indicating much success in life, and that you will soon hear some good news. If you see anybody running quickly along, it is a sign of hearing of their death soon after. *(GD)*

If anyone dreams he is running, it is a good sign, especially if he imagines he runs away in fear, as that signifies security. When someone believes he runs after his enemy, that denotes victory and profit. To dream people run into one another signifies wrangling and arguments; if they are little children, that indicates happiness and good weather; nevertheless if those children are armed with sticks or staves, that suggests war and disagreements. *(T)*

To dream that you are running from a relentless pursuer is a warning that you will need to have all your wits about you to withstand some temptation which will be put in your way. To dream that you are running in pursuit of something or somebody indicates that you are too fond of relying on your own judgement. Unless you listen to the advice of your friends when it is offered, you will one day regret your obstinacy. *(M)*

───────── ♦ ─────────

RUST

To dream of rust means approaching sorrow, the decay of health, bad debts in business, separation from friends, loss of popularity, and many other evils which will be hard even for a philosophic mind to bear.   *(O)*

   To see rust on any bright object denotes a big disappointment in store for you; probably just when you are looking forward to attaining some long-desired goal, for something will occur to snatch success from your grasp.   *(M)*

SACKS

To dream of sacks foretells an unexpected happening which will cause you much uneasiness. *(M)*

———— ◆ ————

SAGE

To dream of sage signifies hard work, trouble, sadness and weakness. *(T)*

———— ◆ ————

SAILING

To dream you are sailing quietly on water denotes a peaceful life. *(P&F)*

To dream of sailing on a rough sea promises prosperity. If the sea is calm, however, beware of enemies who will seek to cause trouble between you and your friends. *(M)*

———— ◆ ————

SAILOR

To dream that you are talking to a sailor promises news from abroad. The girl who dreams she is engaged to a sailor will marry a shy man and she will have to take charge of things. *(M)*

———— ◆ ————

SAINTS

To dream you see a saint signifies consolation, and is a warning to live well and honestly. It also denotes good news, increase of reputation and authority. *(T)*

———— ◆ ————

SALAD

To dream of a salad signifies trouble and difficulty in the management of affairs. To dream you eat a salad signifies evil or sickness. *(T)*

———— ◆ ————

SALMON

A dream in which salmon play a prominent part, whether being caught or eaten, denotes that you are likely to see much of the world before finally settling down to marriage. *(O)*

———— ◆ ————

SALT

A bad omen. If you know of any enemies, it will be better to pacify them rather than arouse their hatred. If you try to harm them, you yourself will suffer. *(M)*

———— ♦ ————

SATIN
To dream you trade in satin signifies loss and misfortune. *(T)*

———— ♦ ————

SAUCEPAN
An omen of misfortune. Many problems will decend on you together, and you will need a stout heart to battle against them. *(M)*

———— ♦ ————

SAUSAGES
To dream you see sausages signifies domestic troubles. If you are making them, it indicates illness. *(OM)*

———— ♦ ————

SAWING
To dream of sawing wood foretells that you will do something that you will afterwards regret. If a young fellow dreams this he will probably offend his sweetheart and find it hard work to get her to overlook the disagreement. *(M)*

———— ♦ ————

SCABS
To dream your arms or elbows are covered in scabs or ulcers signifies annoyance, sadness and failure in business. To dream your legs are scabby signifies fruitless anxiety. If anyone dreams their skin is scabby, they will grow rich proportionately to the number of scabs. *(T)*

To dream that you are covered in scabs is the forerunner of great success and riches. You may marry someone rich, or receive a gift of a considerable sum of money. *(DSG)*

———— ♦ ————

SCHOOL
To dream of attending school means that you are ashamed of your ignorance and will set to work in earnest. A golden opportunity will shortly occur of which you will only be able to avail yourself if you add to your present stock of knowledge. *(O)*

To dream you go back to school but cannot learn your lessons shows you are about to undertake something you do not understand. *(OM)*

———— ♦ ————

SCIENCES
To dream you study the sciences signifies cheerfulness. *(T)*

———— ♦ ————

SCISSORS
To merely see a pair of scissors is a sign of an early marriage. To dream of

using scissors is a warning that, by dividing your attention between two ambitions, you will realise neither. You must make up your mind which of the two you would prefer, and concentrate your energy on attaining it. To see many pairs of scissors together denotes that you will suffer much through unrequited love. *(M)*

────── ◆ ──────

SCRATCH

To dream that you have been scratched with nails signifies that you will repay your debts; or that you will be hurt by the people who scratched you. *(A)*

To dream that anyone scratches the soles of their feet indicates loss through flattery. *(T)*

────── ◆ ──────

SCREAMING

To dream that you hear screaming is a sign that someone you know will meet with a serious accident. If the screams are prolonged, that person will never really recover from the injuries received. To dream that you are screaming is a sign that you will receive a proposal, which it will be in your interest to accept. *(M)*

────── ◆ ──────

SCREW

To dream of a small screw is a good sign and indicates success in all you undertake; but to dream of a large screw indicates trouble brought about by love affairs. *(M)*

────── ◆ ──────

SCYTHE

Time's fatal weapon proves troubles approaching
Some family sickness or false friends encroaching. *(MS)*

To dream of a scythe foretells injuries from enemies and disappointments in love. *(DSG)*

────── ◆ ──────

SEA

To dream you see the sea blue and gently waving signifies joy, and the successful performance of business; but if the sea is calm, it signifies problems and delays; and when it is tempestuous, it denotes anxiety, losses and adversity. To dream you fall into the water or into the sea, and that you wake suddenly signifies that you will become involved with a married woman, and that you will find it hard to disengage yourself from the hands of envious enemies. *(T)*

For a young man to dream that he walks on the sea signifies the love of a delightful woman; but to a woman it foretells a dissolute life. This dream is good also to those who are employed looking after people or in government, for they will receive a good salary and be well regarded. *(A)*

To dream you are sailing on a smooth sea is a good omen. In love, it foretells that you and your partner will be happy together and live comfortably. To dream you are sailing on a rough sea foretells many difficulties in life, particularly a disappointment in love. To dream you are cast away on a deserted, rocky shore indicates that after many troubles and difficulties, you will become rich and happy.   *(GD)*

To dream that you are surrounded by the sea indicates that someone is nursing a grudge against you, and you must be careful to contradict in no uncertain terms any malicious scandal you may hear against yourself. To dream that you witness a storm at sea is a sign that a close relative will bring disgrace and disagreement to your family.   *(M)*

───────── ♦ ─────────

SEA BIRDS

To see sea birds such as cormorants indicates danger to mariners, but not death. To others they signify their supposed friends, who are either whores, liars or thieves, and if the dreamer loses anything, he will never recover it again.   *(A)*

───────── ♦ ─────────

SEASHORE

To dream of sitting by the seashore or of walking on it means that you can shortly expect to take a long voyage. Should you be sitting on a stone, it means many pleasant adventures, but to be seated on grass indicates shipwreck and disaster.   *(O)*

───────── ♦ ─────────

SEAT

To dream that you have fallen off your seat signifies that you will lose your job.   *(OM)*

───────── ♦ ─────────

SEWING

For a young woman to dream of sewing is a favourable omen, indicating that she will shortly marry one of the most loving husbands, whose home she will make happy and comfortable by her good sense and industry. *(O)*

───────── ♦ ─────────

SHADOW

To dream that you see a shadow denotes that you will do something of which you will be ashamed.   *(M)*

───────── ♦ ─────────

SHAVING

To dream you are shaving or cutting someone's hair signifies profit to the person whose hair is being cut, and bad luck to the dreamer.   *(T)*

To dream you are being shaved or that your head has been shaved is a very unfavourable omen. In love, it denotes treachery and disappointment and unfaithfulness and arguments in marriage. To the tradesman it augurs loss of goods and business; to the sailor, an unpleasant and stormy voyage; to the farmer, bad crops and diseases among his livestock.   *(OM)*

———— ♦ ————

SHAWL
If a girl dreams of getting a new shawl it foretells that she will soon have a new boyfriend who will be very attentive and likeable. If she dreams that her lover gives her a shawl, that interesting young man is currently thinking of his next partner, and will soon be involved elsewhere. *(M)*

———— ♦ ————

SHEARING SHEEP
To dream you see sheep-shearing is indicative of loss of property, the affections of the person you love and even your liberty; though to dream that you are shearing them yourself shows that you will gain an advantage over someone who meant to harm you.   *(GD2)*

———— ♦ ————

SHEEP
To dream you see or have many sheep signifies wealth and plenty. *(T)*

To dream of sheep signifies advancement, especially to those who want to be in government or for those who are already in powerful positions. It is also a good dream for academics and schoolmasters.   *(A)*

To dream you see a flock of sheep feeding is a very favourable omen since it denotes success in life. To the lover, it indicates your sweetheart is faithful, good-tempered and inclined to marry you; for those who are married, it denotes children, who will be very happy, become rich, and be great comforts in your later life; to tradesmen, it foretells increase of business and wealth, but also warns that one of his employees is untrustworthy; to the sailor, nothing can be a greater sign of good luck, his next voyage will be pleasant and lucrative, and his sweetheart kind and true. To dream you see sheep running away from you shows that pretended friends are endeavouring to do you an injury, and that your children will meet with persecutions and great troubles. In love, such a dream shows your sweetheart is fickle and unlikely to make you happy.   *(GD)*

To dream of seeing sheep indicates general prosperity in your affairs, but also that success will not be the result of great ability on your part.   *(O)*

A flock of sheep promises wealth; one sheep alone, an easy life.   *(M)*

———— ♦ ————

SHEPHERD
To dream of a shepherd is a bad omen.   *(OM)*

———— ♦ ————

SHERRY
If a man dreams he is drunk on sherry, or another sweet and pleasant

wine, it is a sign he will have powerful friends who will help him grow rich.
(T)

SHIP

To dream you are in a ship and see a clear light a long way off indicated that you will not experience many problems and will achieve your ambitions. If you dream you are walking in a boat or ship and entertaining yourself, you will have comfort and success in your affairs; but if the water is rough it indicates the opposite. To dream of being in a boat or ship in danger of overturning is a sign of danger, unless the dreamer is a prisoner in which case it denotes liberty and freedom. To sail in a ship or see ships sailing is a good sign. To see ships laden with goods signifies prosperity. To see ships endangered by a storm signifies peril. *(T)*

To dream that you are on a ship predicts that you will not take any really long journey by water. To see a ship is a warning not to jump at an offer which will shortly be made to you. It will be to your advantage to reject it. *(M)*

See also **BOAT, SAILING, WATER.**

SHIPWRECK

To dream of a voyage in which you are shipwrecked means that you and a companion will shortly start on a journey liking each other, but you will return hating each other intensely. *(O)*

To dream that you are on a sinking ship denotes false friends. You must be on your guard against confiding any secret for some time. *(M)*

SHIRT

To dream of putting on a shirt signifies travelling in foreign countries. *(A)*

To dream of a shirt is an omen of good fortune. Whatever happens you can always keep smiling. No serious troubles will happen to you. *(M)*

SHOES

To dream you are wearing good shoes signifies financial advantages and a good reputation. The opposite signifies damage, disdain and dishonour. To dream you make shoes or slippers signifies poverty, except to artists. To dream you have new shoes on signifies comfort. To dream you see old shoes signifies loss. *(T)*

To dream of shoes falling off your feet or being old denotes poverty and distress; that you go barefooted signifies you will suffer much pain and affliction. *(D&M)*

To dream you have a new pair of shoes denotes triumph over enemies. *(GD)*

To dream of your shoes being in need of repair is not a good dream, because it signifies that you will often be short of money. *(O)*

If a man dreams of losing his shoes and walking barefoot, it signifies that he will encounter reproaches, especially if he dreams it on the first day of the new moon. *(OM)*

The lover who dreams that he or she is wearing new shoes will suffer from fickleness in the opposite sex, and will not marry his or her present sweetheart. Old shoes promise success in marriage. To married people, new shoes warn of coming financial problems, while old ones indicate that a stroke of good luck is coming to the dreamer. *(M)*

SHOOTING

To dream you shoot with a bow signifies comfort; that you fire a gun indicates profit, deceit and grief through anger. *(T)*

To dream you are out shooting is very favourable if you kill plenty of game. But if you dream you kill nothing, then it indicates bad luck and disappointment in love. *(OM)*

See also **FIREARMS**.

SHOOTING STAR

To dream of seeing a shooting star means that lovers will be ardent in their affection. *(O)*

SHOPS

When a man believes a shop is destroyed by fire, it signifies loss of goods and possessions. *(T)*

SHOULDERS

If anyone dreams he has large shoulders which are more brawny than usual, that signifies good luck, strength and prosperity, although such a dream is bad for prisoners as it denotes annoyance and grief. and that they are in danger of enduring much pain. To dream that your shoulders are painful or swollen signifies trouble and displeasure from relations. *(T)*

SHOWER

To dream of a light shower signifies gain and profit to labourers, but quite the opposite to business men, mechanics or craftsmen to whom it denotes obstruction, loss and damage to their merchandise. *(T)*

See also **RAIN**.

SICKNESS

To dream of sickness is only fortunate to those in captivity or want. *(D&M)*

To the young, dreaming of sickness means marriage, although not always happy; the old dreaming of sickness may expect to receive money, often after it has ceased to be or much use to them. *(O)*

SIGHS

To dream of hearing sighs denotes trouble and anguish.   *(D&M)*

———— ♦ ————

SIGHT

If anyone dreams he has lost his sight, he will violate his word, or else he or some of his children are in danger of death, or he will never see his friends again. To dream you have good and quick sight is an extraordinarily good dream, and indicates success; but a troubled and weak sight signifies want of money, and failure in business.   *(T)*

———— ♦ ————

SIGNPOST

If you see a signpost, you must change your business methods or you will lose out. If you are in love, you will never succeed unless you are friendly and honest with your partner's parents.

———— ♦ ————

SILK

To dream you trade with a stranger in silk signifies profit and joy.   *(T)*
   To dream of silk either in pieces or for sewing signifies prosperity.   *(GD)*
   For a married woman to dream of being dressed in silk shows her husband is fond of a whore, who will almost ruin him.   *(DSG)*
   To dream you are dressed in silk foretells that you will become rich. If a girl dreams of it she will soon see her lover.   *(OM)*

———— ♦ ————

SILKWORMS

      These insects are good and productive to see;
      For while they instruct, stimulative they'll be
      To industrious habits and sobriety.   *(MS)*

———— ♦ ————

SILVER

If anyone dreams he gathers up gold and silver, it signifies deceit and loss. To dream you eat silver signifies anger.   *(T)*
   If a pregnant woman dreams of silver, it shows she will have a girl and a straightforward delivery, but the child will not be wealthy.   *(DSG)*
   To dream of silver shows false friends are around you and will try to ruin you; in love, it denotes falsehood in your sweetheart. To dream you are receiving or packing up pieces of silver or money, if they are of little value, denotes want and a prison; if they are worth slightly more they indicate the receipt of a small sum of money, and the acquisition of some new friends; but if they are coins of value, they denote lack of success in all your undertakings.   *(GD)*
   To dream you are looking at silver means that you are in danger of an attack of illness, only to be warded off by the greatest attention to cleanliness. If the silver is given to you in a dream it denotes sorrow.   *(O)*

SINGING

If anyone dreams he is singing, it signifies he will have reason to weep. To dream you hear singing or people playing music signifies consolation in adversity, and recovery of health to those who are sick. To dream you sing a hymn or psalm signifies problems in business. *(T)*

To hear singing in dreams signifies deceit. *(E)*

To dream that you are singing a solo is not a good dream, and signifies at best that you will soon try to shout your own praises, but that the attempt will not bring the success you expect. Dreaming of taking part in a duet foretells that you are shortly to be reconciled to someone you argued with some time ago. *(O)*

━━━━━━ ♦ ━━━━━━

SISTERS

To dream you see your dead brothers and sisters signifies a long life for the dreamer. *(OM)*

━━━━━━ ♦ ━━━━━━

SKELETON

If you see a skeleton it is a sign of anxiety and domestic troubles. *(OM)*

━━━━━━ ♦ ━━━━━━

SKINS

To dream you see a dark-skinned stranger is a sign of achievement and success. *(T)*

To dream you have any disease or irritation of the skin signifies wealth and achievement; but to dream you see others with skin diseases signifies anger and worries. *(A)*

━━━━━━ ♦ ━━━━━━

SKY

To see the sky clear and beautiful means that you will be loved and esteemed by everyone, and that even those who envy you will come to like you. If you dream of the sky, you are probably of a calm and affable character. Some eminent authors affirm that to dream of seeing the air clear and free from clouds signifies that something which has been lost or stolen will be discovered, and you will be respected and liked by everyone, and make a successful voyage or journey, if you are planning this. But on the contrary, if you dream of a cloudy sky, that signifies sadness, sickness, melancholy and business problems. *(T)*

━━━━━━ ♦ ━━━━━━

SLAUGHTER

To see people sacrificed or killed is good for it is a sign that your business is accomplished or near completion. *(A)*

━━━━━━ ♦ ━━━━━━

SLEEP

To sleep under shady trees with a beautiful woman means success in love. *(D&M)*

To dream you sleep is an evil sign. *(OM)*

SLIPPERS

For a bachelor to dream of a pair of slippers portends he will soon marry; for a young woman it signifies that she has recently met the man who in all probability will be her partner for life. *(O)*

————— ♦ —————

SMELLING

To dream of sweet-smelling flowers in season signifies joy, pleasure and consolation. To dream of smelling them out of season, if they are white, signifies business problems and lack of success; if yellow, the difficulties will not be as severe; if red, the difficulty will be extreme, and it may even signify death. To dream of smelling roses in season is a good sign to anyone except those who are sick or criminals as they are in danger of death or severe illness. Roses out of season indicate the opposite. To dream that you smell marjoram, hyssop, rosemary, sage or other herbs signifies hard work, trouble, sadness and weakness, except to doctors to whom such dreams are propitious. To dream you smell lilies out of season signifies your hopes and ambitions will be frustrated. For a woman to smell laurel, olive or palm means she will have children. A girl will soon be married, a man will experience joy, prosperity, abundance and success in his enterprises. To dream your feet smell bad signifies problems. *(T)*

————— ♦ —————

SMOKE

To dream of smoke signifies that you will meet with success at an early date but it will be very short lived. *(OM)*

————— ♦ —————

SNAILS

To dream of snails signifies intemperance and inconstancy. *(OM)*

————— ♦ —————

SNAKES OR SERPENTS

To dream you see a coiled snake signifies danger and imprisonment; it also denotes sickness and hatred. To dream you see a snake signifies you will be deceived by your wife. To dream you kill a snake is a sign you will overcome your enemies and anyone who envies you. To dream you see a snake that tries to bite your feet signifies envy; and if the creature bites painfully, that signifies sadness and discontent. To dream you see a serpent or seven-headed hydra signifies sin and temptation. To fight with serpents and adders signifies the overthrow of enemies. To dream you see many serpents signifies that you will be deceived by a woman. *(T)*

To dream you are bitten by a serpent shows danger from unknown and subtle enemies. *(P&F)*

To be bitten by a snake indicates that your adversaries will hurt you. If the snake hisses, however, they will have no power over you. *(D&M)*

To see a large serpent rise up to attack you indicates a powerful female enemy whom it will be very hard to avoid. If it tries to hurt you but cannot, beware of false praise. If you kill it, you will defeat your adversaries.   *(GA)*

———————— ♦ ————————

SNOW
To dream of snow in winter has no particular meaning because your mind is recalling the cold of the preceding day. If it is in another season, however, that denotes a good harvest to farmers; to business men, it signifies problems; and to soldiers, that their intentions will be frustrated.   *(T)*

To dream you see the ground covered with snow, or that it is snowing out of season, is a very favourable dream.   *(GD)*

To dream of snow lying on the ground denotes prosperity, but to see it melting away means that you are in danger of losing money which you have worked hard to make.   *(O)*

> The snow will conduce to the most pleasant scenes;
> But forbear, and sin not when loose love would infringe
> Lest your fingers should meet a most confounded singe.   *(MS)*

———————— ♦ ————————

SOIL
To dream that the soil is black signifies sorrow, melancholy and lack of intelligence.   *(A)*

———————— ♦ ————————

SOLD
To dream of being sold is a good sign unless you are rich or sick.   *(OM)*

———————— ♦ ————————

SOLDIERS
To dream you see soldiers is a good sign. To see them come against you signifies sadness.   *(T)*

To dream of seeing soldiers denotes to the lover that your lover's father will force you to move.   *(D&M2)*

To dream of soldiers means that you have a considerable number of enemies, and from their actions in your dream you will be able to conclude whether they are to beat you, or vice versa.   *(O)*

A young woman engaged to be married will go abroad soon after her wedding if she dreams that she has talked to a soldier.   *(M)*

———————— ♦ ————————

SOLES
To dream of soles means misfortune and anxiety.   *(OM)*

———————— ♦ ————————

SORROW
To dream of sorrow and being comforted means accidents and injury to the rich, but aid and assistance to the poor.   *(D&M)*

———————— ♦ ————————

SPARROW
To dream of sparrows denotes that you will not receive much assistance

from others in life, but will have to rely mainly on your own exertions. These however, will enable you to get a full share of what is available.   *(O)*

These birds are omens of little good. You will never make a great success in life, and will always have to work hard to keep the wolf from the door.
(M)

———— ♦ ————

SPARROW HAWK
A dream in which a sparrow hawk predominates is a warning to the dreamer against enemies who are conspiring against him or her.   *(OM)*

———— ♦ ————

SPECTRE
Few dreams are more certain of good luck to the dreamer than to dream of spectres.   *(OM)*

———— ♦ ————

SPIDER
Should you dream of a spider you can infer that the failure of efforts you recently made must not discourage you because, by continued perseverance, you will in the long run be sure to succeed.   *(O)*

Always omens of good luck. If you dream that the spiders are crawling over you, you may expect to receive a large sum of money before you are much older.   *(M)*

Spiders appearing in a dream signify good fortune. If you kill one it foretells future enjoyment for you. To see one spinning is a sign that much money is to come to you.   *(OM)*

———— ♦ ————

SPINNING
To dream of spinning is good and shows a person to be diligent and industrious.   *(OM)*

———— ♦ ————

SPIT
To dream you are in a kitchen turning a spit is the forerunner of troubles and misfortunes. Expect to be robbed, to lose your trade or money and that your friends will desert you. If you are in love, it shows your lover is bad-tempered, lazy and doomed to misfortune and poverty.   *(GD)*

———— ♦ ————

SPLEEN
The spleen denotes the pleasure and content between friends. If anyone dreams his spleen is enlarged and very healthy, he will be invited to a feast or celebration which will be very enjoyable. If, on the contrary, he imagines his spleen is swollen or diseased, some business or other of great importance will fall into his hands, which will bring him problems and anxiety.   *(T)*

———— ♦ ————

SPRAIN
To dream of a sprain means that you can expect an attempt to be made to

borrow money from you under false pretences, and if you yield, you will
experience financial problems. *(O)*

SQUIRRELS

To dream of squirrels signifies that the dreamer will love a bad-tempered
woman by whom he will be bewitched. *(T)*

To dream of a squirrel shows that enemies are endeavouring to slander
your reputation; to the lover, it shows your sweetheart is bad-tempered
and drinks too much; if you have a law-suit, it will be decided against you;
if in trade, con men will try to defraud you, and you will quarrel with your
principal creditor. *(GD)*

A sign that you will be wise to be contented with your situation.
Although you may never be rich, you will be loved by your family and
lead, on the whole, a quiet life. To a girl this dream indicates that someone
has fallen in love with her, but will be too shy to approach her. *(M)*

STAG

To dream of a stag signifies that your investments will prove profitable. If
you chase one it foretells losses in business. *(OM)*

STAR

To dream you see a clear starry sky signifies prosperity and advantage in a
voyage or journey, good news and profit in everything you do. If the stars
are pale, it indicates all kinds of problems. To dream you see the stars
disappear signifies loss and great anxiety or even death. Such a dream is
only good to criminals who will escape punishment. To dream you see the
stars fall on top of your house signifies sickness, or that the house will be
empty, or destroyed by fire. If you see the stars shining into the house, it
signifies that the chief person of the family will be in danger of death. To
dream you see stars with streaming tails signifies future evils by war and
famine. *(T)*

To dream you see the stars shining very brightly is success to the lover,
and good news from a distant country; to see them fall denotes health.
(GD)

To dream of watching a star means that you will soon meet a beautiful or
handsome lover. *(O)*

STARCHING

To dream you are starching clothes signifies profit. *(T)*

To dream you are starching linen shows that you will be married to an
industrious person, that you will be successful in life and save money,
perhaps also that you are about to receive a letter containing some
pleasant news. *(GD)*

STARLING
To dream you see a starling signifies a small discontent.　　　　*(T)*

———— ♦ ————

STATUES
To dream you make statues, whether of clay or anything else, is good for teachers and those who look after children. Statues also signify children to those who are married.　　　　*(A)*

To dream of seeing a bronze statue moving signifies riches.　　*(OM)*

———— ♦ ————

STINGS
To dream of stings signifies grief and anxiety. To many they have signified love and also injuries by wicked people.　　　　*(A)*

To dream of being stung by bees is unlucky, for it means that you are about to enter on a succession of difficulties.　　　　*(O)*

———— ♦ ————

STOMACH
If anyone dreams that his stomach is bigger and fatter than usual, his family and property will increase proportionately to the size of his stomach. If you dream that your stomach has grown thin, you will escape a bad accident. If anyone dreams that their stomach is swollen but still empty, they will become poor, though they will be well regarded by many people.　　　　*(T)*

To be wounded in the stomach by anyone you know signifies bad news to old women; but to young men and women it indicates good news.　　*(A)*

———— ♦ ————

STONE
To dream of having a stone thrown at you denotes that you are in danger through the too-free use of speech, and is a hint that to call people fools and expect that they will applaud you as intelligent is a mistake.　　*(O)*

———— ♦ ————

STORKS
To dream you see storks in flocks in the air foretells the approach of enemies and thieves. In winter it signifies bad weather. To dream you see two storks together signifies marriage and procreation of good and helpful children to their parents.　　　　*(T)*

———— ♦ ————

STORM
To dream of a storm is an omen of dangers and difficulties.　　*(OM)*

———— ♦ ————

STOUTNESS
To dream of growing stout signifies that you are on the way to considerable wealth.　　　　*(O)*

STRANGE PLACES

To dream of being in a strange place denotes a good legacy from a relation while you are in prison. *(DSG)*

———— ♦ ————

STRANGERS

If anyone dreams he strikes a stranger with a sword, it signifies victory, assurance and success in his affairs; if it is with a stick, it signifies command and profit. To dream you trade with a stranger signifies profit. *(T)*

To dream of a complete stranger indicates the return of a long-absent friend. *(OM)*

———— ♦ ————

STRAW

To dream of straw signifies misfortune and losses. *(OM)*

———— ♦ ————

STRAWBERRIES

To dream of strawberries denotes to pregnant women, a straightforward delivery of a boy. To a girl, it means marriage with a man who will become rich and make her happy, while to a young man they denote that his wife will be sweet-tempered and they will have many children, all boys.

(D&M2)

The young woman who dreams that she is eating strawberries will receive a proposal of marriage from a wealthy man. If she dreams that she is gathering strawberries, her love will be unrequited. The married person who dreams of eating strawberries will shortly receive an invitation to attend a social function; but if she dreams she is gathering the fruit, she will have cause to lose hope of ever realising her dearest desire. *(M)*

———— ♦ ————

STREET

To dream of a street in the heart of a great city is a sign that you will soon move to the country to find more peace and happiness there than is possible in the town. *(O)*

———— ♦ ————

STRIKING

To dream you strike someone on the ear with your hand or punch them with your fist signifies peace and love between a man and his wife. If the dreamer is unmarried, it means he will soon court a lady for whom he has great respect, and that he will defeat his enemies. If a woman dreams that she strikes her lover, that signifies she is not secure, and that her lover will by some accident or other get into trouble. *(T)*

———— ♦ ————

STUMBLING

Dreaming of stumbling means that a business in which you are interested is about to sustain severe losses through quite innocent misfortune. *(O)*

SUGAR
A dream into which sugar enters, whether eaten or seen only, denotes approaching illness, but not of a severe nature. *(O)*

———— ♦ ————

SUN
The sun represents unity, truth, light, fruitfulness, heat, abundance and wealth. To dream you see the sun rise above the horizon signifies good news and success in your designs. To dream you see the sun set signifies the opposite. If a woman has such a dream, it signifies she will have a son. To dream you see the sun signifies completion of business and revelation of secret things; to the sick it indicates recovery, to the prisoner liberty, and a cure to anyone with an eye problem. To dream you see the sun clouded, red or hot, signifies obstruction in business, death to your children, or danger to yourself; but such a dream is good to criminals. To dream that the sun descends upon your house signifies danger from fire. To dream the sun shines in your bedroom signifies gain, profit and happiness, and a son to married people. To dream you see the sun obscured, or disappear, is a very bad sign, except to a criminal, for to others it usually signifies death or at least loss of sight through an accident or illness. To see the sun shine around your head signifies pardon to criminals and good reputation to others. To dream you enter a house where the sun shines signifies acquiring property. To see the sun clear signifies that you will achieve your ambitions. To dream you see the sun in a cloud signifies danger. To see the sun and moon fall together is a bad sign. *(T)*

To dream the sun rises or sets in a clear sky is a very good augury to those who are just going to law. To dream of the sun rising and setting in a cloudy sky is bad. *(D&M)*

To dream you see the sun shine shows accumulation of riches, and enjoying a responsible job. *(GD)*

Should the sun go behind a cloud and then emerge again, you may take it that even if you experience some problems all will come good in the end. *(O)*

If you are in love and dream that you see the sun shining brilliantly, your lover will make you a good partner in life. For a married person, the dream promises an improvement in domestic and business affairs. *(M)*

———— ♦ ————

SUNBEAMS
To dream you see sunbeams come into your bed signifies a fever. *(T)*

———— ♦ ————

SUNDAY
For a young woman to dream of it being Sunday means that she is about to form an alliance with a clergyman, and the happiness or discontent of that alliance many be gathered from the brightness or otherwise of the day seen in the dream. *(O)*

SUNRISE

To dream of seeing the sun rise denotes that you are about to take a step up in the world, perhaps by being offered a partnership in a company in which you are at present only an employee. *(O)*

To dream you see the sun rise is an omen that all through your life you will suffer trials through conceit and vanity. *(M)*

———— ♦ ————

SUNSET

To dream that you are watching a particularly fine sunset is an omen of lingering illness, and should the sun disappear suddenly the illness will end only in death. *(M)*

———— ♦ ————

SUPPER

To dream that this meal foretells news of a birth. *(OM)*

———— ♦ ————

SWALLOW

To dream of a swallow signifies good works, weddings and music, and promises a practical wife or compliant housekeeper. *(A)*

To dream of a swallow signifies good news and good luck to those in whose houses they build their nests. *(T)*

To dream you see a swallow is a sign that you will be forced by unforeseen circumstances to undertake a long journey. If several of these birds appear you will return much richer than you were when you started out. *(M)*

———— ♦ ————

SWANS

To dream that you see a swan signifies joy, revealing of secrets and health to the dreamer, but if it sings it foretells death. *(T)*

To dream of seeing swans denotes a happy marriage and many children, who will do well and become rich, and fill your old age with joy and happiness; to the lover, they denote constancy and affection in your sweetheart, in trade they show success but much anxiety from the disclosure of secrets. *(GD)*

> Complicate models of pomp and placidity,
> Matrimonial content and jealous acidity. *(MS)*

To dream of a swan signifies the birth of a male musician and the creation of beautiful music. *(A)*

These graceful birds are in all circumstances proof that your love is well placed and highly esteemed. *(M)*

———— ♦ ————

SWEARING

To dream that you hear violent arguments and swearing is a sign that you will go down in the world, and be short of money. *(M)*

SWEEPING

To dream of sweeping means that the death of a relative, though at first a sorrow, will eventually prove of advantage in improving your worldly position.

(O)

The unmarried woman who dreams that she is sweeping will one day be wealthy and have everything she wants. To a married woman the dream promises a dutiful family, who will more than repay her for her care and attention.

(M)

━━━━ ◆ ━━━━

SWEETS

To dream you taste sweets signifies subtlety.

(T)

━━━━ ◆ ━━━━

SWELLING

To dream that your face is swollen shows that you will accumulate wealth; or if in love, that your sweetheart will come into money and marry you.

(DSG)

━━━━ ◆ ━━━━

SWIMMING

To dream of swimming in a large river signifies future peril and danger.

(T)

To dream of swimming denotes much hardwork, sadness and sickness.

(D&M)

To dream you are swimming with your head above the water denotes great success in your undertakings, whether they are in love, trade, sea or farming. To dream of swimming with your head under water shows that you will experience a great trouble, and hear some very unpleasant news from a person thought dead. In trade it shows loss of business, and that you may be imprisoned for debt; in love it denotes disappointment. *(GD)*

━━━━ ◆ ━━━━

SWORDS

If anyone dreams he has been stabbed with a sword, he will receive an extraordinary kindness from the person who attacked him. If blood is not drawn, the advantage and delight will be the less. If anyone dreams that he is mortally wounded with a sword, it is a sign that he will receive several good turns from whoever wounded him, according to the proportion, number and size of the wounds. If a woman dreams she is stabbed by a sword or that she herself either out of courage or in her own self defence, strikes anyone, she will be honoured and if married have a male child. If anyone dreams that his friend strikes him over the breast with a sword, it signifies bad news to the old, but friendship to the young. *(T)*

To dream of having a sword is a sign of poverty; if you dream you see a man flourish a sword it indicates that you will make a loss. A young girl who imagines her lover wears a sword will marry a poor man. *(M)*

TABLE
A dream in which a table is the most prominent object means that your life is to be calm and methodical, without startling events, and almost entirely destitute of ups and downs. *(O)*

---◆---

TABLEAU
If a young lady dreams that she is appearing in a tableau it is a sign that her future husband will be fond of showy dress, and not very intelligent. *(M)*

---◆---

TABLECLOTH
To dream of a dirty tablecloth foretells that you will have plenty to eat. *(M)*

---◆---

TAFFETA
To dream of taffeta signifies that you will have wealth but that it will bring you no satisfaction. *(OM)*

---◆---

TAILOR
If a young girl dreams that her boyfriend is a tailor and she likes him it is a sign that she will marry an easy-going chap, who will allow her to be both master and mistress after marriage. The married woman who dreams of a tailor will do well to give less thought to dress than before. Vanity is causing her to be talked about and snubbed. *(M)*

---◆---

TALKING
To dream you talk idly at church and are a daydream signifies envy and sin. To talk with your brother signifies anxiety. With powerful men signifies honour, profit and gain. To dream you talk with an enemy signifies you must beware of him. To talk with your son signifies damage. *(T)*

To dream you see many people in debate shows some design against you, and that you will argue with relations. *(D&M)*

---◆---

TAMARIND TREE
To dream of tamarinds shows much anxiety and uneasiness caused by a woman; failure in trade; also, a rainy season, and bad news from abroad. *(D&M2)*

TAMING
To dream you tame wild beasts signifies damage. *(T)*

———— ♦ ————

TARTS
To dream you make tarts signifies joy and profit. *(T)*

———— ♦ ————

TEA
After dreaming that you have received an invitation to tea with a friend, be wary of new friends. You will probably meet someone it will be well to avoid. To dream you are drinking tea is a sign that, although many joys will come to you during life, they wsill be interspersed with troubles, which will give you rather more than your share of worries. The girl who dreams she is taking tea with her lover will not find much favour with the young man's family, although there will not be any serious opposition to the match. *(M)*

To dream of sitting drinking tea means that gossip will soon be busy with your reputation, and that you will in consequence be caused a great deal of annoyance. *(O)*

———— ♦ ————

TEAM
To dream of a team denotes death in your family, a bad-tempered lover and lack of success in undertakings. *(DSG)*

———— ♦ ————

TEA POT
To dream of a tea pot signifies that you will soon form new friendships. *(OM)*

———— ♦ ————

TEARS
To dream of tears has the opposite meaning. You will have joy and pleasure on the on the day following your dream. *(OM)*

———— ♦ ————

TEETH
The teeth are taken for the closest relations and best friends; the front teeth are applied to children, brother and other close relations, the upper teeth signify the males, and the lower the females. If anyone dreams they have lost or damaged one of their teeth, that indicates injury or death to a relation. But if you dream that your teeth are more attractive and whiter than usual that signifies joy, prosperity, good news and friendship among relations. If a person dreams that one of their teeth has grown longer than the rest, they will be in trouble with some of their relations. The upper eye-tooth signifies the father and the lower the mother. If anyone dreams that one of his front teeth is loose, or turned black, or that it is painful, one of his friends or relations will be sick, or in trouble. If anyone dreams their

teeth have grown more attractive, white and firm than usual, they will enjoy happiness and profit from their relations and friends. If anyone imagines they are cleaning their teeth they will give money to their relations or friends. If some of the teeth are larger than the rest, so that the dreamer is hindered from speaking and eating, that signifies arguments among relations. To dream you pull out your teeth signifies death. *(T)*

To dream your teeth are taken out or fall out denotes loss of children or some relations. *(P&F)*

To dream you have lost your teeth shows the death of friends; to dream that you have no teeth at all signifies profit, but to dream of false teeth shows sudden death. *(D&M2)*

The mouth represents the house, and the teeth the inhabitants; those of the right side, the men, the other, the women. The right side also signifies the elder, the left the younger. The eye-teeth signify those of middle age. The front teeth signify the old people. If you dream you lose a tooth, it indicates the death of a relation. Teeth can also signify possessions. By the front teeth are meant hidden treasures, by others a vessel or some such thing of little importance. To anyone in debt, loss of a tooth can mean loss of possessions. The teeth falling out in one go signifies that everyone will leave you. For the sick to dream they lose any teeth signifies long illness but not death. To dream you have black or rotten teeth and that you lose them signifies that the dreamer shall be delivered from problems and anger. Also by this dream some have lost their old people. To dream you have gold teeth is good for anyone who studies public speaking, but to others it can mean fire damage to their house or sickness. To dream you have wax teeth signifies sudden death. To dream you have lead or tin teeth signifies shame or dishonour; teeth of glass or wood signify a violent death; silver teeth signify money earned by eloquence. To dream you lose your teeth and grow new ones signifies a change of condition for good or bad, according to the number of the teeth. To dream that your teeth are in your hand signifies loss of children. To dream of grating your teeth signifies you will end your pain and misery by eloquence. *(A)*

———————— ◆ ————————

TELEGRAM

For a young woman to dream of receiving or sending a telegram means that she is about to form a close relationship with a young man which will ripen into love, and end in happy marriage. *(O)*

To dream that you are sending a telegram is a sign that before very long you will be giving serious news to your friends. To dream that you receive a telegram indicates that you will be concerned at the silence of a friend from whom you have heard regularly. *(M)*

———————— ◆ ————————

TELEPHONE

To dream of receiving or making a telephone call signifies that you are on the eve of making a considerable sum by a lucky invention.   *(O)*

After dreaming that you are speaking over the telephone be prepared to hear that someone for whom you have had a great respect will be saying unkind things behind your back.   *(M)*

---◆---

TELESCOPE

A young man dreaming of looking through a telescope learns from it that his lover has another admirer of whom he should beware. If the telescope be seen pointing to the right it is an indication that at present she cares nothing for the rival.   *(O)*

To dream that you are looking through a telescope indicates that you will have trouble with your eyesight.   *(M)*

---◆---

TEMPESTS

To dream you are in a storm or a tempest shows that you will, after many difficulties, be very happy, that you will become extremely rich, and marry exceedingly well. For a lover to dream of being in a violent temper denotes that you will have many formidable rivals who, after causing you a great deal of anxiety and uneasiness, you will triumph over. It also indicates that you will receive good news from a long-absent friend abroad and who will have overcome many hardships and extreme difficulties.   *(GD)*

---◆---

TEMPTATION

If you dream you are tempted to do some foolish action you will experience much unrest through being the object of unjust suspicions. *(M)*

---◆---

THEATRE

To dream that you are in a theatre is a sign that you will shed many tears of repentance for some action which cannot be undone.   *(M)*

To dream of being in a theatre means that the realities of life will soon cease to interest you, that you will take refuge in dreamland and live on illusions till your last hour.   *(O)*

The theatre in a dream signifies sorrow caused by losses of money and of friends.   *(OM)*

> To dream you are in one forerunneth much glee
> And proves bliss from marriage, the produce will be. *(MS)*

---◆---

THEFT

To dream that you steal is only good to someone who is trying to deceive another.   *(A)*

---◆---

THIEVES

To dream of thieves denotes loss and trouble.   *(A)*

THIGHS

The thighs represent the relations. If anyone dreams that both his thighs are broken, or beaten black and blue, he will die in a foreign country alone, without the assistance of his relations. If a girl dreams this, she will be married to a stranger, and lead her life in some remote country, far away from her relations. If she is a wife, she will become a widow and lose her children. If anyone dreams that their thighs have grown bigger and stronger than usual, their relations will be promoted to an important position which will prove advantageous. If anyone dreams that he has been wounded on the thigh, he will not accomplish his desires, but be annoyed by his relations. To dream you see the fair and white thighs of a woman signifies health and joy. If a man dreams he has well-proportioned thighs it signifies a happy voyage. *(T)*

━━━━━━━━ ◆ ━━━━━━━━

THIMBLE

The girl who dreams that she has received a present of a thimble will never marry. To dream that you lose your thimble promises continued happiness in your home. *(M)*

To dream of a thimble signifies that your occupation will improve. *(OM)*

━━━━━━━━ ◆ ━━━━━━━━

THIRST

If anyone dreams his thirst is quenched with clear, fresh water, he will live happily and become very wealthy; if the water was luke warm or dirty, he will end his days ill and unhappy. *(T)*

To dream you are thirsty and cannot find a drink is a bad omen and a sign that the dreamer will not finish his business. *(A)*

It is extremely unlucky to dream that you are suffering from thirst; you will lose your money, and know what it is to be without a penny in your pocket. *(M)*

To be troubled in a dream by thirst means that you will shortly discover in yourself a craving for money, which will be a misfortune, as you are never likely to have more than is absolutely necessary. *(O)*

━━━━━━━━ ◆ ━━━━━━━━

THORNS

In dreams, thorns signify problems. *(DSG)*

To dream that you have a thorn in your foot indicates that you will move to another district, and will not like the people with whom you will have to associate. *(M)*

━━━━━━━━ ◆ ━━━━━━━━

THOUGHTS

To dream that you are unsettled in your thoughts signifies joy. *(DSG)*

THRESHING

Should you dream that you are threshing corn you will rise to an important position, and will have the satisfaction of knowing that you have achieved the success solely by your own efforts. *(M)*

———— ♦ ————

THROAT

If anyone dreams that his throat is cut with a knife, he will be injured by someone. If he dreams he cuts the throat of an acquaintance he will do him an injury; if he does not know the person, he will injure a stranger. To dream your throat is cut and you are not dead signifies hope and success in business. *(T)*

To dream that you have anything wrong with your throat may generally be taken to mean that you will have a good voice, if only you will take the trouble to develop it. *(M)*

———— ♦ ————

THRONE

After seeing an empty throne you must be prepared to hear that the head of your family has met with a serious accident. *(M)*

———— ♦ ————

THUMB

To dream that you have injured your thumb indicates that you will shortly be in a serious quandary. You will have to choose between giving offence to someone whom it would pay you to please, and making yourself look ridiculous in the eyes of your acquaintances. *(M)*

———— ♦ ————

THUNDER

To dream you hear thunder signifies that you will suffer from envious people spreading unkind rumours about you. *(T)*

To dream you hear thunder and see lightning is a very good omen; it denotes success in trade, good crops to the farmer, and a speedy and happy marriage to the lover. If you are looking for a job you will get it; if you have a law-suit, it will go in your favour; it also indicates news from a distant country, intimating that a close relative has oibtained a very lucrative situation, in which he will have an opportunity of doing his friends a great deal of good. *(GD)*

Be careful to keep clear of strangers of the opposite sex. If you ignore the warning, your sweetheart or partner in life will become jealous, and cause you much unhappiness. *(M)*

To hear thunder in a dream is unlucky for the unmarried as it indicates that all their love affairs are likely to have an unfortunate termination. To the married, middle aged and old it means the receipt of unexpected news. *(O)*

THUNDER BOLT

To dream you see a thunder bolt fall near you without a storm signifies that the dreamer will be forced to run away and live elsewhere. To dream that a thunder bolt falls on your head or on your house signifies loss of life and goods. *(T)*

———— ♦ ————

TIGER

If you dream that you escape from a tiger it is a good omen but it signifies great danger if you are caught by one. *(OM)*

———— ♦ ————

TIME

To dream of anyone playing music out of time indicates that if you persevere, you will become a musician, perhaps even a professional one. *(O)*

———— ♦ ————

TOADS

To dream of fighting with toads indicates success. *(D&M)*

———— ♦ ————

TOBACCO

To dream of smoking indicates waste, but is not exactly an omen of poverty, though waste always preceeds shortages. If you dream of seeing large piles of tobacco it is a sign of bad luck and loss in speculation. To dream you take snuff is a bad omen in love affairs, but if you dream you sneeze when you take it, it is a sign of long life. *(M)*

———— ♦ ————

TOMB

To dream you build or see a tomb is in general a good dream, but fallen and ill-kept graves are the opposite. *(A)*

To dream of tombs or skeletons denotes plenty of money. *(D&M)*

To dream of wandering among tombs denotes that you will shortly receive money through the death of a relation. *(O)*

To dream that you are erecting a tomb signifies marriages, weddings and the birth of children; but if the dreamer imagines that he sees the tomb fall to ruin, that signifies sickness and problems to him and his family. *(T)*

———— ♦ ————

TONGUE

If a lady dreams of having a sore on her tongue it is a sign that she has either spoken slander or will be tempted to do so. *(M)*

———— ♦ ————

TOP

To dream that you play with a spinning top signifies pain and travel which will lead to some advantage. *(A)*

TORCH

If you see a torch put out, it signifies sadness, sickness and financial problems. If you hold a burning torch it is a good sign, especially to the young, for it signifies that they will enjoy their lives, achieve their ambitions, overcome their enemies and be respected and liked. *(T)*

To dream of holding a torch or firebrand at night is good, especially to the young, to whom it most often signifies love; but to see someone else hold a torch is bad news to anyone who wants to conceal a secret. *(A)*

———— ◆ ————

TORTOISE

To dream of seeing a tortoise crawling along, especially if crawling up a hill, means for a man that he will reach a high position in life through hard work and perseverance. *(O)*

This animal signifies long life and success. *(OM)*

———— ◆ ————

TOWER

To dream that you are ascending a tower signifies that you will experience reverses in the fortune of your affairs. *(OM)*

———— ◆ ————

TOWN CLERK

To dream of being a town clerk signifies that you will do someone else's work with difficulty and without payment. *(A)*

———— ◆ ————

TRADING

To dream you are trading in wool with a stranger signifies profit; in iron, loss and misfortune; in silk, satin, velvet and other fine fabrics, profit and joy. *(T)*

———— ◆ ————

TRAGEDY

To dream you see a tragedy acted signifies hard work, loss of friends and money, with grief and anxiety. *(T)*

———— ◆ ————

TRAIN

To dream that you carry a young bride's train is a sign that you will meet a young man at a wedding who will fall in love with you. He will ask to see more of you, and even hint that he would like to marry you, but behind your back he will make inquiries whether you are likely to inherit any property or money. After dreaming that you see a train travelling quickly be careful not to undertake a long journey for at least a week. You will be in danger of losing your life if you ignore the warning. *(M)*

———— ◆ ————

TRANSFIGURATION

To dream that you are changed from small to large and then even larger is a good sign signifying increase of business and goods, but to be much larger than a man signifies death. For a man to dream he is a woman means that you will find a woman to love, or that your work will become easier. If a woman dreams that she is an unmarried man she will find a husband, or if she has no children she will have a son, but if she is both married and has a son, she will be a widow. To dream that you are made of gold means you will become very rich. To the sick, however, it means death. To dream that you are made of brass indicates success. To dream that you are made of iron foretells infinite miseries. To dream that you are made of earth indicates death, except to potters or anyone who earns their living through the earth. To be made of stone is a sign you will receive injuries and wounds. If you dream that you have been changed into a beast the significance depends on the animal in question. *(A)*

TRANSFORMATION

To dream you see yourself transformed into a tree signifies joy and profit. *(T)*

TRAPS

To dream of traps and anything used to catch animals is a bad omen, unless you are looking for employees. *(A)*

TRAVELLING

If you travel through a wood and catch yourself on the briars and bushes, it means that you will encounter many troubles and hindrances. To travel over high hills, and rocky places signifies advancement. *(OM)*

TREASURE

To dream you find a treasure shows you will be betrayed by your closest friend. *(GD)*

To dream you are seeking treasure is a sign that you will travel abroad and perhaps settle in a foreign country. To dream that you have found treasure is a sign that you will place confidence in someone unworthy of your regard. *(M)*

TREES

To dream you see all sorts of green or blossoming trees is a sign of of comfort and enjoyment; but if you dream they are dry, or without leaves, uprooted, burned or struck by thunder, that denotes annoyance, fear, displeasure and grief. If someone dreams he has gathered the fruit of an old tree, that indicates he will be heir to an elderly person. To dream you fell trees signifies loss. To see trees, or climb them signifies future honour. To see withered trees signifies deceit. To see trees bearing fruit signifies gain and profit. To see trees without blossom signifies completion of business. *(T)*

To dream you see trees in blossom denotes a happy marriage with your present lover and many children who will all do extremely well in life. To the tradesman it denotes success in business, and to the sailor, pleasant and lucrative voyages. To dream you are cutting down trees foretells heavy losses by trade and by sea; and also the death of a close relation or very dear friend. *(GD)*

To dream that you are planting trees foretells that, although at present there may seem little promise of your ever reaching a high position, your affairs will gradually improve until you will have nothing to worry you. *(M)*

To dream of seeing a tree growing means that though comparatively unimportant now, you will in the end be the most important person where you live. Should the tree seen in your dream be in leaf, it signifies that you will be happy in your children when you have them, and that some of them at least will rise to distinction. *(O)*

TROUT
To dream of trout signifies that your troubles will vanish. *(OM)*

TRUMPETS
To dream you play or hear trumpets played signifies trouble and arguments. *(T)*

To the tradesman it indicates the loss of business; to the farmer, bad crops; to the lover, insincerity in his lover. *(GD)*

To dream of playing the trumpet is good for anyone who fights, but it indicates the revealing of secrets, and means death to the sick. *(A)*

It is bad to dream you hear the sound of trumpets. Sickness and death will cause you to shed many tears during the following year. *(M)*

TUMBLER
To dream that you drink from a clean tumbler denotes health and activity; from a dirty one, the reverse. *(OM)*

TUMOURS
To dream you have a tumour in your shoulder signifies trouble and displeasure from relations. *(T)*

TUNNEL
To dream that you are in a tunnel and experience fear is a sign that you will shortly make a wrong decision in a matter of some importance. To a girl in love it foretells that she will have reason to mistrust her sweetheart. If,

however, she can see light at the end of the tunnel, he will reform and make her a good husband if she reasons with him. *(M)*

To dream of going through a tunnel with a light at the end is a good dream for the depressed, for it signifies that if their lives are now dull and gloomy they will brighten up in the long run into peace and joy. *(O)*

————— ♦ —————

TURKEY
This bird brings a warning of sickness. Take good care of your health, or you will have a serious breakdown. *(M)*

To dream you see a turkey strutting about is a sign you will overcome your enemies. To dream of dead turkeys denotes that you will encounter trouble. *(OM)*

————— ♦ —————

TURNIPS
To dream of being in a turnip field denotes the acquisition of money and if you marry you will be happy and thrive in the world. *(OM)*

————— ♦ —————

TURTLE
A promise of wishes to be fulfilled. The lover who dreams of eating a turtle will marry into a good family. *(M)*

————— ♦ —————

TURTLE DOVES
To dream of turtle doves signifies that much affection will be given to the dreamer. *(OM)*

————— ♦ —————

TWINS
To dream that you see twins is a sign that you will have to work for your own upkeep to the end of your life. *(M)*

UGLY

The girl who dreams that she has received a proposal of marriage from an ugly man will marry a handsome one. *(M)*

———— ♦ ————

ULCERS

To dream you have ulcers on your arms signifies annoyance, sadness and failure in business. If anyone dreams that his flesh is swollen by an ulcer, that indicates money. *(T)*

If a parent dreams that one of her children is troubled with mouth ulcers, it is a good sign that the child will be eloquent. A boy may grow up to be a lecturer or a preacher, or a girl may become an actress or singer. *(M)*

———— ♦ ————

UMBRELLA

To dream that you lose your umbrella is a sure sign that you will receive a gift from an unexpected quarter. To dream that you break or tear your umbrella indicates that you will be blamed for a misdeed which you have not committed, and will find it difficult to prove your innocence. *(M)*

> If business of moment shall press to decide,
> Take advice from your friend and upon it abide. *(MS)*

———— ♦ ————

UNDERTAKER

To dream of an undertaker is a promising omen. You will enjoy good health for some time to come. *(M)*

———— ♦ ————

UNFORTUNATE

To dream that you are unfortunate foretells that your hard work will bring you success. *(OM)*

VALLEY
To dream of a valley signifies a temporary sickness. *(OM)*

———— ◆ ————

VAULTS
To dream of being in hollow vaults, deep cellars or the bottom of deep pits signifies a marriage for a widow; her husband will work hard and never understand her. *(DSG)*

———— ◆ ————

VEAL
Dreaming of veal foretells good luck. *(OM)*

———— ◆ ————

VEGETABLES
To dream of vegetables is an indication of unrewarded work; to gather vegetables signifies quarrels, and to eat them indicates loss in business. *(OM)*

———— ◆ ————

VEIL
To dream you are wearing a veil predicts that you will have reason to hide from someone who seeks you for revenge. For a young woman to dream that she sees a bridal veil is a sign that someone will soon fall ill and die in her house. To dream that she sees a bride wearing a veil means that a female cousin of hers will be engaged to a young man, but when everything is ready for the wedding her lover will elope with another woman he knew before. *(M)*

This dream signifies news of a wedding, but a black veil foretells a separation. *(OM)*

———— ◆ ————

VELVET
To dream you trade with a stranger in velvet signifies profit and joy. *(T)*

You will talk with a powerful person after dreaming of velvet. To dream you are wearing a velvet dress promises wealth and enjoyment. *(M)*

To dream of buying, wearing or looking at velvet, indicates that you will shortly make a considerable profit. If the velvet is black, it will be in a business transaction or if it is red, it will be a personal gain. *(O)*

VENISON
To dream about venison denotes change in affairs. To dream you eat it signifies misfortune. *(OM)*

------ ◆ ------

VERMIN
To dream of vermin indicates that you will soon be entertaining a person who, while pretending to do you a favour, will do his or her best to make trouble between you and your husband or partner. *(M)*

------ ◆ ------

VICAR
To dream that the vicar of the parish calls upon you is a sign that you will shortly call upon him, to ask him to officiate at a wedding, baptism or funeral. *(M)*

------ ◆ ------

VILLA
To dream of buying a villa denotes a marriage as soon as you have saved enough. Selling a villa in a dream is unfortunate and indicates losses. *(O)*

------ ◆ ------

VINEGAR
To dream that you drink vinegar signifies sickness. *(T)*

Denotes treachery and deceit. The girl in love will find that her sweetheart is unfaithful. *(M)*

------ ◆ ------

VINES
To dream you see a vine signifies abundance, riches and fertility. *(M)*

An especially good omen. A dream of a vine is a sure indication that things will go well with you. Your dearest wish will be fulfilled, and you will not suffer any problems for some time to come. *(M)*

------ ◆ ------

VINTAGE
This dream foretells successful business operations and affection rewarded. *(OM)*

------ ◆ ------

VIOLETS
Omens of good. You have no enemies, and your love is fully returned. *(M)*

To dream of violets when they are out of season signifies a newly-awakened affection. *(OM)*

------ ◆ ------

VIOLIN
To dream you play or see someone else play a violin signifies good news, harmony and a good relationship between man and wife, employer and employee. *(T)*

To dream that you hear the music of a violin is a sign that you will receive an invitation to join in a celebration, probably a wedding. To dream that you are playing the instrument promises a rapid rise to a life of ease. *(M)*

---◆---

VIRGIN

A virgin discoursing is good in a dream,
Joy and delight on your hours, now, shall beam. *(N)*
A virgin dreaming that she has lost her virginity signifies great danger. *(OM)*

---◆---

VIRGINALS

To dream you play or see someone else play the virginals signifies the death of relations. *(T)*

---◆---

VIRGIN MARY

To dream that you speak to the Holy Virgin Mary signifies consolation, recovery of health, and all good fortune. To dream you talk with the Virgin Mary signifies joy. *(T)*

---◆---

VISION

Danger is in store to the person who appears to you. *(OM)*

---◆---

VISIT

To dream of receiving a visit means that you ought to cultivate the art of being friendly with everyone you meet, because a stranger will shortly be introduced to you who will have it in his power to make your fortune. Dreaming of paying a visit indicates that before long you will see the need to leave your present locality and trying a new one, which will be a great change for the better. *(O)*

---◆---

VISITOR

To dream you receive an unexpected visitor indicates that you will soon hear of a birth, probably in your family. *(M)*

---◆---

VOICES

To dream you hear a voice, but cannot see who is speaking shows that you will be deluded by a con man. *(P&F)*

If in your dream you hear voices it is a very significant dream. If they are angelic voices, a friend who is ill will die. If you hear voices of horror or dismay some of your friends or relatives will meet with an accident, either on the railway or at sea. If you hear voices of harmony you will have peace and joy in all your relationships. *(M)*

To hear voices signifies the reverse of what it implies; if cheerful, the sorrow is to come; if sad, then joy may be expected. *(OM)*

◆

VOLCANO
If anyone dreams of a volcano that signifies that someone powerful will oppress and destroy good men. *(T)*

To dream about volcanoes forebodes peace and happiness. *(OM)*

◆

VOMIT
To dream of vomiting signifies profit to the poor; or problems to the rich. *(OM)*

◆

VOW
To dream of a broken vow is a bad omen. *(OM)*

◆

VULTURE
A vulture signifies a dangerous enemy. If you kill one it foretells conquest of misfortune. To see one eating its prey means that your troubles will cease and you will be fortunate. *(OM)*

WADING
If a girl dreams of wading in clear water it is a sign that she will soon marry happily. If the water is muddy it foretells that she will only be happy for a short time, then will experience problems. If a man dreams of wading it denotes that he will be engaged in an intrigue which will land him in the law-courts. *(M)*

———— ◆ ————

WAGON
A bad omen. Your life will be shadowed by trouble and you will never improve your position. *(M)*

———— ◆ ————

WALKING
To dream of walking in the dirt or among thorns signifies sickness. To dream you walk in rushing water signifies adversity and grief. To dream you walk at night signifies trouble and melancholy. To dream you walk in a forest signifies trouble. To walk in a garden signifies joy. To walk on holy ground is a good sign. Walking on thorns signifies the destruction of enemies. To walk when your feet are sore signifies lack of food. To walk with four-footed animals signifies sickness. *(T)*

To dream that you are walking a long distance is a sign that you will one day find it difficult to get a job. The girl who dreams she is walking with her sweetheart will do well not to rush into marriage before carefully considering her prospective husband's position. *(M)*

To dream of walking first with friends then alone signifies that in pursuit of what you think your duty you will give offence to many, but that everything will come right in the end, your unfriendly critics coming to see that you were, in fact, in the right and they in the wrong. *(O)*

———— ◆ ————

WALLS
To dream of walls signifies dangerous enterprises and lack of success; if you climb them and the ascent is easy it foretells success in business. *(OM)*

———— ◆ ————

WALNUTS
To dream you see and eat walnuts signifies difficulty and trouble. *(T)*

WANDERED

Dreaming of wandering aimlessly is a sign of approaching trouble, sometimes about a love affair of the heart, but more often about money. To judge whether the problem is to be of long or short duration try to remember if it was broad daylight or in the dark. If dark, the trouble will be long-lasting. *(O)*

———— ♦ ————

WAR

To dream of war signifies trouble and anger to everyone except to captains and soldiers. *(DSG)*

To dream of fighting and winning shows danger avoided. *(D&M)*

To dream of war is a sign that very shortly you will become the object of unjust suspicion and suffer much from the sneers of your so-called friends. *(M)*

———— ♦ ————

WARTS

To dream you have warts signifies you will become rich. *(T)*

———— ♦ ————

WASHING

To dream you wash your face signifies repentance of your sin. To wash your feet signifies disturbance. To wash your hands signifies disquiet and anxiety. To wash your head signifies avoidance of danger. To wash yourself in the sea signifies loss and damage. *(T)*

To dream of washing clothes signifies that you will sustain or escape an injury. *(A)*

> This of course among women can only apply,
> And removals will clearly the dream testify,
> Yet it oft has been known to the female sterile
> To presage in due time, cogent reason to smile. *(MS)*

To dream of washing your face signifies that you will settle a quarrel to your advantage. *(DSG)*

To dream of washing in a fountain, pond or brook of running water, or in a clean stream denotes happiness and joy. *(D&M)*

To dream of washing is a sign that you will soon have reason to defend a friend's character. *(M)*

For a man to dream he is washing himself signifies riches and prosperity, but to dream he washes or bathes himself in his clothes is evil and indicates sickness and great danger. *(OM)*

———— ♦ ————

WASPS

To dream you are stung by a wasp, signifies anxiety and trouble caused by envious people. *(T)*

To dream of wasps is a warning of strife to come. *(M)*

WASTING

If anyone dreams he has grown thin and wasted, he will suffer problems of one kind or another, either illness or loss of money. If a woman dreams that her tongue has grown small and wasted, it signifies she will show wisdom, prudence and discretion for which she will be respected by everyone.   *(T)*

---◆---

WATCH

To dream that your watch has stopped often indicates death, but to a young man means that his love will end in nothing.

> Early and late he will sue in vain,
> The maiden's love he will not gain.   *(O)*

To dream of a watch signifies a journey by land.   *(OM)*

---◆---

WATCHDOG

To dream of a dog signifies farms, servants and possessions to come. *(A)*

---◆---

WATER

To dream that you see a clear, calm river indicates good. To dream you see a rough river signifies that you will be threatened by someone powerful. To dream of being in a rushing river signifies the danger of sickness or other problems. To dream of swimming in a large river signifies future peril and danger. To dream you see a clear river run by your bedroom indicates the arrival of a rich and generous person, who will do something to your advantage; but if the water is troubled, and spoils the furniture of the room that signifies violence, quarrels and disorder in the family. To see a stream of clear water running by your house, you will be unexpectedly offered a promotion which will be financially advantageous, and in which post you will be able to help the oppressed. To dream you see a rough stream signifies loss and damage by fire, law-suits and enemies. It is a good sign to dream you see a pond full of clear water in a field because it signifies that you will thrive, and soon be married, if you are not so already, and will have good and obedient children. To dream you see a pond whose water overflows the banks predicts loss of money and death of wife and children; and if the wife has the same dream, that denotes her death, or the loss of her money. To dream that you see a small pond signifies that you will enjoy the love of a beautiful woman or handsome man. To dream that you are in a boat on a river, lake or pond of clear water is very good, and signifies joy, prosperity and success. If a sick person dreams that he sees a river or fountain of clear running water, that indicates his recovery, but if the water is rough and muddy, it signifies the opposite. If a young man dreams that he draws water out of a clear well, it signifies he will soon be married to an attractive girl; if the water is troubled, he will not be happily married and will fall ill. If he seems to give others clear well-water to drink he will enrich others, or afflict them if the water is troubled. If anyone dreams that his river, pond or fountain is dried up, that signifies poverty or death. If anyone dreams that he sees water flow from a place where it could not possibly come, that signifies problems. If he imagines that he has taken up some of that water, the mischief will be of a longer duration, according to the quantity he has drawn; if the water dries up, the problem will be solved. To drink warm water means that someone who has been offended by your behaviour will try to harm you. To see a bath signifies affliction or grief. If a person dreams he gets into a bath which is too hot or too cold, he will be troubled by his family; the problems will be greater if the water is very hot. To undress without getting into the bath indicates a minor problem. If the water is comfortably warm it is a good dream, indicating prosperity, pleasure, joy and health. To carry water in a garment, broken vessel, cloth, or anything else which could not hold water denotes loss and damage, and that you will be deceived by people to whom you have trusted your money or property. If the water in these impossible vessels is not spilt, then you will keep your property, though with much difficulty; but if the water is spilt, you will lose it. If you think you have hidden the vessel and water underground, you will experience severe problems, be in danger of being made a public spectacle, and of dying a shameful death. If you dream someone gives you a glass full of water that signifies he will soon marry and have children. If the glass seems to be broken, but the water unspilt that signifies the death of his wife, but that his child will live, and vice versa. If a minister dreams he gives his people clear water to drink, it signifies that he will teach them the word of God faithfully, and will be instrumental in their salvation; if the water is troubled, he will teach them heretical and false doctrine. If anyone dreams that he has spilt water in his house, that denotes care and problems according to the quantity of water.   *(T)*

To dream you are drinking water denotes great trouble and adversity; in trade, loss of business and being arrested; to the lover it shows your sweetheart is false, prefers another, and will never marry you.   *(GD)*

> To drink is inverse to the line of success,
> Troubles crowd on to failure, arrest and distress.   *(MS)*

When water enters into a dream it may have several meanings. If you are entering water it is an evil sign, indicating that you will shortly have many difficulties to surmount, if you can surmount them. Should you be given a glass of water it means marriage, but if the water is well-water you may be sure that the marriage will occur soon. Standing beside a clear stream in a dream foretells good luck; if the water is muddy it means misfortune. If the water is muddy but fast-running it indicates that you are likely to have personal experience of bankruptcy unless you take warning in time.   *(O)*

WATER CARRIER
To dream of a water carrier signifies increases in money.　　　*(OM)*

———————◆———————

WATERMILL
To dream of being in a watermill is a favourable omen. To the tradesman it denotes great increase of business; to the farmer, abundant crops; in love, success and a rich sweetheart and a happy marriage.　　　*(OM)*

———————◆———————

WAVES
To dream of waves foretells that you must be prepared to fight for fortune.
　　　(OM)

———————◆———————

WEASEL
To dream of a weasel signifies that you have or will have a bad and wicked wife.　　　*(A)*

　To dream of a weasel means you must beware of those who would appear to befriend you without reason.　　　*(OM)*

———————◆———————

WEDDING
If a man dreams he is married to an ugly woman, that signifies death, or great discontent; if to a handsome woman, that denotes joy and profit. *(T)*

　For the sick to dream they are married or celebrate their wedding is a sign of death.　　　*(A)*

　To dream of being married, or a wedding, is a very unfavourable dream especially for lovers. It denotes the death of a near friend or relation, with loss of property and severe disappointments.　　　*(GD)*

　It is unlucky for a girl to dream of a wedding. She will remain single for most of her life, and will have reason to distrust the male sex. To a married person the dream gives warning of sickness and death.　　　*(M)*

　For a man who is sick to dream that he is married to a young girl shows he will die quickly.　　　*(OM)*

———————◆———————

WEDDING RING
For a woman to dream that she has lost her wedding ring signifies that she does not have much love for her husband; but if she dreams that she has found it again, it is a sign that her love is not wholly lost.　　　*(OM)*

———————◆———————

WEEDS
To dream that you are weeding a garden is a sign that your children will cause you much trouble and anxiety. To see weeds growing in profusion is indicative of blighted hopes.　　　*(M)*

　To dream of weeds or of weeding a garden means that, however fond of ease you may be, you must become wise enough to face continual exertion cheerfully, because your work will never be completed.　　　*(O)*

WEEPING

To dream you weep and grieve whether for a lost friend or for any reason signifies joy for a good action you will perform. *(A)*

The meaning of a dream in which you weep is directly the opposite of what you might expect. You are on the eve of hearing something which will excite in you the deepest joy. *(O)*

◆

WEIGHING

To dream of weighing anything in scales denotes that you will soon experience the truth of the remark that it is better to have a grain of fortune than a pound of wisdom. *(O)*

◆

WELL

If a young man dreams he draws water out of a clear well, it signifies he will soon be married to a beautiful girl; if the water is troubled, he will be disturbed by her and suddenly fall sick. If he seems to give others clear well-water to drink, he will enrich others by this girl's means or if the water is troubled he will harm them. To dream you cleanse a well or fall into it, signifies injury. *(T)*

The person who dreams of a well will either be renowned for learning and wisdom, or will marry someone who will gain fame through the same acquirements. *(M)*

◆

WHEAT

To dream you see the land sown with wheat signifies money and profit with difficulty and hard work. *(T)*

To dream you see or are walking in a field of wheat is a very favourable omen, and denotes great prosperity and riches; in love, it predicts a completion of your dearest wishes, and foretells much happiness with fine children, when you marry; if you have a law-suit you will gain it, and you will be successful in all your undertakings. *(GD)*

◆

WHEEL

To dream you see a wheel come off a carriage, or coming off, is a warning that if you have arranged for a railway journey you ought to postpone it, for to you, at least, it will result in mishap. *(O)*

◆

WHEELBARROW

A dream of pushing a wheelbarrow means for a man that he will marry soon and have a considerable family, and that he will gladly work long hours for the sake of his children. *(O)*

WHIP

To dream that you whip someone is good. To dream you are whipped by the gods or the dead is not good. It is always good to be whipped with rods, or with the hand, for it signifies profit; but with leather, reeds or cudgels indicates evil. *(A)*

For a young woman to dream of seeing a whip means that she will marry a fool and a spendthrift. For a young man to dream of seeing a whip means that he will marry a woman who will be slovenly in her habits and careless and unmanageable in her house; she will drive him from home to seek company elsewhere, and his life will be miserable in consequence. *(M)*

◆

WHIPPING

If anyone dreams that his hips are black and blue with whipping, that indicates his death in a short time or at least that he will hate his wife and have several grievances. *(T)*

◆

WHIRLWIND

A dream in which a whirlwind appears warns you to beware of dangerous reports. *(OM)*

◆

WHISPERING

To hear whispering in a dream means that many people are talking ill of you, and that on consideration of your conduct you will find that they are not doing so quite without reason. *(O)*

◆

WIDOW

To dream that you are a widow is a sign that there is a rival striving to gain your affections. The single man who dreams that he has married a widow will receive more than one disappointment in love. *(M)*

For a woman to dream of a widow signifies that her husband or lover will desert her. *(O)*

◆

WIDOWER

The girl who dreams that she has married, or is about to marry a widower will give her love to the wrong man, and only find out her mistake when it is too late. If a man dreams that he is a widower it is a sign that his wife will out-live him by many years. *(M)*

A man dreaming of a widower may safely infer that he is about, if a husband, to be deserted by his wife, and if single, that the young woman he is going out with is going to play him false. *(O)*

◆

WIFE

To dream you hear your wife scold signifies great torment. *(T)*

It is extremely unfortunate for a man to dream of his wife. He will be separated from her by death or quarrelling and live to regret the day they met.
(M)

If a man dreams he sees his wife married to another, it denotes change of affairs or condition.
(OM)

———— ♦ ————

WILL

To dream you make your will is a bad sign.
(T)

To dream that you make your will is a sign of long life.
(M)

To dream of making a will is one of the most reliable indications that you are destined to have a long, contented and prosperous life.
(O)

For a pregnant woman to dream that she has made her will is unfortunate as it denotes a difficult labour.
(OM)

———— ♦ ————

WIND

To dream that you are out in a strong breeze is a sign that you will have a hard battle to fight in life, but providing you can endure and conquer, ease and happiness will follow. When the wind blows high it signifies that you have to encounter several perils, but that you are destined to emerge safely from them all.
(O)

———— ♦ ————

WIND INSTRUMENTS

To dream of any instrument you can blow signifies trouble, with the exception of the bagpipe and reed.
(A)

———— ♦ ————

WINDMILL

Problematical e'er of vicissitudes various
Of incidents painful and pleasures vagarious,
Tells youth due employ of abilities given,
And age to repose on the mercy of heaven.
(MS)

Gives promise of a short holiday in a strange district or a change of home.
(M)

———— ♦ ————

WINDOWS

To dream you see the windows at the front of the house destroyed by fire signifies the death of brothers; if they are those at the back of the house, it means the death of a sister.
(T)

To dream of looking out of a window means that you will shortly travel through many foreign countries, get acquainted with many strange faces, and return home without having contracted even the ghost of an attachment for anyone.
(O)

WINE

To dream that you drink white wine signifies health to the dreamer.   *(T)*

> This beverage admits of a treach'rous solution,
> And predicts, I conjecture, some fatal delusion,
> The mind's eye has formed of a friend or relation,
> And incurs disappointments' severe castigation.   *(MS)*

To dream that you are drinking wine means that you are about to suffer in health from too eagerly pursuing your duty, but that the injury will not be permanent.   *(O)*

————— ♦ —————

WITCH

To dream of a witch foretells that you will leave your home and live among strangers; if the witch attempts to injure you it denotes that you will be dependent upon strangers for your support.   *(M)*

————— ♦ —————

WOLVES

The wolf signifies an avaricious, cruel and disloyal person; and if anyone dreams he has overcome a wolf, he will conquer an enemy with the same qualities, and on the contrary, if he is bitten by the wolf, he will be injured in some way by a cruel and disloyal enemy. To dream you have the head of a wolf is a good sign as it means you will achieve your ambitions. To dream you see many wolves signifies that you will be robbed.   *(T)*

————— ♦ —————

WOMAN

To dream you see a woman naked signifies the death of someone.   *(T)*

To dream you see a woman is beneficial as it means love and no problems.   *(D&M)*

A dream in which an old woman figures largely is good. It means safety, prosperity and comfort. To dream of a young woman means much the same thing, but these good features will be combined with not a few worries and distractions. Should a man dream of parting from a young woman it signifies that he will fall in love.   *(O)*

————— ♦ —————

WOOD and WOODS

To dream you are carrying wood signifies profit. To dream you are in woods signifies disgrace and loss.   *(T)*

To dream you are cutting or chopping wood shows that you will be happy in your family, and become rich and respectable in life. To dream you are carrying wood on your back shows that you will rise to affluence by your hard work, but that your partner will be bad tempered, and your children unloving. If you dream you are walking in an extensive wood, it denotes that you will be married several times.   *(GD)*

To dream of travelling through a wood and striking the briars and the bushes as you pass is an evil sign for it means many troubles and hindrances in important affairs. *(A)*

────── ♦ ──────

WOOD PIGEON

To dream of these birds signifies the dreamer keeps company with wild and dissolute women. *(A)*

────── ♦ ──────

WOOL

To dream you trade in wool signifies profit. *(T)*

To dream you are buying and selling wool denotes prosperity and great affluence by means of industry and trade. *(DSG)*

A promise of plenty throughout life. *(M)*

────── ♦ ──────

WORKING

To dream of being hard at work anywhere or at anything means that you are in danger of losing your present job and you should take the utmost care to please your employer, for his attitude towards you is just now none of the best. *(O)*

────── ♦ ──────

WORKMAN

To dream of a workman signifies that your enterprises will bring great profit. *(OM)*

────── ♦ ──────

WORKSHOP

To dream of a workshop signifies good fortune. *(OM)*

────── ♦ ──────

WORMS

To dream of earth worms signifies enemies that try to ruin you. *(T)*

To dream that you vomit long worms or see them on your feet signifies that you will discover your enemies and will overcome them. Little worms signify care and anger and often displeasure which you will have because of your wife or family. *(A)*

────── ♦ ──────

WORRY

To dream you are worried and unsettled in your thoughts signifies joy. *(T)*

────── ♦ ──────

WORSHIP

To dream you worship God signifies joy. *(T)*

────── ♦ ──────

WOUNDS

If anyone dreams that he has been stabbed with a sword in the front of his body and draws blood, the injured person will receive an extraordinary kindness from the attacker; if blood is not spilled, the advantage will be less. If anyone dreams that he is fatally wounded with a sword, that is a sign that he will receive several courtesies and good turns from the person who wounded him. If anyone has a wound which he dreams is healed, he will boast of his valour and gain honour by it in public opinion.   *(T)*

To dream of being wounded in the palm of the right hand signifies debt of war.   *(A)*

To dream of wounds in the stomach foretells joy to young people.

(D&M2)

> To dream you are wounded to lovers is naught
> Since experience is good, when not too dearly bought,
> But if wounds should incline to a mortification
> Your sorrows should tire me by amplification.   *(MS)*

WREATH

To dream of a wreath foretells a wedding and much happiness for the dreamer.   *(M.)*

WREN

To dream of these pretty birds denotes great happiness and content through life; to the lover they are particularly favourable; they show your sweetheart is kind and amiable, much attached to you, and one who will make you very happy.   *(GD)*

WRESTLING

To dream you wrestle with a stranger signifies danger of sickness. To wrestle with a child, and throw him on the ground signifies that you will lose a child by death, while to be beaten by the child foretells mockery and sickness. To dream you see a little child wrestle with a man is good, for the child will do greater things than you imagine; but if you wrestle or fight with a champion this is not good. To dream you wrestle with death indicates sickness. A woman who dreams she wrestles with her husband will bring sorrow into the family. Wrestling in a dream with death denotes a long sickness and law-suits.   *(OM)*

WRIST

To dream that your wrists are broken is very good. It foretells that you will marry your present lover and be happy.   *(OM)*

WRITING

To dream you write to your friends signifies good news. To dream you write on paper signifies accusation.   *(T)*

> Dreaming of writing, ever means news
> 'Twill grant or deny, will give or refuse.   *(M)*

To dream of writing with the left hand means you will disgrace someone through a secret deceit. *(A)*

To dream that you are writing is a sign that someone is worrying because he or she has not heard from you recently. For a girl this dream also warns of a proposal of marriage which she will have to reject. *(M)*

To dream of writing a letter means that a friend from whom you have been separated for a long time, and whose whereabouts you do not know, it about to call on you, and to bring good news about himself. *(O)*

WRY NECK

To dream your neck is turned so that you look backwards warns you not to go out of the country or engage in new business in case they turn out badly. Anyone in a distant country will return home. *(A)*

YACHT

The person who dreams of sailing on a yacht will bring trouble on his or her own head through being too much inclined to put business before pleasure. *(M)*

To dream either of watching a yacht sailing or of being on board is a dream of change in which there will be a considerable element of risk. *(O)*

———————— ◆ ————————

YARN

Brings promise of a busy but happy life. The girl who dreams she is using yarn will marry a working class man who will prove to be a much better husband than many far above him in the social scale. *(M)*

To dream of yarn, of whatever type, is a good omen, meaning that you will have a long life and that your experience will be mainly pleasant, even if somewhat monotonous. *(O)*

———————— ◆ ————————

YAWN

To dream that you yawn is a sign that you will one day grow tired of your present occupation and go abroad to seek your fortune. To a married woman yawning predicts sickness in the family. *(M)*

To dream that you are yawning foretells that you will have to show more energy in order to succeed. *(OM)*

———————— ◆ ————————

YEW

To have a yew tree as a prominent feature in a dream points to the approaching loss of friends, and also to the probable loss of money. *(O)*

———————— ◆ ————————

YOKE

To dream of a yoke is unfavourable, unless it is broken, then it denotes a rising above your present situation. *(DSG)*

For a young woman to dream of seeing a yoke of oxen ploughing is a sign that she will marry a young man who, though poor, will make her a good husband; but circumstances will require her to work at some daily employment that they may together better their condition. *(M)*

YORKSHIRE PUDDING

To dream of eating Yorkshire pudding means for a young man that, though at present much taken up with the idea of good living, he is shortly to meet one who will alter the current of his thoughts and convince him that it is love after all that makes for the happiness of life. *(O)*

ZEBRA

To dream of a zebra is a sign that you will strive for a long time to gain something on which you have set your heart, and will be disappointed when you finally reach your goal. *(M)*

To dream of a zebra foretells disagreement with friends. *(OM)*

———— ◆ ————

ZINC

To dream that you see a quantity of zinc is a sign that you will emigrate to a foreign country before many years are over. You will have inducements offered to you to join some of your old friends who have emigrated before you. *(M)*

———— ◆ ————

ZOO

To dream that you pay a visit to a zoo is a sign of happy, prosperous and eventful times. To a young man it means that he will meet with a marriage partner who will greatly enhance his wealth. He will rise in the world through his wife's wealth, but will be under her thumb because of it and have to do what she wants all the time. For a young woman to dream that she visits a zoo is a sign that she will fall in love with a young man who will be fond of botany and natural history. He will study both subjects, and will gain eminence in learning both, and acquire fame and reputation as a proficient geologist and medical botanist. *(M)*

Everyday Eating made more exciting

Foulsham books are available from all good bookshops:
or you can telephone Macmillan Direct on 01256 329242
or order on our website www.foulsham.com